JAMAICA
ABSOLUTELY

EDITED BY ARIF ALI

HANSIB

Published in Great Britain, 2012
by Hansib Publications Limited

Email: info@hansib-books.com
Website: www.hansib-books.com

ISBN 978-1-906190-31-6 (Hardback)
ISBN 978-1-906190-32-3 (Paperback)

First published in 2010

Design and production by Hansib Publications Limited
Printed and bound in Great Britain

Foreword

"Enough for every need, but not for everyone's greed."

This is Hansib's second attempt at producing a book on Jamaica. The idea was inspired some thirty-five years ago when Evon Blake approached me to assist with the distribution of his book *Beautiful Jamaica* in 1974-5 for the UK market.

Jamaica: Absolutely is the twenty-first book in our 'Nation's Series'. Hansib has taken much criticism from Jamaican nationals in the UK, USA, Canada and Jamaica for not producing what our readers felt was a necessary book for the largest of the Caribbean diaspora communities in the UK, USA and Canada.

As one Jamaican living in Barbados said: "How can you produce six book for Antigua and Barbuda and none for Jamaica." He added that, "there are more Jamaicans than all the English-speaking Caribbean countries put together."

Working in Jamaica over the past year has given me an insight into a country and its people that is far beyond my expectations. The kindness, sense of humour and courtesy is experienced within minutes of your arrival.

Like most people of the Caribbean, when they laugh their eyes light up; but the Jamaican has a mischievous twinkle that lingers on.

Jamaica has opened its doors with many incentives and opportunities for investors both large and small.

The island attracts in excess of 2.7 million visitors every year, hosting them in some of the most stylish hotels anywhere in the world and offering some thought provoking attractions, mouth watering food and some way-out ideas for fun and frolics.

As you travel around the country, during what is probably the worst recession for a century, you get a feeling that the country is gearing up to be ready to take advantage as the recession eases.

One should never forget that Jamaica is the land of the Maroons; the land that inspired Marcus Garvey and Bob Marley; a country whose people have chalked up many achievements in any country they have domiciled.

Jamaica has given the world many things and people for us to remember. But, just in case we have a lapse in our memory, they recently threw onto the world stage some of the most amazing athletes headed by Usain Bolt. And, as for the country itself, even Christopher Columbus said it was, "the fairest isle I have ever laid eyes on."

It is, therefore, no wonder that my friend, Ken Campbell, thought that the book should be called, "Jamaica: Absolutely".

Arif Ali
Kingston, Jamaica

Contents

Thank you to the following for their help and support towards the publication of *Jamaica: Absolutely*.

Director of Tourism John D Lynch, Deputy Director David Shields who gradually steered the project to fruition, Essie Gardner for her sterling support throughout the project, Sharille Pink, Beverley Johnson, Terry Ann Campbell, Matthew Blake and other members of the Jamaica Tourist Board and former Director of Tourism Basil Smith.

To senior members of Hansib's UK team, Managing Editor, Kash Ali, Project Coordinator, the ubiquitous Isha Persaud, Co-ordinating Editor, Earle Robinson, Richard Painter and Shareef Ali, Alan Cross, Ella Barnes, Fidel Persaud, Zahid Ali, Chandani Persaud;

Tony Matthews, whose invaluable support never wavered and Hermin Yorke who was always there whatever the task;

Bindley Sangster and Douglas Brooks for pointing us in the right direction on so many occasions. Joe and Angela Whitter and their staff at their home and office; Lascelles Poyser for ensuring I visited so many places;

Mohan Jagnarine, Anand James for the visits to the Ackee canning plant in St Catherine, the food production unit near Spur Tree in Manchester, the 20/20 cricket finals at Sabina Park and of course the bars and restaurant wherever we can find them and your own respective business operations.

WRITERS (*in alphabetical order*): Sharon Atkin-O'Brien, Barbara Makeda Blake Hannah, Myrna Hague Bradshaw, Sonny Bradshaw, David Buckley, Carolyn Cooper, Fae Ellington, John Fletcher, Delano Franklyn, Christopher Gentles, Sandra Graham, Jamaica Information Service, Aldrick Allie McNab, Herbi Miller, Janneth Mornan-Green, Rex Nettleford, Noelle Khalila Nicolls, Lascelles J. Poyser, Stacy Rose, Alfred Sangster, Verene A. Shepherd, Joanne Simpson, Andrew P. Smith, Mark Thompson, Ainsley Walters, Steven K. Widener, Denise Williams, Klaus Wolf.

PHOTOGRAPHERS *(in alphabetical order)*: African Caribbean Institute of Jamaica / Jamaica Memory Bank, Robert Davis, Geejam Productions, Josh Hunter, Jamaica Information Service, Jamaica Trade & Investment, Jamaica Tourist Board, Tony Matthews, Earle Robinson, Brian Rosen, Andrew P. Smith, Steven K. Widener, Klaus Wolf.

I apologise for articles submitted and not used because of deadlines or other reasons. I take this opportunity to thank the many writers who returned our telephone calls and with whom we were unable to make a connection.

A book like the one you are now reading or glancing through cannot be completed without the significant support from scores of people:

Shireen Aga, Ricardo Allicock, Asgar Ally, Jodi Ann Spencer, Noel Badly, Jon Baker, Howard Baugh, Sheila Benjamin-McNeill, Ian Boyne, Eldon Bremner, Zuleikha Budhan, Virginia Chin, Taniesha Clarke, Wayne Cummings, Robert Davis (aerial photos: www.JamaicaByAir.com), Godfrey Dyer, Wilton Dyer, Karen Edwards, Claude Espeut, Jennifer Francis, Sherlock Glenister, Dave Gordon, Lois Grant, Carol Guntley, Barbara Blake Hannah, Ainsley Henriques, Nicola Hussein, Clinton Hutton, Muna Issa, Bernard Jankee, Alexander Jones, Dale Jones, Mark and Paula Kerr-Jarrett, Cookie Kincaide, David Lee, Suzanne Lee, Junior Lincoln, Michael Look Tong, Michael (Miguel) Lorne, Jean Lowrie Chin, Millicent Lynch, Celia Lindsay, Beverly McCook, Christine McCook, Oral McCook, Derrick McKoy, Ian Marsh, Julia Mendonca, Leon Mitchell, Eula Morgan, Gillian Morgan, Denroy Mullings, Yvonnie Myrie, National Land Agency (map), Camille Needham, Earl Patrick, Carmen Patterson, Joe Pereira, Horace Phillips, Susan Pitter, Donna Rambaran, Anika Repole, Hon. Roddy Spencer, Michelle Rousseau, Robert Russell, Tresha Samuda, Maxine Shrouder, Elizabeth Stair, Diana Stewart, Becky Stockhausen, Mark Thomas, Heron Thompson, UPS Translators, Mark Thompson, Winston Tolan, Tony Wade, Valerie Walcott, Barbara Walker, Stewart Weathers, Dale Westin.

Ambassador Jesus Silva, Chinese Embassy (Jamaica), staff at Jamaica Information Service; management and staff at Hilton Hotel (Kingston), Pegasus Hotel (Kingston), Courtleigh Hotel (Kingston), Ritz Carlton – Montego Bay; staff of British Airways and Virgin Atlantic (London Gatwick) and the staff at Norman Manley International Airport (Kingston).

Kenneth Campbell, former editor of West Indian Digest, who with much pride named this book Jamaica: Absolutely.

Humble apologies to anyone whom I may have inadvertently left out.

And finally to Pamela Mary for caring so much.

Arif Ali

Supporters

Hansib Publications is grateful to the following businesses and organisations for their support:

Bellefield Great House
P.O. Box 876, Granville, Montego Bay
Tel/Fax: 952 2382. Email: info@bellefieldgreathouse.com

Bowen Pen Farmers Association
Milbank District, Rio Grande Valley, Portland
Tel: 395 5351. Email: BPFA_ecotourism@yahoo.com

Capital & Credit Financial Group
4 St Lucia Avenue, Kingston 5. Tel: 968 7000. Fax: 920 1055
Email: info@capital-credit.com

Caribbean Flavours and Fragrances Limited
226 Spanish Town Road, Kingston 11
Tel: 923 5111 / 923 5256 / 937 0366. Fax: 923 4323
Email: cff@mail.infochan.com

Coffee Industry Board
1 Willie Henry Drive, Kingston 13. Tel: 758 1442. Fax: 758 3907
Email: cgentles@ciboj.org

Forres Park
23 Liguanea Avenue, Kingston 6
Tel: 927 8275
Email: mlyn@cwjamaica.com

Geejam Productions
San San, Port Antonio, P.O. Box 7312, Portland
Tel: Reservations 993 7000 / 993 7246
Email: rose@geejam.com

Gold Cup Coffee Co. Limited
Unit 3, Blaise Industrial Park, 69-75 Constant Spring Road, Kingston 10. Tel: 905 3879. Fax: 931 9038
Email: goldcup@cwjamaica.com

Guardsman Group Limited
107 Old Hope Road, Kingston 6
Tel: 978 5760-6. Fax: 927 6613
Email: info@guardsmangroup.com

Ironshore Construction Co Limited
1139 Morgan Road, Ironshore, P.O. Box 822, Montego Bay, #1 St James. Tel: 953 3107. Fax: 953 9619
Email: whittergroup@cwjamaica.com

Jamaica Caves Organisation
Windsor District, Trelawny
Email: admin@jamaicancaves.org

Jamaica Tourist Board
64 Knutsford Boulevard, P.O. Box 360, Kingston 5
Tel: 929 9200-19. Fax: 929 9375
Email: info@visitjamaica.com

Jamaica Trade and Invest (Jamaica Promotions Corporation)
18 Trafalgar Road, Kingston 10
Tel: 978 7755. Tel: 978 3337
Toll Free: +1 877 INVEST JA (468 4352)
Fax: 946 0090. Email: info@jti.org.jm

Novelty Trading
53 Hanover Street, Kingston. Tel: 922 5661.
Fax: 922 4743. Email: novtraco@cwjamaica.com

Pier One
Howard Cook Boulevard, Montego Bay
Tel: 952 2452. Fax: 940 5408
Email: info@pieronejamaica.com

River Breeze Cottage
Green Hill P.A., Portland
Tel: 477 4493. Email: riverbreezejm@gmail.com

Sandals
For more information on Sandals Luxury Included vacations, please contact our worldwide marketing representatives Unique Vacations as follows:

United States: 4950 SW 72nd Avenue, Miami, FL 33155
Tel: 1-800-SANDALS. Fax: 305-667-8996
Canada: Tel: 1-800-545-8283. Fax: 416-223-3306
United Kingdom: 0800-742-742. Fax: 0207-823-8758

Spur Tree Spices Jamaica Limited
1 Woodglen Drive, ,Kingston 10. Tel: 929 4536
Email: mj.spurtree@cwjamaica.com

Sun Venture Tours Limited
30 Balmoral Avenue, Kingston 10. Tel: 960 6685 / 469 4444
Email: sunventure@hotmail.com

Superclubs
www.superclubs.com

From Jamaica to the world – celebrating fifty years of achievement

SIMON LEE

W hat impact can a small island, with a land mass of little more than 4,000 sq miles and a population of less than three million, have on the wider world beyond its shores? After fifty years of Independence, Jamaica is synonymous in the minds of many, with reggae, Rasta, Red Stripe and runners; Blue Mountain coffee, patties, jerk pork, ackee and saltfish; household names like Marcus Garvey, Bob Marley and Usain Bolt. A major musical global presence since the 1970s, Jamaica can boast more recording studios per square mile and capita than any other territory on the planet.

Besides its current domination of international athletic sprint events, Jamaican cricketers have long been the backbone of the West Indies cricket team, while the Sunshine Girls netball team have rained (sic) long over all-comers and the Reggae Boys football team became the first Caribbean representatives in the World Cup finals of 1998. Paradoxically for a tropical country where snow is a no-show, Jamaica perplexed the world by entering a bobsled team in the 1988 Olympic Winter Games. In 1994, in the four-man event, the Jamaican team surprised everyone by finishing 14th, joining the elite 'Top Fifteen' best bobsled teams in the world, ahead of the Americans, French, Russians and Italians.

Frontrunners in sports and culture, Jamaicans have also made seminal contributions to regional and international intellectual and political development. Renaissance man, the multi-talented Rex Nettleford, and Louise 'Miss Lou' Bennett-Coverly rank foremost in winning recognition for Creole artforms and language; Stuart Hall revolutionised intellectual discourse and put the new academic discipline of Cultural Studies on the map from his UK base, while Jamaican-born Colin Powell served as American Secretary of State 2001-2004.

The country's natural beauty – from the towering Blue Mountains to the idyllic twenty-mile swathe of white sand which is Negril beach, and its languorous rivers and stunning waterfalls – is also manifest in its women, three of whom became Miss World winners: Carole Crawford (1963), Cindy Breakspear (1976) and Lisa Hanna (1979).

The feisty Jamaican 'talawa' spirit, which is seemingly encoded in the national genes, has a long and distinguished pedigree. Foremost among officially recognised National Heroes, is the legendary Nanny of the Maroons, an exceptional leader despite her diminutive size. Long before Haiti became the first Caribbean slave colony to wrest freedom from its French masters, Nanny opposed the British military, confounding them with her guerrilla warfare tactics during the First Maroon War of 1720-1739. It is likely that Nanny drew on her African heritage for both her guerrilla strategy and her obeah powers, in similar fashion to the Haitian rebels fifty years later.

Another of the early heroes who displayed characteristic indomitable spirit was Samuel Sharpe, main instigator of the 1831 Slave Rebellion, which paved the way for the abolition of slavery. Although like Gandhi an advocate of passive resistance, Sharpe's plan to halt all slave labour from Christmas Day 1831 until grievances and abolition were addressed, was swiftly overtaken by an armed rebellion. Crushed by superior numbers and firepower, Sharpe went to the gallows with other insurrectionary slaves, declaring he'd rather die than live in slavery.

An iconic episode in the struggle of the Jamaican people against post-Emancipation oppression was the Morant Bay Rebellion of 1865, which was led by attorney and landowner George William Gordon (himself the son of a slave mother ▷

FACING PAGE: Stunning waterfalls, such as YS Falls in St Elizabeth, are among Jamaica's many natural wonders. Photo: Brian Rosen

RIGHT: Usain Bolt is now a household name throughout the globe. Photo: Andrew P. Smith

Culture and music have put independent Jamaica on the world map. Photo: Josh Hunter

and a planter father) and Baptist deacon Paul Bogle. The protest march on the Morant Bay courthouse was brutally suppressed; five hundred protesters were shot, Bogle and Gordon tried and executed. But the talawa spirit lived on, to be immortalised in song by arguably the most famous Jamaican of the twentieth century, Bob Marley, in his 'Small Axe' lyrics.

Another man whose influence has reverberated through world history is Jamaica's first National Hero, Marcus Garvey, born in 1887, who instilled pride and agency in all people of the African diaspora, long before the days of Black Power. His Universal Negro Improvement Association founded in 1914, rapidly mushroomed into an international organisation promoting self-government and self-help economics for the Black race, while contesting racial prejudice and discrimination. Garvey is rightly considered a man before his time, whose ideology and practice would inform such movements as Pan-Africanism, Negritude and Rastafarianism.

Other champions of the people who helped forge the politics which would launch independent, self-governing Jamaica, were Sir Alexander Bustamante and Norman Manley. Bustamante rose to prominence during the 1930s World Depression when social unrest swept the Caribbean. After serving seventeen months detention for leading workers' protests, Bustamante founded the Jamaican Labour Party in 1943, which went on to win the first universal adult suffrage general election of 1944. Fittingly, Bustamante was to become the first Prime Minister of Independent Jamaica in 1962.

It was the brilliant lawyer and athlete Norman Manley who founded the People's National Party in 1938 and led the campaign for universal adult suffrage, while supporting Bustamante's trade union movement. When the JLP leader, then in opposition, called for withdrawal from the Federation of the West Indies, established in 1958, Manley took the decision to the people with an unprecedented referendum. After withdrawal, Manley steered Jamaica to Independence declaring at the end of his long political career, "... the mission of my generation was to win self-government for Jamaica, to win political power which is the final power for the black masses of my country from which I spring."

Independent Jamaica has continued the talawa tradition of its early days and can now be considered as the 'fastest' country in the world. Whether the secret to Jamaican sprint speed lies in the humble yam, as some have speculated, or even in the cross-country dashes of the Maroons, there's no doubt that every world-class sprinter is now getting accustomed to watching the back of the green, yellow and black vest bolting in front. The mighty Usain, who has all the performance brio of a dancehall don on and off the track, comes from a noble lineage of great Jamaican athletes: Herb Mckinley, Lennox 'Billy' Miller, Don Quarrie, Merlene Ottey, Veronica Campbell and Asafa Powell. It seems likely that Jamaicans' response to historical and geographical conditions, their 'lived environment', has gifted them not only in athletics but also in many other sporting fields. There have been world champion boxers (including middle weight Mike McCallum in 1984; heavyweight Trevor Burbick in 1986) and many cricketers who have brought grace, power, devastating fast bowling, hard hitting and acrobatic fielding, to pitches across the globe. From

George Headley (the 'Black Bradman') to 'Whispering Death' Michael Holding, Courtney Walsh and current master blaster Chris Gayle, Jamaican cricketers are a force to be reckoned with.

Even more than sports, culture and especially music have put independent Jamaica on the world map. While dancehall now dominates island airwaves, it is its older relative, reggae, which introduced 'the island in the sun' to a global audience. From the Sahara Desert to the Himalayas, reggae has become a lingua franca, spawning Latin American, African and even Japanese versions. Many superb musicians (Roland Alphonso, Tommy McCook, Jackie Mittoo, Don Drummond, Ernest Ranglin, to mention just a handful) were instrumental in developing reggae's antecedent – the fast skanking ska, but by the time the tempo slowed into rocksteady and then the bass-locked offbeat of classic roots reggae, one man scaled the deprivations of Kingston's notorious Trenchtown slum to carry a universal message of 'One Love' to the world. The Honourable Robert 'Bob' Nesta Marley popularised not only reggae but also Jamaica's indigenous Rastafari religion, so that the 'red, gold and green' is now more readily recognised than many national flags.

Although music has tended to eclipse the other arts in terms of popularity and exposure, Jamaica has consistently made sterling contributions in literature, drama and the visual arts. From early twentieth century figures like Claude McKay (a prominent member of the Harlem Renaissance) and H.G. De Lisser, to pre and post Independence writers Una Marson, Vic Reid, Roger Mais, Orlando Patterson, Andrew Salkey, Sylvia Wynter, Louise Bennett-Coverly, playwrights Dennis Scott and Trevor Rhone and contemporaries Olive Senior, Patricia Powell, Nalo Hopkinson and Kei

The red, gold and green colours of Rastafari, as displayed at the entrance to the Bob Marley museum, are now more readily recognised than many national flags. Photo: Jamaica Tourist Board

Miller, Jamaican writers have brought island and diasporic experience to a world audience. The Calabash Literary Festival, inaugurated in 2001, has also become an important showcase for regional writing and publishing.

It was the wife of one of the founding fathers of modern Jamaica who galvanised the visual arts. Norman Manley's wife Edna, was responsible for establishing the Jamaica School of Art (subsequently renamed in her honour) and encouraging the development of both mainstream and intuitive artists, with her own work, particularly in the fields of carving and sculpture. Thanks to her efforts the works of such artists as Albert Huie, Ralph Campbell, Osmond and Barrington Watson reached island and then international audiences.

Gifted with natural and man-made, ready-to-shoot film sets, Jamaica, since Independence, has developed a film and TV industry which is the envy of the English-speaking Caribbean. Perry Henzell's 1971 movie 'The Harder They Come' not only launched Jimmy Cliff as an international artiste but introduced Jamaica and its signature reggae music to the silver screens and imagination of the world. His nephew, Chris Browne, emulated Perry's success with his take on dancehall and ghetto reality with 'Third World Cop' and young filmmaker Alrick Brown walked away with the 2011 World Cinema Award at the prestigious Sundance Film Festival.

Fifty years on, little talawa Jamaica, is going strong. ∎

Out of many, one people

REX NETTLEFORD

Jamaica has long been described as the microcosm of Planet Earth. Never mind its efforts in the not so distant past to remind the world that it is far more than sun, sand and sea. "It is more than a beach – it is a country", wailed the advertisements addressing potential visitors. It indeed remains a country with a rich history, admittedly of severance and suffering but, above all, with the will and a demonstrated capacity for survival and beyond.

This, of course, is the result of the stream of 'rainbow' arrivals from Caucasian Europe, Black sub-Saharan Africa (largely West Africa), of Brown and Mongoloid mortals from India's Decan plateau and China's Cantonese Valley respectively. Still later came arrivals from the eastern Mediterranean. They all came over four centuries to perform a variety of functions which admittedly harboured dilemmas of difference. They ranged from royal administrators, adventurers and plantation owners to exploited labour (over two centuries the property of those who imported them) and indentured contract labourers when slave abolition resulted in an intense labour shortage. They were followed by entrepreneurial, eastern Mediterranean migrants who no doubt heard that Jamaica, already a brand name among many in the wider world, could offer a better and more tolerable life than they had at home.

Remarkably, the diversity of souls endowed with their varied cultures (involving language and art, diet and philosophy) challenged the polyglot hordes of transplanted peoples to shape appropriate designs for social living. It allowed them to mix, share, explore each other, 'cross-fertilise' and create a native-born, native-bred Jamaican sense and sensibility which is now the common heritage of all, whether he or she is of Caucasian stock, of African, East Indian, Chinese and Lebanese ancestry or is of the several ethnic mixtures that all together bring texture and cross-fertilised dynamism to Jamaica's population.

In many ways, all this matches the very diverse and kaleidoscopic splendour of the natural landscape, not only with respect to the flora but also the variety of soil structures, mountain ranges, undulating hillocks, cockscomb hills, valleys, streams, springs, rivers and the surrounding – sometimes raging, sometimes calm and still – Caribbean Sea. The beauty is no absolute guarantee for a problem-free existence. Natural disasters have frequent enough visitations, and social disorders, as are evident everywhere else on earth, threaten to negate the oft-repeated invocation, "Jamaica, No Problem".

Temperaments are, indeed, as varied. Stiff upper-lip Anglo-Saxon attitudes vie with ebullient, high spirited and, just as easily, cool-tempered supposedly African traits. Alongside these, inscrutable Asian (Indian and Chinese) calm co-exists with intertextual relish to produce a multi-layered, multifaceted, contrary and contradictory aggregation of souls. Electoral inflammability sometimes places Jamaica's enduringly promising parliamentary democratic governance on edge. The seeming unpredictability is nonetheless fascinating.

All great civilisations, it is said, are the result of cross-fertilisation. And contemporary Jamaica represents the cross-fertilisation of Europe, Africa, Asia and the eastern Mediterranean along with the original Native American settlers (Tainos) on foreign soil. They are therefore responsible for Jamaica's cultural diversity, richness and energy. ▷

FACING PAGE: Basic School graduation ceremony at Comfort Castle Seventh-Day Adventist church.

RIGHT: Blue Mountain Coffee 'higgler' in Port Antonio. Photos: Josh Hunter

CLOCKWISE FROM TOP: Jack Sprat's Record Shop & Restaurant in Treasure Beach. Photo: Josh Hunter

Shy pose from a six-year-old. Photo: Josh Hunter

Official opening of Parliament. Photo: Brian Rosen

Maroon farmer in Moore Town. Photo: Josh Hunter

FACING PAGE, TOP: A game of dominoes against a backdrop of the John Crow and Blue Mountains. Photo: Josh Hunter

FACING PAGE, BOTTOM: Sisters in Port Maria. Photo: Andrew P. Smith

These traits are evident in the music, dance, visual and culinary art and the sense of style of the ordinary people who offer the world and themselves a rainbow crew not only of artists, sports persons (in track and field, cricket and soccer), but also of Westminster-style political leaders, well educated academics and highly trained professionals, all individually and collectively descendants of their many different ancestors.

If Europe with its plenitude of cultural traits ranging from Anglo-Saxon governance through Celtic (Welsh and Scots) vitality and Sephardic Jewish ancestral musings are evident, Africa surviving the Middle Passage gives its musical and performance arts, its religious animism, its innate distaste for racial oppression and its sense of community, while India strengthens the encounters with its Hindu and Muslim customs (culinary, festive and philosophical), while China sends its concentration on discipline and hard work matched by a not dissimilar Levantine contribution seen among the "Syrians".

Such are the regulative principles which underlie the inescapable changes that come with the now "globalised" world and the onslaught of the electronic communications technology revolution exported by North America through its newscasts, talk-shows and entertainment programmes, albeit reconfigured, re-interpreted and duly adapted by the mass of the population to their own liking.

The encounters through mutual engagement, compliance and resistance, collaboration and confrontation, irreverent wit and screw-face solemnity have produced distinctive Jamaican elements of social and cultural significance evident in the language that most Jamaicans speak most of the time along with Standard English, religion (complete with saints and sinners, the sacred and the profane, good and evil, God and the Devil), kinship patterns celebrating the offspring of parents with and without the benefit of confetti, artistic manifestations (traditional, contemporary and classic) and a delicately balanced sense and sensibility.

So 'Jamaica Talk', greatly influenced by the Standard English lexicon and African (Akan) grammar and structure, has come to be rated as one of the major Creole tongues of the Western Hemisphere. Zion Revivalism, pukkumina (Pocomania) and convince cult are variants of the 'syncretised' religious expressions resulting from the mix of Christian liturgy and African ritual preserved as such in Kumina, the kikongo rite, followed more recently by Rastafari, which innovatively draws on the Old Testament and on the Judaic theological trajectory of Scattering, Exile ▷

and Return on the road to redemption in the quest for social justice, freedom and human dignity which Christian Orthodoxy, inherited from a colonising Europe, failed to deliver. Kinship involving the mutual caring among cousins many times removed or non-consanguineous adoption, without the benefit of formal legal sanction, assures the ideal of family cohesion, the brotherhood of Man and the application of caring and compassion especially among Jamaican women, the culture bearers, whatever their class, race or creed.

The arts draw on the ancestral sources of Africa, Europe and Asia to produce music, dance, theatre, drama and choral theatre of world class rather than as exotica, as some would mistakenly see it. Jamaican popular music, from mento through ska and rocksteady to reggae and dancehall, has produced the likes of Bob Marley, Jimmy Cliff, Peter Tosh and Toots Hibbert, with Beenie Man and Buju Banton, among others, of more recent vintage. They can all boast an extensive global reach and are all the beneficiaries of the confluence of many traditions and cultures which spawned them and brought a uniqueness to Jamaica.

The various arrivals have done another thing which again fuels the artistic outpourings of the society. If the phenomenon gave to the southern Caribbean the pre-Lenten Carnival (now a post-Lenten Easter feature in Jamaica's calendar), it gave to Jamaica, from as far back as the early 19th century, the jonkonnu (or masquerade), where European revels interact with African masquerade at Christmas time to produce a distinctively Jamaican festival. It has variations which continue to find expression in dance and musical theatre and in the cultural programmes of post-Independence Jamaica.

Meanwhile, the (East) Indians have made a significant contribution in the festival art of Hosay – the Mohammedan celebration entered into with gusto by both Hindu and Christian Jamaicans with African-Jamaicans doing the drumming while the Indians do the dancing.

Such is the result of the cross-fertilisation in the limited space shared by the different arrivals over time. Everyone is, after all, part of everyone else regardless of race, colour, class, creed or political persuasion. This, however, is not to deny the persistence of differences among Jamaicans. But greater than those differences is the proven capacity to deal creatively and positively with the dilemma such differences engender, thus making utterly true and incontrovertible the saying that all Jamaicans are part-African, part-European, part-Asian, part-Native American, while being absolutely Jamaican.

CLOCKWISE FROM TOP: Sentries standing guard at National Heroes Park. Photo: Tony Matthews

A welcoming smile in St Thomas. Photo: Andrew P. Smith

A moment of distraction in Long Bay. Photo: Josh Hunter

Pots and pans to go! Photo: Tony Matthews

FACING PAGE: Early morning in Falmouth. Photo: Josh Hunter

CLOCKWISE FROM TOP: Fort Charles in Port Royal. Photo: Tony Matthews

Ward Theatre. Photo: Tony Matthews

Coke Memorial Methodist Church. Photo: Tony Matthews

Synagogue in Kingston. Photo: Andrew P. Smith

FACING PAGE, TOP: Jetty with an international flavour. Photo: Brian Rosen

FACING PAGE, BOTTOM: Trident Castle is one of the largest private homes in the Caribbean. Photo: Josh Hunter

CLOCKWISE FROM TOP: A refreshing plunge into Kingston Harbour. Photo: Arif Ali

Hindu mandir in Kingston. Photo: Tony Matthews

A typical fishing village. Photo: Tony Matthews

Schoolgirls in St Thomas. Photo: Andrew P. Smith

FACING PAGE: Local community in the Rio Grande valley in Portland. Photo: Josh Hunter

Culture

FAE ELLINGTON

Q uaint yet cosmopolitan, this is Jamaica; Absolutely! It is a society of mesmeric cultural contradictions. From Bob Marley's social and revolutionary commentary pulsating, to the hypnotic reggae beat to the penetrative ancestral counter-rhythms of the traditional dances of Kumina or Dinki Mini. It's mento, the original folk music with lyrics that tackle the most taboo subjects. Jamaica is Usain Bolt setting the 'Bird's Nest' at the 2008 Beijing Olympics on fire. She is sweaty school children racing along an unpaved road, shoes in hand, to see who's first to get to the mango tree. Jamaica is Rum, Red Stripe beer, Blue Mountain coffee and jerk. She is racy, sexually

---

FACING PAGE: Jamaica is the birthplace of the Rastafarian culture. Photo: Josh Hunter

BELOW: It is claimed that Jamaica has the largest number of churches per sq mile. Photo: Brian Rosen

explicit dancehall lyrics rattling your brains at five o'clock on a Sunday morning as pious looking women with weary looks of disapproval ready themselves and their children for church.

'Towards Jamaica the Cultural Superstate', that's the stated vision of the National Cultural Policy of Jamaica. This document was adopted by Cabinet in 2003. In addition, the Planning Institute of Jamaica's Vision 2030 Jamaica National Development Plan puts culture, or the creative industries, at the top of the capital stocks of a nation on a new model for Jamaica's road to prosperity.

Jamaica's population is close to 2.7 million. Just over 90 per cent of Jamaicans are of African descent. The national motto "Out of Many, One People" captures Jamaica's diverse cultural heritage with influences of the Spanish, British, Chinese, Indian, Lebanese, Syrian, Irish, German, Scottish and Welsh to name the dominant ethnic groups. It is this cultural cocktail that defines Jamaican uniqueness.

RELIGION

It is said that Jamaica has the largest number of churches per square mile. The predominant religion is Christianity in its various interpretations. From the Eurocentric traditional expressions to the home grown revivalist or pocomania groups with the palpable African influences. Every religion is represented on this small island. But perhaps the religion or ideology that has both captured and intrigued Jamaicans and non-Jamaican alike would be that of Rastafari. It is a potent force expressed through music, food, fashion and language. The colours of Rastafari are also big business the world over. ▷

FOOD AND DRINK

Jerk is synonymous with Jamaica. It's a well-guarded secret combination of seasonings and spices with the trademark scotch bonnet pepper. Just about anything can be jerked: chicken, fish, pork, and shrimp. Jerk is relatively new but Blue Mountain coffee, rum and Red Stripe beer blazed the trail decades before.

The national dish is a curious pairing of codfish imported originally from Newfoundland with the national fruit, ackee - brought from West Africa. Having a meal of ackee and saltfish with roasted breadfruit – brought to the island from Tahiti by English sea Captain William Bligh; boiled bananas, fried plantains – both brought from the Canary Islands by the Spaniards; bammie – made from cassava a staple of the Tainos – Jamaica's native people; escoveitched fish – a way of pickling fish introduced by the Spanish; steamed callaloo (Jamaica's spinach) - with a cup of Blue Mountain Coffee is the stuff of which paradise is made. If you visit at Christmastime do ask for a glass of sorrel. Be sure to say with or without rum. Our natural fruit juices are to die for – soursop, papaya, guava, garden cherry, mango and tamarind, just to name a few. Coconut water is a must so too (sugar) cane juice.

Vegetarian? Then the Rastafarian Ital stew is just for you. A rich stew of beans and vegetables seasoned with fresh garden herbs and simmered in coconut milk. Or you may want to try our pepper-pot soup made from callaloo or that finger-licking turn cornmeal (polenta).

We boast some of the best Indian and Chinese restaurants. Our gourmet restaurants are world renowned.

Jerk chicken is synonymous with Jamaica. Photo: Brian Rosen

Carnival is a mass of socalypso, colour and rhythm. Photo: Andrew P. Smith

FESTIVALS AND CELEBRATIONS

Many folk songs depict the social and political conditions that laid the foundation for Jamaica's celebrations. The Bruckins Party with their dance and Jubilee song were performed to celebrate the anniversary of Emancipation and the ultimate Abolition of slavery, 1838. Queen Victoria was the reigning sovereign then. "Augus mawnin come again. Dis is di year of Jubilee'. Queen Victoria gi (set) wi free."

Jamaica is home to several music and food festivals. Reggae Sunsplash (now defunct) and Sumfest are known for their widespread international appeal. Jamaica Carnival is a mass of socalypso colour and rhythm imported from the Eastern Caribbean. East Fest and Rebel Salute showcase popular reggae and dancehall acts. The Jazz and Blues Festival staged in Montego Bay attracts foreign and local acts so does the Ocho Rios Jazz Festival staged in mid June each year. Kingston on the Edge is a relatively new arts festival (2009 the 3rd year) held at end of June into the first few days of July.

The Jamaica Cultural Development Commission, (JCDC) started in 1963 the year after Jamaica gained her Independence, as the Jamaica Festival Commission. This agency has played a significant role in helping Jamaica preserve its national identity and cultural heritage in a world that morphs cultures and distinctiveness. Its mission is "To enhance national development through cultural practices by creating opportunities that unearth, develop, preserve and promote creative talents and expressions of the Jamaican people."

The JCDC partners with schools, communities, individuals and corporate Jamaica in the planning and facilitating of year-long training workshops, running competitions and staging events in traditional folk forms, dance, music, culinary arts, speech and drama, the fine arts, photography and the literary arts.

The Calabash Literary Festival first staged in 2001 at Treasure Beach on the island's South coast during the final weekend of May features local and international writers. This is an adult festival that is free to patrons. Established and new writers read excerpts of their work: Beverly Anderson Manley, broadcaster and former wife of Michael Manley, former Prime Minister Edward Seaga, novelist Anthony Winkler, Nobel Laureate Derek Walcott, Stacy Ann Chin and internationally acclaimed poet Lorna Goodison are just a few who have participated. Festival organisers are Colin Channer, Kwame Dawes and Justine Henzel.

The Chinese community celebrate Chinese New Year and the Indians stage the traditional Hosay festival. There are annual craft, agricultural, horticultural and orchid shows.

FOOD FESTIVALS

The food festivals are usually identified with specific parishes. There is the Trelawny Yam festival (birth parish of Usain Bolt), Portland Jerk Festival (home of the famous Boston Jerk), Little Ochi Seafood carnival in Manchester, Hanover and St Mary host Breadfruit festivals. There are seafood festivals; a Curry Festival in Westmoreland; and the Banana Festival in St Mary and Hanover.

CUSTOMS

Jamaica is a nation of customs. Here are a few. At the family and community levels Jamaicans celebrate weddings and deaths rather elaborately. 'Wake', 'Set-up', 'Ni-night', 'Singing' are occasions used to bring cheer to the family of the deceased. These often occur every night between death and the burial, going on for upwards of a week at times. The old hymn-singing has given way to thumping sound systems blaring, the latest local music, predominantly dancehall. It's a party atmosphere with, domino playing, liquor drinking, dancing, noisy chatter and laughter. Some inner-city urban funerals of community folk heroes are a display of ornate caskets and dancehall fashions.

At Easter Jamaicans eat Bun (sweet dough with raisons, currants, cherries) and cheese and fried fish. Christmas pudding and cake made of fruit and rum is standard in most Jamaican homes. ▷

BELOW: The burial of a deceased relative or friend often heralds a week-long series of events which aim to bring cheer to the bereaved. Photo: Josh Hunter

THEATRE ARTS

Theatre in Jamaica has a rich heritage. You might be surprised to know that 'When theatres reopened in the United States after the War of Independence (1775- 1783) the best advertisement for a play opening in New York was that it had just had a successful run in Jamaica' (Louis Marriott). Most productions take place in the capital city Kingston. Many productions tour the island's major towns. Several are taken to Jamaicans in the diaspora in the USA, Canada, England, and throughout the Caribbean. There are usually between four and six plays from which you can choose.

Jamaica boasts several awarding winning choirs and folk groups. Groups participate in competitions at home and abroad. There is a television competition for high school choirs, which is keenly contested and supported. The Carifolk Singers formed in 1973 was awarded one gold and two silver medals at the inaugural Choir Olympics held in Linz, Austria, in the year 2000, a feat that was repeated at the third choir Olympics in Germany in 2004. The Jamaican Folk Singers, The University Singers, (UWI) the internationally acclaimed National Dance Theatre Company singers are not to be missed.

DANCE COMPANIES

The National Dance Theatre Company (NDTC) formerly led by founder, academician and cultural icon Professor Rex Nettleford (died 2 February 2010) is the most well known. Movements Dance Company, L'Acadco, the Company Dance Theatre and Xaymaca are other well-established groups. There are annual company seasons. Jamaicans dance just about anywhere, even in church!

NATIONAL DRESS

Jamaica's national dress! Now here's a predicament. The 21st century Jamaican has 'colours': The black, green and gold, the colours in our National Flag which signify 'brand Jamaica'. These colours are also the trademark of our outstanding track and field athletes and our Reggae Boyz footballers.

The 'Ites' (red), green and gold of Rastafari are powerful emotional signifiers and identifiers. But the 'official' national fabric is the 'bandana'; a red, blue, yellow and white plaid. Author extraordinaire and social commentator Louise Bennett Coverley is credited with popularising the bandana, Jamaica's national fabric.

Some Jamaicans still refer to the national fabric as 'market cloth'. It was used mainly by market women as 'head ties' and aprons and by some revivalist religious groups as an essential part of their headgear. Groups such as the Jamaican Folk Singers and the National Dance Theatre Company (NDTC) have used the bandana for costumes.

It is also a staple for the annual festival of the performing arts organised by the Jamaica Cultural Development Commission (JCDC).

Our representatives in local and international beauty contests, Miss World and Miss Universe have over the years worn gowns made of bandana combined with other fabrics and colours depicting the ethos of the people.

The bandana originally from Madraspatnam, India, is sometimes called 'Madras'. It is not manufactured in Jamaica. It is imported from India or China. Intriguing…that's Jamaica!

JAMAICAN LANGUAGE

Jamaica is a bi-lingual society. English is Jamaica's official language but it is not the first language or native tongue. 'Jamaican', 'Jamaica Talk' or 'Patwa' is our lingua franca. The Jamaican language is influenced primarily by African languages. It is not English, nor is it a corruption of English.

The best-known proponent of the Jamaican language, Louise 'Miss Lou' Bennett Coverley, gives her perspective of Jamaican as a corruption of English. "For if dat be de case, den dem shoulda call English Language corruption of Norman French an Latin an all dem tarra language what dem seh dat English is derived from."

The language has been immortalised in our popular music – reggae and dancehall, our dub poetry, our playwrights and poets, some broadcast announcers and disc jockeys. Jamaican is much more than "Irie; Yeah Man; No problem!"

'Jamaican' is an oral language. Very few persons are able to write and read it. Many attempts at writing Jamaican result in words being spelt the English way. This shouldn't be, because back in 1961, Jamaican linguist Frederic Cassidy developed a method of writing our language. In June 2009 Di Jamiekan Langwij Unit (The Jamaica Language Unit) Department of Language, Linguistics & Philosophy, Faculty of Humanities at the University of the West Indies, (UWI) Mona launched the book and CD, *Ou fi Rait Jamiekan: Writing Jamaican the Jamaican Way*. You may wish to pick up a copy.

In England translators of 'Jamaican' are often needed to assist with immigration and court cases involving Jamaicans.

It's the rhythm; it's the taste. It's the colours; it's the place. It's the people: It's the Culture. Jamaica: Absolutely! "Once you go, you know." ∎

Facts & Figures

Full Name: Jamaica
Capital: Kingston (pop. 660,000)
Area: 10,991 sq km (4,243 sq miles)
Location: Jamaica is the third largest island in the Caribbean region and is one of the four main islands that comprise the Greater Antilles group of islands. Its two closest neighbours are Cuba (approx. 90 miles to the north) and Haiti (approx. 115 miles to the east)

Nationality: Jamaican(s)
Population: 2.7 million (UN, 2005 est.)
People: African origin 90.9%, East Indian origin 1.3%, Chinese origin 0.2%, White 0.2%, Mixed 7.3%, Other 0.1%
Language: English, Patois
Religion(s): Roman Catholic, Anglican, Baptist and other Protestant, Seventh Day Adventist, Rastafarian, Jewish, Muslim, Hindu, Bahai
Life Expectancy: 71.5 male; 75 female (2006 est.)

Government: Constitutional, Westminster-style, parliamentary democracy
Main Political Parties
Jamaica Labour Party (JLP)
People's National Party (PNP)
National Democratic Movement (NDM)
Head of State: HM Queen Elizabeth II, represented by the Governor-General, HE The Most Hon. Sir Patrick Allen
Prime Minister: The Most Hon. Portia Simpson Miller
Administrative Divisions (14 Parishes):
Hanover, Saint Elizabeth, Saint James, Trelawny, Westmoreland, Clarendon, Manchester, Saint Ann, Saint Catherine, Saint Mary, Kingston, Portland, Saint Andrew, Saint Thomas

Currency: Jamaican Dollar (JMD)
Exchange Rates (July 2009): US $1 = JMD $88; GBP £1 = JMD $142; EUR 1 = JMD $123
GDP: US $9.86 billion (IMF, 2006)
GNI per capita: US $4,600 (2006 est.)
Labour Force: total 1.1 million (2006); services 64.6%; agriculture 18.1%; industry 17.3%

MAIN ECONOMIC SECTORS
INDUSTRY: tourism, bauxite/alumina, agro processing, light manufacturing, rum, cement, metal, paper, chemical products, telecommunications
AGRICULTURE: sugarcane, bananas, coffee, citrus, yams, ackees, vegetables, poultry, goats, milk, crustaceans, molluscs

Exports: US $2 billion (2006 est.)
MAIN EXPORTS
Alumina, bauxite, sugar, bananas, rum, coffee, yams, beverages, chemicals, clothing, mineral fuels
EXPORT PARTNERS
US 25.8%, Canada 19.3%, UK 10.7%, Netherlands 8.6%, China 7%, Norway 6.4%, Germany 5.6% (2005)

Imports: US $4.6 billion (2006 est.)
MAIN IMPORTS
Food and other consumer goods, industrial supplies, fuel, parts and accessories for capital goods, machinery and transport equipment, construction materials
IMPORT PARTNERS
US 41.4%, Trinidad and Tobago 14%, Venezuela 5.5%, Japan 4.6% (2005)

Participation with International Organisations
African, Caribbean and Pacific Group of States (ACP), CARICOM, Caribbean Development Bank (CDB), Commonwealth, Food and Agriculture Organisation (FAO), G-15, G-77, Inter-American Development Bank (IADB), International Agricultural Exchange Association (IAEA), IBRD, ICAO, International Criminal Court (ICC), ICRM, International Fund for Agricultural Development (IFAD), IFC, IFRCS, IHO, ILO, IMF, International Maritime Organisation (IMO), Interpol, International Olympic Committee (IOC), IOM, ISO, International Telecommunications Union (ITU), LAES, MIGA, NAM, Organisation of American States (OAS), OPANAL, OPCW, United Nations (UN), UN Conference on Trade & Development (UNCTAD), UNESCO, UN

Industrial Development Organisation (UNIDO), UN World Trade Organisation (UNWTO), Universal Postal Union (UPU), WCO, WFTU, World Health Organisation (WHO), WIPO, WMO

MEDIA
PRESS: The Gleaner, The Sunday Gleaner, The Star, Daily Observer, Observer on Sunday, Weekend Mirror, The Western Mirror, Xtra News
RADIO: Hot 102 FM, Irie FM, Klas Sports Radio, Kool 97 FM, Love 101, Megajamz 98 FM, Nationwide News Network, News Talk 93 FM, Power 106 FM, Radio Jamaica, Zip 103 FM
TELEVISION: Cable News & Sports, CVM TV, Hype TV, Love TV, Reggae Sun TV, RETV, Sportsmax, Television Jamaica (TVJ), Tempo

PUBLIC HOLIDAYS
New Year's Day
Ash Wednesday
Good Friday
Easter Monday
Labour Day – 23rd May
Emancipation Day – 1st August
Independence Day – 6th August
National Heroes Day – mid-October
Christmas Day
Boxing Day

SPECIAL EVENTS
Maroon Celebrations – January
Rebel Salute – January
Jamaica Jazz & Blues Festival – January
National Prayer Breakfast – 3rd week of January
Holocaust Memorial Day – January
Chinese New Year – January/February
Black History Month – February
Reggae Month – February
Reggae Village – February
Bob Marley's Birthday – 6th February
Annual Bob Marley Lecture – February
Bob Marley Week – February
Marcus Garvey Event – February
Africa Unite – Smile Jamaica – February
Reggae Film Festival – February
Birthday of Sir Alexander Bustamante, National Hero – February
Jamaica Reggae Music Awards – February
White Cane Month – March
Edna Manley's Birthday – March
Commonwealth Day – 2nd Monday of March
International Day for the Commemoration of the Anniversary of the Abolition of the Trans-Atlantic Slave Trade – March
Carnival – March/April
Trelawny Yam Festival – April
Jamaica Horticultural Society Annual Flower Show – April
Calabash Literary Festival – May
Indian Heritage Day – May
Mothers' Day – 2nd Sunday of May
Children's Day (Jamaica) – May
Labour Day – May
Ocho Rios Jazz & Blues Festival – June
Diaspora Day – June
Fathers' Day – 3rd Sunday of June
Birthday of Norman Manley, National Hero – 4th July
Portland Jerk Festival – July
Reggae SumFest – July
Caricom Day – July
Emancipation Day – 1st August
Independence Day – 6th August
Birthday of Marcus Garvey, National Hero – 17th August
International Day for the Remembrance of the Slave Trade and its Abolition – 23rd August
Indigence Celebrations – August
Birthday of Louise "Miss Lou" Bennett Coverley – 7th September
Maritime Week – September
Heritage Month – October
National Heritage Week – October
National Heroes Day – 20th October
Kingston and Negril Restaurant Week – November
Eat Across Jamaica Day – 25th November
Kumba Mi Yaba – December
Reggae Marathon – December
Fireworks on the Waterfront – 31st December

IMPORTANT DATES
Independence from Britain – 6th August 1962
Joined the Commonwealth in 1962

National Flower: Lignum Vitae (Guiacum officinale)
National Bird: The Doctor Bird (Trochilus polytmus) or Swallowtail Hummingbird
National Fruit: Ackee (Blighia sapida)
National Tree: The Blue Mahoe (Hibiscus elatus)
National Motto: "Out of Many, One People"
Time Zone: GMT -5 hours
Highest Point: Blue Mountain Peak (2,256 m / 7445 ft)
Internet Country Code: .jm
International Dialling Code: 1-876

National Symbols

Lignum vitae was found in Jamaica by Christopher Columbus. Its name, when translated from Latin, means "wood of life" – probably adopted because of its medicinal qualities. The short, compact tree is native to continental tropical America and the West Indies. In Jamaica it grows best in the dry woodland along the north and south coasts of the island.

The plant produces an attractive blue flower and orange-yellow fruit, while its crown has an attractive rounded shape. The tree is one of the most useful in the world. The body, gum, bark, fruit, leaves and blossom all serve some useful purpose. In fact, the tree has been regarded for its medicinal properties. A gum (gum guaiac) obtained from its resin was once regarded as a purgative. It was exported to Europe from the early sixteenth century as a remedy (combined with mercury) for syphilis and has also been used as a remedy for gout.

The wood was once used as propeller shaft bearings in nearly all the ships sailing the 'Seven Seas'. Because of this, lignum vitae and Jamaica are closely associated with shipyards worldwide. It is a very heavy wood which will sink in water. Because of its toughness it is used for items such as mortars, mallets, pulleys and batons carried by policemen. It is sometimes used in the manufacture of furniture.

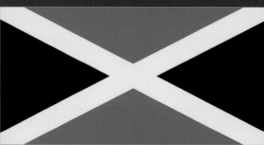

NATIONAL FLAG

The Jamaica National Flag was designed by a bipartisan committee of the Jamaica House of Representatives and was first raised on Independence Day, 6th August 1962.

It consists of a diagonal cross in gold which, itself, creates four triangles – two in green and two in black. The symbolism of the flag invokes the phrase: "The sun shineth, the land is green and the people are strong and creative." Black depicts the strength and creativity of the people; gold reflects the natural wealth and beauty of sunlight; and green symbolises hope and the country's agricultural resources.

COAT OF ARMS

The Jamaican Coat of Arms carries the national motto, "Out of Many, One People", which is an affirmation of the multi-racial origins of the Jamaican people. Above the motto stand two figures: a male and female member of the Taino tribe. They are standing either side of a shield which bears a red cross upon which are five golden pineapples. A crest above the shield depicts a Jamaican crocodile mounted on top of a Royal Helmet and mantling of the British Monarchy.

BRIAN ROSEN

BRIAN ROSEN

NATIONAL BIRD (ABOVE)
DOCTOR BIRD (*TROCHILUS POLYTMUS*) OR SWALLOW TAIL HUMMINGBIRD

The doctor bird or swallow tail humming bird, is one of the most outstanding of the 320 species of hummingbird and lives only in Jamaica. Its iridescent colours and streamer-like tail make it a distinctive member of the hummingbird family.

The origins of the name 'doctor bird' are somewhat unsettled. One theory is that its erect black crest and tail resembled the top hat and tailcoats of early doctors. Another suggests that the name refers to the way the birds 'lance' the flowers with their bills to extract nectar.

NATIONAL FRUIT (RIGHT)
ACKEE (*BLIGHIA SAPIDA*)

Although the ackee is not indigenous to Jamaica, it has remarkable historic associations. Originally imported to the island from West Africa – probably on a slave ship – it now grows luxuriantly, producing large quantities of edible fruit each year.

The name is derived from the original name 'ankye' which comes from the Twi language of Ghana. The botanical name was given in honour of Captain William Bligh (notorious for the mutiny on the Bounty) who, in 1793, took the plant from Jamaica to England. Captain Bligh also brought the first breadfruit to Jamaica.

The ackee tree grows up to 50 ft in favourable conditions and bears large red and yellow fruit 3-4 in. long. When ripe these fruits burst into sections revealing shiny black round seeds on top of a yellow aril (flesh) which is partially edible. Jamaica is the only place where the fruit is widely eaten.

TONY MATTHEWS

NATIONAL TREE
BLUE MAHOE (*HIBISCUS ELATUS*)

The blue mahoe is indigenous to the island and grows quite rapidly, often attaining 20m (66 ft) or more in height. In wetter districts it will grow in a wide range of elevations, up to 1200m (4000 ft) and is often used in reforestation. It is an attractive tree with a straight trunk, broad green leaves and hibiscus-like flowers. The flowers change colour as it matures, going from bright yellow to orange red and finally to crimson.

The name 'mahoe' is derived from a Carib Indian word; the 'blue' refers to the blue-green streaks in the polished wood, giving it a distinctive appearance. It is considered so beautiful and durable that it is widely used for cabinet making and also for making decorative objects such as picture frames, bowls and carvings.

The inner bark of the tree is often referred to as 'Cuba bark' because it was formerly used for tying bundles of Havana cigars. Cuba is the only other place where the tree grows naturally.

NATIONAL ANTHEM (Above)

Eternal Father bless our land.
Guard us with Thy Mighty Hand.
Keep us free from evil powers,
Be our light through countless hours.
To our Leaders, Great Defender,
Grant true wisdom from above.
Justice truth be ours forever,
Jamaica, land we love.
Jamaica, Jamaica, Jamaica, land we love.

Teach us true respect for all.
Stir response to duty's call.
Strengthen us the weak to cherish,
Give us vision lest we perish.
Knowledge, send us heavenly Father,
Grant true wisdom from above.
Justice truth be ours forever,
Jamaica, land we love.
Jamaica, Jamaica, Jamaica, land we love.

NATIONAL PLEDGE

Before God and all mankind,
I pledge the love and loyalty of my heart,
The wisdom and courage of my mind,
The strength and vigour of my body,
In the service of my fellow citizens,
I promise to stand up for justice,
Brotherhood and peace,
To work diligently and creatively
To think generously and honestly,
So that, Jamaica may, under God,
Increase in beauty, fellowship
And prosperity and play her part
In advancing the welfare,
Of the whole human race.

NATIONAL SONG (Above)

I pledge my heart forever
To serve with humble pride
This shinning homeland, ever
So long as earth abide.

I pledge my heart this island
As God and faith shall live

My work, my strength, my love
And my loyalty to give

O green isle of the Indies,
Jamaica, strong and free,
Our vows and loyal promises,
O heartland, 'tis to thee

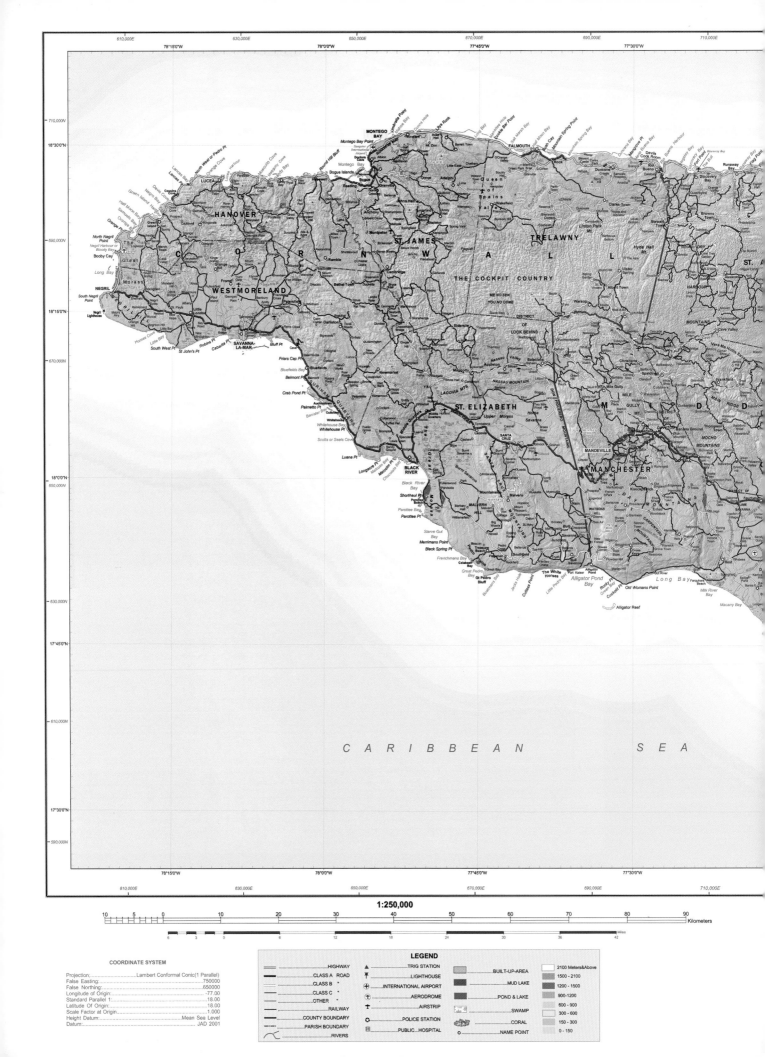

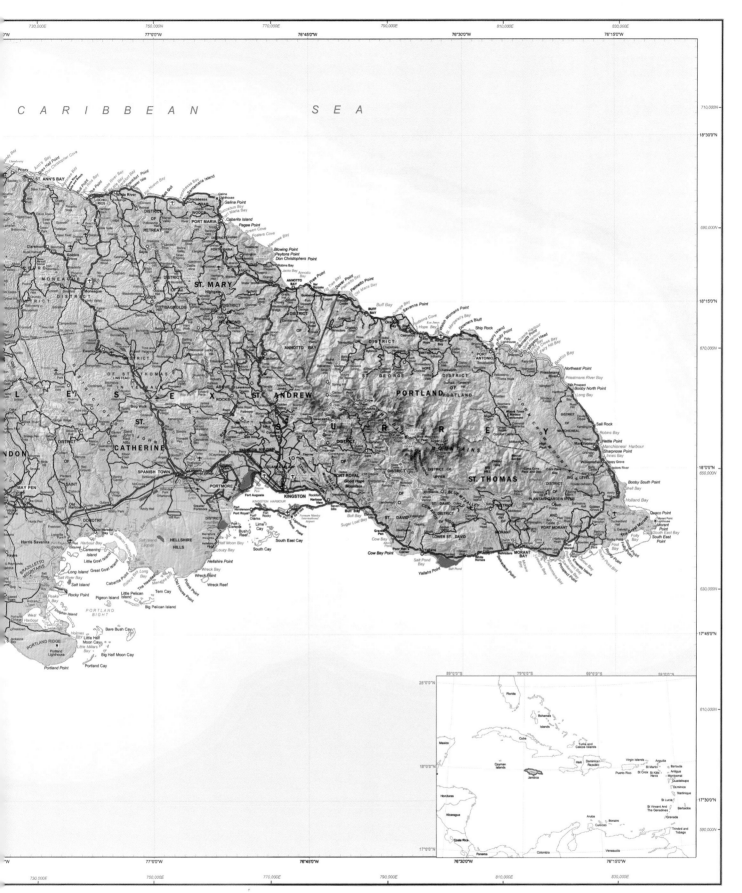

This Edition has been prepared by The Survey & Mapping Division of
The National Land Agency, 231/2 Charles Street Kingston, Jamaica W.I.
Compiled in 2007 by Digital method from the 1982 1:250,000 edition ,
1:50,000m(1992) map series, 2000 Ikonos and 2006-2007 Quick Bird images.

Jamaican history: 1400 years in the making

VERENE A. SHEPHERD

Jamaica has a rich and textured history that is often buried beneath its sand and sea and hidden behind its sunshine glow. A growing interest in heritage tourism, however, requires that we showcase this important past, so critical to our sense of identity and nationhood. The island has been home to many civilisations and ethnic groups: Africans, Ciboneys, Chinese, Europeans (including English, Germans, Irish, Scots, Spanish, Welsh); Indians, Jews, Lebanese/Syrians and Tainos. These groups have contributed to the island's multi-cultural and multi-religious reality, with a co-existence of Buddhists, Christians, Confucians, Hindus, Muslims, Rastafarians and people of no faith at all. Its earliest inhabitants were the Ciboneys and Tainos, the latter giving the island the name Xaymaca, later changed by Europeans to Jamaica.

The Ciboney were a nomadic shell culture which predated the Tainos. As hunter-gatherers, they developed no village life around agriculture and artisan technologies. The more numerous and technologically developed Taino dominated and enslaved the Ciboney as the latter were not organised for military activity.

The Taino, from the Arawakan language group (a reason they have been previously called 'Arawaks'), migrated northwards from the Guianas and Venezuela, reaching Jamaica somewhere between AD 600 and 900, with settlements stretching along the north coast from Priestman's River in the east of the island to Montego Bay and Negril in the west. They were a highly developed civilisation with standards of industrial technology in textiles and ceramics that were on par with the rural communities of Asia and Europe. They lived by trading, fishing, hunting and growing fruits and crops of sweet potato, tobacco, corn (maize) and cassava (yucca). The bammy, now loved by Jamaicans, was first made by the Tainos. The women also participated in weaving and craftwork.

Tainos lived in loosely structured family groups, with a separation of males and females. They were ruled by their local cacique (chief) who in turn came under the jurisdiction of a regional cacique.

CONQUEST, COLONISATION AND RESISTANCE

In May, 1494, the lives of Jamaica's first inhabitants were disrupted when Christopher Columbus and his crew, operating under the Spanish flag, invaded the island, landing off the north coast near the Taino village of Maima near Seville in St Ann, now one of the island's premier tourist parishes. Columbus returned nine years later and was shipwrecked and marooned on the island for just over a year with his base at Santa Gloria.

Contact between Taino and European invaders varied from peaceful to violent. Tolerance levels were severely tested during Columbus's more extended stay when the Tainos had to supply food beyond their means. Under Spanish occupation, Taino economic, social and political life was

RIGHT: Maroons waged wars against British domination and eventually won Treaty Rights in 1739/40.

Enslaved Africans were brutally herded throughout the plantations of Jamaica.

disrupted. Their caciques lost power and influence and they were subjected to forced labour, sexual exploitation and other abuses that eventually decimated their population.

Taino heritage, however, survived in the Maroons (many Tainos ran away to interior hideouts and later mixed with the former enslaved Africans) and in the artefacts they left behind.

Ownership of Jamaica fluctuated between Columbus and his heirs, and the Spanish crown between 1504 and 1655. The first Spanish Jamaican capital was at Seville in St Ann, but in 1534 shifted to Villa de la Vega in St Catherine, near present-day Spanish Town. As the island lacked mineral wealth, the Spanish developed its agricultural potential, establishing many hatos (cattle ranches) on the southern plains, planting some sugarcane for local sugar production, and growing tobacco, indigo, pimento, hardwoods, cotton, food crops and a variety of fruits and vegetables. Animals, animal products, food and cotton products were exported regionally as well as to Spain, though the infrequent shipping created trading problems for the colony.

ENGLISH INVASION

In 1655, Jamaica was seized from the Spanish colonisers by the English under an expedition led by Admiral William Penn and General Robert Venables. By then, the Spanish population had declined so considerably that fewer than 200 men defended Fort Caguaya, making conquest easy for the English.

By 1663, the island had established civil government. Gradually, the English (and later Irish, Scots and Welsh), developed a diversified economy in Jamaica, embarking on livestock farming and the cultivation of crops like cocoa, cotton, tobacco and indigo for export. By 1750, sugar had become the dominant export crop, but other crops continued to be planted on lands that were topographically unsuitable for sugarcane cultivation.

Coffee became a significant crop in the hilly regions of St Andrew. The cultivation in Jamaica expanded after the successful Haitian Revolution in 1791 as many planters fled Haiti with their enslaved Africans and established coffee plantations in Jamaica.

Livestock farming also continued to be important and by 1782 there were three hundred livestock 'pens' on the island. By 1832, Jamaica had 176 coffee plantations employing more than twenty-two thousand enslaved people, and fifteen pimento plantations employing nearly thirteen hundred enslaved workers. The labour force on the sugar plantations accounted for nearly half of the enslaved population and nearly fifteen per cent on the coffee plantations.

SUGAR AND SLAVERY

With no exploitable indigenous populations, English, Irish and Scottish indentured servants and later enslaved Africans formed the main labour force in Jamaica after 1655, especially for the expanding sugar industry.

▷

39

Historians differ on the numbers of Africans who were sold into slavery in the Americas and the Caribbean, although it is generally acknowledged that at least twelve million, and possibly up to twenty million, mostly male, Africans were traded. More than one million enslaved Africans were landed in Jamaica between 1519 and 1867. They were taken from many regions of West Africa, but largely from the Bight of Biafra, the Gold Coast, West-Central Africa, the Bight of Benin, Sierra Leone and Senegambia. The island, therefore, had a strong Igbo (Nigerian), Akan (Ghanaian) and Congo/Angola presence.

AFRICAN LABOUR

Enslaved Africans were used in all sectors of the economy in Jamaica: field labour, artisan labour, domestic labour; and they worked in both rural and urban locations. The enslaved worked on sugar estates as well as on pens and coffee plantations. In every case, enslaved females dominated the field gangs, working as hard as males.

Women, especially those of mixed-race, dominated the domestic arena, though it was not an exclusive female preserve. The managerial, supervisory and artisan fields were dominated by men (most mixed-race), a reflection of the patriarchal nature of society and the gender and race ideology of the day. When they were not working in the formal plantation sector, producing sugar and other commodities for developing the European economy, they cultivated their 'provision grounds' and reared animals, using the produce for their own subsistence, marketing the surplus.

CONTROL AND RESISTANCE

The brutality of plantation society, together with the sexual abuse of females, led to sustained resistance by enslaved Africans. Maroons like Cudjoe, Nanny and Queen Cubah waged wars against British domination and eventually won Treaty Rights in 1739/40. The treaty dictated that they had to promise to end all wars and to discontinue harbouring new runaways. Some kept the treaty, and some did not, and many other armed revolts erupted across the island. The most significant of these was the war led by chief Tacky in St Mary in 1760, the 1824 plot in Hanover, and the war led by Sam Sharpe in 1831/32. Sharpe and other rebels (whose names are inscribed on a monument in Montego Bay) were eventually captured and hanged.

Day-to-day non-violent strategies also undermined the plantation system. Activism combined with humanitarianism in Britain and local and international economic forces eventually led to the abolition of the slave trade in 1807 and of slavery itself in 1838, after a brief transitional Apprenticeship System from 1834 to 1838.

EMANCIPATION AND "FREE SOCIETY"

"Full Free" in 1838 did not end systems of domination. Anti-labour tactics caused the formerly enslaved Africans to leave the plantations. Some squatted on unoccupied land, rented or purchased land for peasant development. Where planters refused to sell land directly to Africans, the missionaries, like William Knibb and James Phillippo, acted as go-between, buying land and then re-selling it. Some of these lands were established as Free Villages, one of the earliest being Sligoville in St Catherine. Some freed people migrated to the urban centres and to countries like Cuba and Panama where wages were higher. The construction of the Panama Canal would not have been possible without thousands of Jamaican migrant labourers.

Intent on maintaining the plantation, the landholding class imported indentured labourers from Europe, Asia, North America and Africa to supplement the declining African-Jamaican labour force. This explains the importation of 'liberated' Africans, Chinese, Indians and a few Germans (associated with Seaford/German Town in Westmoreland), in the 19th century.

As the 20th century approached, Jamaicans also used education as a route to upward social mobility and higher-status occupations, thus distancing themselves further from the plantation past.

Indian indentured labourers gradually replaced Africans as the majority labour force, especially in Westmoreland, St Catherine, St Mary, St Thomas, Portland and Clarendon. Jamaica imported around 38,000 Indians between 1845 and 1916. Chinese indentured labourers, arriving since 1854, were fewer, and many of the Chinese opted out of plantation labour from very early on to establish themselves in the retail trade.

Despite the landholders' belief that contract labourers would be more controllable, Africans, Chinese and Indians resisted their status as exploited labourers using some of the same strategies as enslaved Africans.

A DISAFFECTED COLONIAL PEOPLE

Jamaican society was ruled by a white minority even after Emancipation. The Old Representative System of government represented mainly the propertied classes. The franchise was gradually

Indian indentured labourers replaced Africans as the majority labour force following the abolitiion of slavery.

lowered to enable more people to vote, but women and non-propertied men (most of whom were African) continued to be disenfranchised. Those in power still engaged in unfair governing practices, ignoring most of the economic, social and political claims of the masses. In 1865, for example, there was less than one in every 200 Jamaicans with the franchise, and all but a handful comprised Europeans. This and other factors determined that mass protest characterised the post-slavery period as it did the previous centuries.

One such protest was the Morant Bay Rebellion, caused by the limited franchise, agrarian distress, compounded by the economic impact of the American Civil War and an absence of broad-based democracy and local accountability by those in power. Paul Bogle of Stony Gut, one of George William Gordon's Black deacons in the Baptist church, led this protest on 11 October 1865. The protest was severely put down by Governor Edward Eyre, a former lieutenant-governor of New Zealand and a former governor of St Vincent. Almost 600 people were killed and as many flogged. The Commission of Enquiry, set up to investigate, concluded that the system of government in Jamaica was unworkable. Eyre was recalled and the Legislature was given a choice: give more people the right to vote or surrender the government to the Crown. They chose to surrender their political power, ushering in direct British/Crown Colony rule.

The imposition of Crown Colony government ushered in a further period of discontent and, predictably, an outright movement for decolonisation, despite several modifications to the Crown Colony system. Marcus Mosiah Garvey (1887-1940) was essential to the decolonisation movement in Jamaica. His Black Power ideology radicalised many, influencing Jamaicans to protest their colonial status, sneer at modifications to Crown Colony government and agitate for self-rule and eventually full independence.

Crown Colony rule was regarded as a wasteful, inefficient and discriminatory system which denied opportunities to the governed, stifled popular initiatives and was based on complete indifference to local public opinion. Others wanted the Caribbean to form itself into a close and unified political structure through federation as a pre-independence step.

THE FEDERAL INTERLUDE

The first conference on British West Indian Federation was held in Montego Bay in 1947. By a majority vote it accepted the principle of political federation and set up a Standing Closer Association Committee to study the possibility of federation and to draft a federal constitution. On 2 August 1956, the Parliament at Westminster passed the British Caribbean Act to establish a federal union between the ten territories. But the federation was not without its problems and eventually collapsed. Individual Caribbean ▷

governments had to accept the recommendation of the London Conferences. Jamaica, for example, suspected that federalism would delay its own progress towards self-government, hamper the development of new industries and force a reduction in its lucrative tariff. Nor did it welcome the idea of absorption in a national state which, at the outset, was less independent than Jamaica itself. The result was that when Norman Manley called for a referendum, the people of Jamaica voted against federation. Manley then resigned as leader of the West Indies Federal Labour Party and Jamaica subsequently withdrew its membership. Eric Williams responded to this by arguing that Jamaica's withdrawal was illegal, that the federation had consequently ceased to exist, and all that was left was a caretaker government; "One from ten left zero, not nine".

With the break-up of the federation, the British-ruled colonies began to move towards independence singly, and to agitate for internal autonomy. The decade of the 1930s had introduced a more radical note, manifested in a spate of labour protests. There was a new preoccupation with people's conditions. It was out of this that the trade union movement had been formed. Alexander Bustamante and A.G.S. Coombs, for example, had in 1934 formed the Jamaica Workers' and Tradesmen Union. Some of these unions became linked to political parties and supported the move to independence.

It should also be noted that returning Jamaicans who had emigrated in search of better conditions but who had been forced to repatriate by a downturn in the global economy in the 1930s, helped in the agitation for collective bargaining, an improvement in workers' conditions and self-government. Those who had contributed to Britain's efforts during the First and Second World Wars, and who had experienced discrimination in the "Mother Country", also helped to shape the anti-imperial struggles.

THE EMERGENCE OF POLITICAL PARTIES

Among the political parties formed in Jamaica to spearhead the struggle for peaceful constitutional changes that would eventually lead to self-government, were the Jamaican Political Reform Association (1921) and the People's Political Party (1929 under Marcus Garvey). Quasi-political parties were the Elected Members' Association (1935); the Federation of Citizens' Association (1935); the Jamaica Progressive League (1937, formed in New York by W. Adolphe Roberts with a branch established in Jamaica); and the Jamaica Democratic Party. All of these parties pressed for internal self-government.

LEFT TO RIGHT: Paul Bogle led the Morant bay Rebellion; Marcus Garvey was essential to the decolonisation movement in Jamaica.

After the achievement of Universal Adult Suffrage in 1944, the Jamaica Liberal Party, the United Rent Payers' Party, the Jamaica Radical Workers' Union and the J.A.G. Smith Party were formed. These were little more than party labels for independent candidates. In fact, 'Third Parties' have generally failed to thrive in Jamaica up to the present time.

The early 20th century saw two major political parties in Jamaica: the People's National Party (formed in 1938 and led by Norman Manley) and the Jamaica Labour Party (formed in 1943 and led by Alexander Bustamante). These were both linked to trade unions (first to the Trade Union Congress and then to the National Workers' Union in the case of the PNP, and the Bustamante Industrial Trade Union, BITU, in the case of the JLP), indicating that they had emerged out of working class militancy in the 1930s. The PNP, under Manley's leadership, struggled against reactionary plantocracy and against the colonial power and advocated full self-government. The Jamaica Progressive League became a 'co-operative affiliate' of the PNP. The struggle of the JLP and the PNP over constitutional changes for Jamaica was eventually able to slowly foster the general idea of a Jamaican national consciousness. The end result of this struggle was the achievement of universal adult suffrage and independence on 6 August 1962. In the first national elections after the achievement of adult suffrage in 1944, the JLP won 22 seats, the PNP won five, and independents won five.

The Jamaica Labour Party remained in power until 1972, though not under Bustamante after 1967. Donald Sangster was Prime Minister in 1967 and Hugh Shearer, who took over after Sangster died, from 1967-1972. The JLP lost the 1972 elections to the PNP's Michael Manley (1924-1997), son of Norman Manley and Edna Manley. The PNP remained in power until 1980 at which time the JLP again came to power under Edward Seaga. The JLP was defeated by the PNP once again in 1989. Percival Patterson succeeded Michael

Manley in 1992 after ill-health forced Manley to give up the reigns of power. The PNP of the 1980s, however, espoused a different political ideology, moving away from the democratic socialist policies of the 1970s. After more than eighteen years in power, the PNP lost to the JLP in the 2007 elections.

The independent nation also joined the United Nations and the Organisation of American States and attempted to forge regional unity with other independent and non-independent territories through CARIFTA (Caribbean Free Trade Association) and CARICOM (Caribbean Common Market and Community) to resolve problems of a regional nature. The Caribbean territories have still not resolved issues such as freedom of travel, work permits and competitive international relations. Nevertheless, CARICOM has survived with new members from the non-English-speaking territories like Haiti and Suriname being admitted, and with renewed resolve to see that the newest regional initiative, the CSME, succeeds. Regionalism is also expressed through the University of the West Indies and the West Indies Cricket Team.

DECOLONISATION AND HERITAGE

As an independent nation with a multi-ethnic population, Jamaica has embarked on a process of forging national unity through encouraging appreciation and respect for all cultures. But some insist on playing the ranking game, elevating those with lighter skin shades above black-skinned people, privileging English over Jamaican, and 'dissing' dancehall, gerreh, dinki-mini and Kumina – all expressions of people with connections to Africa, who form the majority ethnic group of the country's 2.7 million population.

The lower economic status of African-descended people when compared to that of Chinese, Indian, European, Jewish and Lebanese/Syrian descent (who dominate the retail trade and the commercial and industrial sectors) often creates tensions. There is also some intolerance of Rastafari (a social movement and religious ideology made popular by Leonard Howell and others in the 1930s), despite the outstanding contribution to the island's economic and cultural development through the creative work of its adherents, among them Bob Marley, Buju Banton, Capleton, Luciano, Queen Ifrika, the I-Threes, Etana and Mutabaruka. But 21st century Jamaicans are working it out!

The island has also sought to replace or supplement the heroes and heroines of the colonial period with its own and showcase its rich heritage on several sites of memory. It has seven declared national heroes and heroines: Nanny of the

LEFT TO RIGHT: The early 20th century saw two major political parties in Jamaica led by Norman Manley (PNP) and Alexander Bustamante (JLP).

Maroons, Samuel Sharpe, Paul Bogle, George William Gordon, Marcus Mosiah Garvey, Alexander Bustamante and Norman Washington Manley. It has established a National Heroes Park in which monuments to these icons have been erected in the Shrine Area. Outside of this area are monuments to other icons like Aggie Bernard of the 1930s Labour Movement, former Prime Ministers Michael Manley, Hugh Shearer and others. In a park named after a 1930s icon, St William Grant, stand monuments including one to Queen Victoria. Edna Manley's 'Negro Aroused' stands where enslaved Africans used to be sold, and our artistic culture is on show at the National Gallery of Jamaica. The Institute of Jamaica (former establishment of Mary Seacole), Liberty Hall (the legacy of Marcus Garvey), the National Library of Jamaica, the National Archives and the various university and parish libraries are repositories of the intellectual wealth of the island. The Park of World Heroes, near Cross Roads, with a bust of Mahatma Gandhi already installed, testifies to Jamaica's internationalism.

In New Kingston, an Emancipation Park exists with a much-contested symbol to emancipation. Streets, buildings and highways carry the names of local and international figures like Nelson Mandela. Simon Bolivar stands tall in front of National Heroes Park and Bob Marley strums his guitar in a monument opposite the National Stadium and Arena. Sports heroes like George Headley, Herb McKinley and Merlene Ottey are not forgotten by a nation obsessed with cricket and athletics.

The statue of Christopher Columbus and the heritage trail storyboards in the colours of the Spanish flag might attract disapproval, but others like those at the various Maroon villages, the birthplaces of the national heroes and heroines and sites important to slavery, resistance and independence, are much celebrated. The process of symbolic decolonisation is well on its way. So, come to Jamaica and be informed! ∎

National Heroes

Nanny of the Maroons

Nanny was a leader of the Maroons at the beginning of the 18th century. She was known by both the Maroons and the British settlers as an outstanding military leader who, during her lifetime and afterwards, became a symbol of unity and strength for her people in times of crisis.

She was particularly important to them in the fierce fight with the British during the First Maroon War from 1720 to 1739. Although she has been immortalised in songs and legends, certain facts about Nanny (or "Granny Nanny", as she was affectionately known) have also been documented.

Both legends and documents refer to her as having exceptional leadership qualities. She was a small, wiry woman with piercing eyes. Her influence over the Maroons was so strong that it seemed to be supernatural and was said to be connected to her powers of obeah. She was particularly skilled in organising the guerrilla warfare carried out by the eastern Maroons to keep away the British troops who attempted to penetrate the mountains to overpower them.

Her cleverness in planning guerrilla warfare confused the British, and their accounts of the fights reflect the surprise and fear which the Maroon traps caused among them.

Besides inspiring her people to ward off the troops, Nanny was also a type of chieftain or wise woman of the village who passed down legends and encouraged the continuation of customs, music and songs, that had come with the people from Africa, and which instilled in them confidence and pride.

Her spirit of freedom was so great that in 1739, when Quao signed the second Treaty (the first was signed by Cudjoe for the Leeward Maroons a few months earlier) with the British, it is reported that Nanny was angry and disagreed with the principle of peace with the British, which she knew would mean another form of subjugation.

FACING PAGE: Nanny engaged in guerrilla warfare to keep away the British troops.

There are many legends about Nanny among the Maroons. Some even claim that there were several women who were leaders of the Maroons during this period of history. But all the legends and documents refer to Nanny of the First Maroon War as the most outstanding of them all, leading her people with courage and inspiring them in their struggle for freedom.

George William Gordon

Born to a slave mother and a planter father who was attorney to several sugar estates in Jamaica, George William Gordon was self-educated and a landowner in the parish of St Thomas.

In the face of attempts to crush the spirit of the freed people of Jamaica and again reduce them to slavery, Gordon entered politics. He faced severe odds, as the people whose interests he sought to serve did not qualify to vote.

He subdivided his own lands, selling farm lots to the people as cheaply as possible, and organised a marketing system, through which they could sell their produce at fair prices.

Gordon urged the people to protest against and resist the oppressive and unjust conditions under which they were forced to live.

Gordon was arrested and charged for complicity in what is now called the Morant Bay Rebellion in 1865. He was illegally tried by Court Martial and, in spite of a lack of evidence, convicted and sentenced to death. He was executed on 23rd October 1865.

Sir Alexander Bustamante

When Alexander Bustamante began to make his presence felt in Jamaica, the country was still a Crown Colony. Under this system, the Governor had the right to veto at all times, which he very often exercised against the wishes of the majority.

Bustamante was quick to realise that the social and economic ills that such a system engendered, had to be countered by mobilisation of the working class.

Pay and working conditions were poor in the 1920s and 1930s. Failing harvests and the lay-off of workers resulted in an influx of unemployed people moving from the rural areas into the city. This mass migration did little to alleviate the unemployment problem.

Bustamante first impressed his name on the society with a series of letters to *The Gleaner* and occasionally to British newspapers, drawing attention to the social and economic problems of the poor and underprivileged in Jamaica.

The years 1937 and 1938 saw the outbreak of widespread discontent and social unrest. In advocating the cause of the masses, Bustamante became the champion of the working class. He also confronted the power of the Colonial Governor, declaring, "Long live the King! But Denham must go."

On 8th September 1940, Bustamante was detained at Up Park Camp, for alleged violation of the Defence of the Realm Act. He was released seventeen months later.

In 1943, he founded the Jamaica Labour Party (JLP), with himself as head. The first general election under Universal Adult Suffrage came in 1944 and the JLP won 22 of the 32 seats.

Sir Alexander became the first Prime Minister of Independent Jamaica in 1962. He retired from active politics in 1967. He died on 6th August 1977, at the age of 93.

Paul Bogle

It is believed that Paul Bogle was born free in 1822. He was a Baptist deacon in Stony Gut, a few miles north of Morant Bay, and was eligible to vote at a time when there were only 104 voters in the parish of St Thomas. He was a firm political supporter of George William Gordon.

Poverty and injustice in the society and lack of public confidence in the central authority, urged Bogle to lead a protest march to the Morant Bay courthouse on 11th October 1865.

In a violent confrontation with full official forces that followed the march, nearly 500 people were killed and a greater number was flogged and punished before order was restored.

Bogle was captured and hanged on 24th October 1865, but his forceful demonstration achieved its objectives. It paved the way for the establishment of just practices in the courts and it brought about a change in official attitude, which made possible the social and economic betterment of the people.

Norman Manley

Norman Washington Manley was born at Roxborough, Manchester, on 4th July 1893. He was a brilliant scholar and athlete, soldier (First World War) and lawyer. He identified himself with the cause of the workers at the time of the labour troubles of 1938 and donated time and advocacy to the cause.

In September 1938, Manley founded the People's National Party (PNP) and was elected its President annually until his retirement in 1969.

Manley and the PNP supported the trade union movement, then led by Alexander Bustamante, while

LEFT TO RIGHT: George William Gordon urged the people to protest against oppressive and unjust conditions.

Alexander Bustamante became the first Prime Minister of Independent Jamaica in 1962.

Norman Manley identified himself with the cause of the workers and was renowned for his integrity and commitment to democracy.

FACING PAGE: Paul Bogle's efforts paved the way for the social and economic betterment of the Jamaican people.

leading the demand for Universal Adult Suffrage. When Suffrage came, Manley had to wait ten years and two terms before his party was elected to office.

He was a strong advocate of the Federation of the West Indies – established in 1958 – but when Bustamante declared that the opposition Jamaica Labour Party (JLP) would take Jamaica out of the Federation, Norman Manley, already renowned for his integrity and commitment to democracy, called a referendum (unprecedented in Jamaica) to let the people decide.

The vote was decisively against Jamaica's continued membership of the Federation. Norman Manley, after arranging Jamaica's orderly withdrawal from the union, set up a joint committee to decide on a constitution for separate Independence for Jamaica.

He chaired the committee with great distinction and then led the team that negotiated the island's Independence from Britain. With the issue settled, Manley again went to the people. He lost the ensuing election to the JLP and gave his last years of service as Leader of the Opposition, establishing definitively the role of the Parliamentary Opposition in a developing nation.

In his last public address to an annual conference of the PNP, he said: "I say that the mission of my generation was to win self-government for Jamaica, to win political power which is the final power for the black masses of my country from which I spring. I am proud to stand

here today and say to you who fought that fight with me, say it with gladness and pride, mission accomplished for my generation.

"And what is the mission of this generation? It is reconstructing the social and economic society and life of Jamaica."

Norman Manley died on 2nd September 1969.

Samuel Sharpe

Samuel Sharpe was the main instigator of the 1831 Slave Rebellion, which began on the Kensington Estate in St James and which was largely instrumental in bringing about the abolition of slavery.

Because of his intelligence and leadership qualities, Sam Sharpe became a 'daddy', or leader of the native Baptists in Montego Bay. Religious meetings were the only permissible forms of organised activities for the slaves. Sam Sharpe was able to communicate his concern and encourage political thought concerning events in England, which affected the slaves and Jamaica.

Sam evolved a plan of passive resistance in 1831, by which the slaves would refuse to work on Christmas Day of 1831 and afterwards, unless their grievances concerning better treatment and the consideration of freedom were accepted by the estate owners and managers.

Sam explained his plan to his chosen supporters after his religious meetings and made them kiss the Bible to show their loyalty. They, in turn, took the plan to the other parishes until the idea had spread throughout St James, Trelawny, Westmoreland, St Elizabeth and Manchester.

Word of the plan reached the ears of some of the planters. Troops were sent into St James and warships were anchored in Montego Bay and Black River, with their guns trained on the towns.

On 27th December 1831, the Kensington Estate Great House was set on fire, as a signal that the Slave Rebellion had begun. A series of other fires broke out in the area and soon it was clear that the plan of non-violent resistance, which Sam Sharpe had originated, was impossible and impractical.

Armed rebellion and seizing of property spread mostly through the western parishes, but the uprising was put down by the first week in January. A terrible retribution followed with more than 500 slaves losing their lives, most of them as a result of the subsequent trials.

Samuel Sharpe was hanged on 23rd May 1832 and he is quoted as saying, "I would rather die upon yonder gallows than live in slavery".

In 1834, the British Parliament passed the Abolition Bill and in 1838 slavery was abolished.

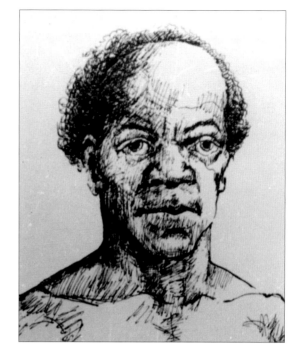

Samuel Sharpe was the main instigator of the 1831 Slave Rebellion.

Marcus Mosiah Garvey

Jamaica's first National Hero was born in St Ann's Bay, St Ann, on 17th August 1887. In his youth Garvey moved to Kingston, where he worked as a printer and later published a small paper *The Watchman*.

During his career, Garvey travelled extensively throughout many countries, observing the poor working and living conditions of Black people.

In 1914, he started the Universal Negro Improvement Association (UNIA) in Jamaica. The UNIA, which grew into an international organisation, encouraged self-government for Black people worldwide, self-help economic projects and protest against racial discrimination.

In 1916, Garvey went to the USA where he preached his doctrine of freedom to the oppressed Black people throughout the country.

However, US officials disapproved of his activities and he was imprisoned and then deported.

Back in Jamaica in 1927, he continued his political activity, forming the People's Political Party in 1929. He was unsuccessful in national elections but won a seat on the Kingston and St Andrew Corporation (KSAC).

But the world of the 1930s was not ready for Garvey's progressive ideas. He left Jamaica again, this time for England where he died in 1940. His body was brought back to Jamaica in 1964 and buried in the National Heroes Park in Kingston.

Garvey's legacy can be summed up in the philosophy he taught: race pride; the need for African unity; self-reliance; the need for Black people to be organised; and for rulers to govern on behalf of the working classes. ■

FACING PAGE: Marcus Garvey advocated self-government for Black people worldwide.

Highway to heritage

DAVID BUCKLEY

N ational heritage consists of everything arising from the history of the country, cultural, natural and manmade. We will concentrate on the manmade, with references to the natural, and in this way look at the visible evidence of our history.

Let us begin an imaginary, but quite feasible, five-day, four-hundred-mile highway trip around Jamaica, starting at the eastern border of St Catherine. The road runs between fields of sugarcane, the cultivation of which was a central element in our history. This was the reason for slavery, with all its attendant horrors, and even today still affects us. But we cannot allow the past to paralyse the present, and we can build on this legacy to strengthen our identity as a people.

White Marl is the site of the largest of the 300 known Taino sites in Jamaica, and was occupied from at least 1000 A.D. The Tainos originated in the rainforests of South America, travelling up the Orinoco River to what is now north-east Venezuela, and settled in Trinidad in about 100 A.D. From there they arrived in Jamaica, perhaps as early as 600 A.D. Hunters, fishers and farmers, they did not survive European civilisation. In the Mountain River Cave just north of Spanish Town they left paintings and carvings from which much has been learned of these first Jamaicans, and at White Marl there is the Taino Museum, preserving this aspect of our heritage.

At the entrance to Spanish Town is the 1801 Iron Bridge, one of only two in the Western Hemisphere; it spans the Rio Cobre and facilitated travel between Spanish Town and Kingston. The Georgian square in the town is one of the finest in the New World, and was built in the 18th century by the English. It includes a courthouse, a ▷

CLOCKWISE FROM TOP: The Georgian square in Spanish Town is home to some fine examples of period architectural; the Iron Bridge into Spanish Town. Photos: Brian Rosen

Governor's residence, a memorial to Admiral George Rodney, and the old Legislative Assembly of Jamaica. This was the second Spanish capital of Jamaica, established in 1523, and was taken by England in 1655. Spanish Town remained the capital of Jamaica until 1872, when Kingston was given that honour. In this place the treaty with the Maroons was signed in 1740, making them the first free people of colour in the New World, and from the steps of the Governor's mansion Emancipation was proclaimed in 1838.

Not far away is the Cathedral of St James, built on the ruins of the Spanish Chapel of the Red Cross, both being the first such places of worship in the hemisphere for the two nations.

The next parish is Clarendon, which has few official heritage sites, the main ones being St Peter's Church and Jamaica's largest mineral spa, the Milk River Baths. Close to the highway is Halse Hall dating from the late 1600s, set near to a Taino site and a Spanish bridle trail.

In Manchester, the Mandeville town centre includes the Parish Church and the Courthouse, both still in service. Just outside the town is the Bloomfield Great House, preserved, refurbished and now a restaurant. A few miles away is Roxborough, birthplace of Norman Washington Manley, a National Hero.

In St Elizabeth, Black River has a Historic District consisting of century-old houses of architectural and historical interest, still serving as guesthouses. Further west is Savanna-La-Mar, where we find what may be called the colonial triad of church, court and fort. All of Jamaica's capital towns had these three; religion, law and military power were the realities of colonialism.

On the western side of the island is the famous Negril with seven miles of white sand beach, a major natural heritage devoted to tourism. We next enter the town of Lucea, and again find the triad of church, court and fort, the beautiful harbour being guarded by Fort Charlotte, and we can visit nearby Blenheim, the birthplace of Sir Alexander Bustamante, another National Hero, who along with his cousin Norman Manley led Jamaica to independence in 1962.

The road to St James brings us to the ruins of Barbican Estate, one of the many which by the second half of the 18th century had made Jamaica the most valuable overseas asset of the British Empire. We may also visit Kenilworth to see another such remnant of the source of significant funding for the industrial Revolution in Britain and her expansion as a naval and colonial power. ▷

Doctors' Cave beach in Montego Bay is a popular tourism destination. Photo: Robert Davis

The waterwheel at Tryall is an example of one method of powering factories, others being animal and wind power. Tryall itself, formerly a sugar estate, is now a luxury hotel.

Montego Bay, the capital of St James, is centred around the Sam Sharpe Square, named after the National Hero. For his part in the Christmas Rebellion of 1831, he was tried, convicted and hanged on the steps of the restored courthouse, after declaring, "I would rather die on yonder gallows than live a slave another day" – stirring words for many people. The Parish Church is close by, and the expected fort a mile or so west, overlooking the harbour. Rose Hall is perhaps the most imposing 'great house' in the Caribbean, and has long been open as an attraction, in which we may be told of the scandalous (but untrue) behaviour of Annie Palmer, the White Witch of Rose Hall. Greenwood and Orange Valley Great Houses follow shortly, both developed sites open to the public.

Falmouth, capital of Trelawny, is undergoing major restoration of its impressive Georgian heritage buildings, and plans exist to make the town a major cruise ship attraction. There is a memorial church to the life and work of William Knibb, the abolitionist who, with other non-conformists, played a vital part in ending slavery. The Parish Church and Fort Balcarres are easily visited, and on the outskirts of the town is the "Persian" waterwheel, which gave Falmouth piped water in 1800, in advance of New York City.

Rio Bueno is on the border of St Ann, and some argue that this is where Columbus landed in 1494,

CLOCKWISE FROM ABOVE: Doctor's Cave beach in Montego Bay. Photo: Klaus Wolf

FACING PAGE, CLOCKWISE FROM TOP: Black River. Photo: Klaus Wolf

De Montevin Lodge in Port Antonio. Photo: Klaus Wolf

Bellefield Great House, built in 1794, is one of the oldest former sugar plantations in Jamaica. Located in Montego Bay, it is available for special events, weddings and conferences.

finding a Taino settlement and a freshwater river, neither of which existed at Discovery Bay. Rio Bueno has its church and fort in common with other coastal towns, further indication of the value of Jamaica and the constant threat of invasion by other powers, not to mention pirate raids on the settlers' livestock and provisions.

Runaway Bay, usually believed to have been the site from which the last Spaniards escaped in 1658, was more likely the place of departure for slaves no longer willing to endure their conditions. At Sevilla la Nueva we come to a very important site in the New World, where three ethnic groups lived, worked and died together. Tainos, Spaniards and Africans all existed here for a number of years until the ravages of disease drove the Spanish to Villa de la Vega, today's Spanish Town, in 1523. Archaeologists have uncovered the remains of Spanish stone buildings, and the property has the 18th century Seville Great House, which houses an exhibition of artefacts relating to the history of the site.

St Ann's Bay is the birthplace of Marcus Garvey, the national hero who founded the Universal

Negro Improvement Association in the 1920s, and contributed immensely to the empowerment of Black people worldwide. The famous Dunn's River Falls is just west of Ocho Rios, and other attractions are Dolphin Cove and the new Mystic Mountain nature attraction.

In St Mary, Harmony Hall is a former Baptist manse, for some years now a flourishing art gallery and restaurant. Further on is Prospect, where tours of this working plantation are available. Rio Nuevo is preserved as the place of the final battle for Jamaica in 1658, ending Spain's attempt to hold on to the island. West of Port Maria, in St Mary, 'Firefly', the home of Noel Coward , is open for tours. We approach Port Maria below the bluff on which sits Fort Haldane, and come to the Parish Church on the seaside across from the courthouse.

In the churchyard is a memorial to Tacky, a Coromantine chieftain who in 1760 organised and led a serious uprising intended to overthrow slavery island-wide, another indication of the unceasing resistance to slavery and oppression seen in Jamaica's history. A few miles from Port Maria we find Brimmer Hall, another plantation tour facility.

A stretch of 45 scenic miles brings us to Port Antonio, to see the Parish Church, Fort George and a new courthouse. The de Montevin Lodge, from the heyday of banana exports, the Bonnie View Hotel overlooking the twin harbours, and the ill-fated Folly Mansion complete this portion. High in the hills to the south, National Hero Nanny and the Maroons defied the might of the British Empire.

Having enjoyed the breathtaking scenery of the east coast, we enter St Thomas, and at Port Morant

see the remains of two forts (defence against French raiders who often came in search of food and water). In Morant Bay stands a monument to Paul Bogle, who was hanged at the courthouse for his role in the 1865 Rebellion. His friend and mentor, George William Gordon, was also executed; they are now National Heroes. Stony Gut from which Bogle and followers set out to their fate, is a few miles north of the main road and is accessible to the public.

We arrive on the eastern edge of St Andrew, and come to the Rockfort and its mineral spa; the fort was one of six or seven which used to guard Kingston and its harbour. In this parish we can drive on a single road and see most of the main sites in the parish. Hope Road will take us from the 1664 St Andrew Parish Church to Devon House, built in 1881 by Jamaica's first Black millionaire.

Next is King's House, followed by the Bob Marley Museum, and then on to the botanical gardens, on the old Hope Estate. The University ▷

ABOVE: Dolphin Cove. Photo: Jamaica Tourist Board

FACING PAGE, CLOCKWISE FROM TOP RIGHT: The Bob Marley Museum celebrates one of Jamaica's greatest gifts to the world. *Photo: Jamaica Tourist Board*

St Andrew Parish Church. Photo: Brian Rosen

The falls at Ocho Rios. Photo: Brian Rosen

Visitors to Emancipation Park in Kingston are greeted by the monument 'Redemption Song'. These two bronze figures stand 10 and 11ft tall and were created by Jamaican sculptor, Laura Facey in 2003. Photo: Klaus Wolf

A rare view of the sprawling city of Kingston. Photo: Robert Davis

of the West Indies has a chapel constructed with the stones of an old sugar warehouse; remnants of an aqueduct are next to it.

We continue to Craigton Great House and on to Newcastle, a military hill station built in the 19th century, where the cool air repelled mosquitoes and saved the lives of many a soldier. It is still in the hands of the Jamaican military forces.

Kingston is the smallest Parish, and King Street is home to the Ward Theatre, the Coke Chapel, the Kingston Parish Church and the St William Grant Park, with statues of Alexander Bustamante and Norman Manley. The courthouse is a little south of the park. North of it is Liberty Hall, established in 1923 by Marcus Garvey, and now dedicated to preserving the work of this remarkable man. Other places of interest in Kingston are the Catholic Cathedral, the Jewish Synagogue, and Museum. Jamaica has a strong heritage of religious freedom and Headquarters House, formerly the seat of Government, is now the office of the Jamaica National Heritage Trust. Heroes Park is a short drive north from the park.

An imaginary ferry ride will take us to Port Royal, old home of the notorious buccaneers and the famous Sir Henry Morgan. Port Royal is the fifth most well known heritage site in the world, and many see great potential for it. The fort itself began as a careenage for Spanish ships and was greatly expanded by the English. Close to the fort is the church, with the tomb of Lewis Galdy, who miraculously survived the 1692 earthquake, unlike many of the residents and much of the town. There is an impressive cast-iron Naval Hospital nearby, said to be unique in the world.

We cross the narrow harbour entrance to where Fort Clarence and Fort Small stood, along with the 'Twelve Apostles' battery, and it is easy to see why no enemy ships, except two prizes of war, ever ventured into the harbour. To the north of Port Royal there is also the formidable Fort Augusta, completing a ring of firepower which was never tested.

Our trip has shown us a fair sampling of national heritage; the official list consists of over 300 natural and built sites. A number of these are in operation as part of what Jamaica has to offer the world. It is easy to see that much more can and likely will be done to enhance the attractiveness of the island, beyond the sun, sea and sand, which are not unique to Jamaica. There is great educational value in these sites for our young citizens, and one hopes greater use will be made of them in this way. ∎

Kingston

PARISHES BY NOELLE KHALILA NICOLLS

Any time of year, anytime of day, step into the streets of Kingston, Jamaica and you will walk onto a five-star buffet of cultural delights. The universal season in this booming capital is 'Positive Vibrations' for business and pleasure.

If you plan a business convention in February you could choose from a host of Reggae Month activities, organised to celebrate Jamaica's musical gift to the world. Not to be missed in April is Jamaica Carnival, a wild and creative street parade.

The treat for June is the world renowned Caribbean Fashion Week, a display of Caribbean couture, street style and fashion flair. Even if you are just visiting for a two-day business meeting in November, plan ahead and take advantage of the fabulous Kingston Restaurant Week.

Kingston is a city that never sleeps. For all of its virtues and vices it has a universal appeal on which many try to capitalise. The character of the city has even surpassed the confines of its geographical area, often being confused with the parishes of Kingston and St Andrew. These parishes are inextricably linked, as they are controlled by one municipality and jointly contain sections of the capital city. But they do have distinct histories, commercial strengths, cultural contributions and environmental attributes.

Kingston, the parish, consists of the notorious seventeenth century city Port Royal and the waterfront communities of Downtown Kingston. Sitting at the mouth of the Kingston Harbour, Port Royal was once considered the wealthiest and wickedest city in the New World. It was originally of greater strategic importance than Kingston, serving as a military and naval base for the British and a thriving commercial centre. A devastating ▷

Kingston is a city that never sleeps. Photo: Jamaica Tourist Board

ABOVE: Some areas in Kingston resemble the high-rise capitals of many developed countries. Photos: Tony Matthews

MAIN PICTURE: Kingston in twilight. Photo: Brian Rosen

Hope Gardens provides a tranquil retreat from the hustle and bustle of Kingston. Photo: Klaus Wolf

earthquake in 1692 plunged half of the city into the ocean, and demolished the other half.

One building withstood the earthquake: Fort Charles. This relic still stands today, just fifteen minutes away from the Norman Manley Airport, along with other colonial remnants.

After the earthquake hit, Kingston was developed in the neighbouring Liguanea Plain, in the shadows of the towering Blue Mountain Range. After surviving a number of calamities – from floods to fires – it took the capital city title from Spanish Town in 1872. Kingston's natural harbour, the seventh largest in the world, made it a prime location for trade in the growing colonial empire.

The waterfront communities of Downtown Kingston are best known as the birthplace of reggae music and Rastafari. There you will find staple attractions like the Gordon House, the National Gallery, Ward Theatre, Coronation Market and Hero's Circle. You will also find hidden treasures like the Downtown Kingston Reggae Music Heritage Tour.

Several international reggae stars hail from Kingston, including Dennis Brown, Buju Banton and Beenie Man. While 'Mr Reggae' himself, Bob Marley, was born in St Ann, he received his first music break at Studio One, one of downtown Kingston's finest recording studios. It is a staple on the music heritage tour, along with other studios, vintage record stores and dancehall spots.

Whether travelling for business or pleasure, an investment of your time in exploring Kingston city and Kingston parish is guaranteed to provide great returns. ∎

St Andrew

NOELLE KHALILA NICOLLS

While Kingston is loaded with political, cultural and economic significance, the Parish of St Andrew is not to be overshadowed. With almost twenty times more physical space than Kingston, St Andrew contains the largest population of all the parishes in Jamaica. It is bordered by four other parishes, St Thomas, Portland, St Mary and St Catherine, and contains diverse places of interest.

Blue Mountain tours are readily available from St Andrew, although the highest peak is located in Portland. The Hollywell National Forest Park is a great alternative to the rugged hike to the top. Nature enthusiasts will love this sanctuary for birds, trees, flowers and ferns, rarely seen anywhere else on the island.

Tucked in the mountain at 3,100 feet is the Strawberry Hill Hotel & Spa, where you can select one of their twelve 19th century Georgian style cottages, with incredible views of the city, or opt to stop by for a scrumptious Sunday brunch.

Competition is stiff in St Andrew on Sunday mornings. Instead of a mountain view brunch, diners might be more interested in a restaurant on the riverside at the Boone Hall Oasis, Stony Hill. The beautifully manicured gardens on this property also make it popular for weddings and special events.

A lot closer to sea level is the modern centre of commerce, New Kingston: a hip strip filled with sky scrapers, bright lights, international cuisine and buzzing night life. Choose from any number of world class hotels: The Jamaica Pegasus, Hilton, Courtleigh, Four Seasons and the newest of them all, the Spanish Court Hotel. All of the hotels are prime venues for conferences, meetings, seminars, and first-class accommodation. ▷

A breathtaking view of the Blue Mountains. Photo: Jamaica Tourist Board

Within walking distance is Christopher's Piano Bar, a chic spot for socialising over cocktails. Upstairs to the bar is Quad, a multi-level nightclub, visited by the rich and famous. Around the corner is Asylum Nightclub, a dancehall queen's dream. Cell phone providers are easily found in New Kingston, along with foreign exchange bureaus and banks.

The National Stadium is close by, where you might be lucky enough to see football superstar and St Andrew native, Ricardo Gardner play for the Reggae Boys to a full house of 30,000 cheering Jamaicans decked out in black, green and gold.

Away from the city, nestled in the hilly Nine Mile region of Bull Bay, on the border of St Thomas, is a commune for the Boboshanti mansion of the Rastafari called Bob Hill. Visitors to this Rastafari community are housed and fed, and only required to respect the strict traditions of the community. Men and women sleep in separate quarters; women cover their heads with head wraps; strictly vegan food is served; and daily devotions are performed.

A pilgrimage to Bob Hill is one of the best ways to learn about some of the traditions of the Rastafari. The daily routine for residents is

FACING PAGE: Devon House was built in 1881 and is a fine example of Jamaican architecture. It has been well restored and is a popular tourist attraction. Photo: Jamaica Tourist Board

ABOVE: Established in 1841, the cantonment at Newcastle was once home to a number of British regiments. Plaques and insignia of the various regiments adorn the northern wall of the parade ground. The facility is now used by the Jamaica Defence Force. Photo: Klaus Wolf

morning devotion and roll call, and three sessions of reading psalms and chanting throughout the day.

Kingston and St Andrew might not have the polish of the more developed tourist cities in St Ann and St Thomas, but they both offer a type of originality like almost no other parishes do.

OVERVIEW

Established: 1867
Land Area: 455 sq km (181 sq miles)
Capital: Halfway Tree
Places of Interest: Devon House, St Andrew Parish Church, Hope Gardens, National Stadium

Portland

There are many truly Jamaican cuisines, like ackee and saltfish with fried johnny cakes, or mackerel rundown with yellow yam and boiled green banana. Only one food has the same level of pepper and spice, flavour and flamboyance as the people of Jamaica. Jerk pork, jerk chicken, jerk fish, jerk lobster, jerk pasta, jerk pizza: you name it and Jamaicans jerk it.

Jerk seasoning is the unofficial national spice of Jamaica, originally engineered by Jamaica's first free Africans, the Maroons. And Portland parish is the unofficial national homestead. Mix together the three main ingredients, crushed pimento, scotch bonnet pepper and salt, and you get the basic jerk formula. Add upwards to thirty different spices, like thyme, garlic, scallion and nutmeg, based on the most secret family recipe, and you get a customised blend of truly Jamaican jerk in the form of a powered seasoning or a saucy marinade.

Food connoisseurs can eat their way across Jamaica on a tasty attraction called the Culinary Jerk Trail. After visiting nine different tasting stops, the feast culminates at the famous Boston Bay Jerk Centre, where it all began in Portland. Every July, thousands of people gather in the parish for a world-class display of culinary creativity at the annual Portland Jerk Festival.

Food is not the only good thing about Portland, although it must be said, the first bananas were exported out of Jamaica from Portland's twin harbours. As many as seventeen steam liners operated from the capital Port Antonio, making it at one time the banana capital of the world. Banana, sugarcane and other fruit crops are still ▷

RIGHT: Villas at San San

OVERLEAF: Rafting on the Rio Grande is Jamaica's equivalent to cruising on a Venetian gondola. Photos: Geejam productions

The Blue Lagoon is a deep blue water hole that is fed by freshwater springs and connects to the sea via a narrow channel. At almost 200 feet deep, it is popular with scuba divers who marvel at its crystal-clear waters. Photo: Geejam productions

harvested along the coastline, and the Blue Mountain Range provides lots of fertile farmland for coffee farming.

Portland's attractions range from mineral spas, waterfalls and caves, to botanical gardens, rivers, beaches and mountain trails. The highest peak of the Blue Mountains is accessible from Portland, sitting at 7,403 feet.

Sport fishing is best enjoyed in October, when anglers from around the world assemble to compete for the prize catch in the annual Port Antonio International Marlin Tournament.

River rafting on the Rio Grande River is Jamaica's equivalent to cruising on a Venetian gondola. The three-hour, six-mile tour on a bamboo raft snakes through Jamaica's rural riverside communities, passing through Lover's Lane, where it is customary to plant a kiss on your partner.

Portland is a rapidly growing parish thanks in part to the work of one native investor, Michael Lee-Chin. Lee-Chin is Portland's most famous resident. Now a multimillionaire with a net worth of some C$1.7 billion, he developed his financial acumen working in Canada's financial sector, ultimately as the chief executive officer of the leading Canadian mutual fund Advantage Investment Council.

In 2000, he stormed through Jamaica acquiring a diverse collection of business entities in the media, health, tourism, telecommunications and financial services, all under the name of the company he founded, Portland Holdings Inc. The future of Portland as an investor's paradise and tourist hot spot continues to look bright.

OVERVIEW

Established: 1723
Name Origin: Duke of Portland
Land Area: 814 sq. km (314.3 sq. miles)
Capital: Port Antonio
Main Towns: Port Antonio, Boston Bay, St Margaret's Bay
Commerce: Tourism, Agriculture
Places of Interest: Nanny Town, Navy Island, Blue Lagoon, Folly Great House, Rio Grande, Boston Beach, Reach Falls, Somerset Falls
Popular Activities & Attractions: mountain climbing, nature tours, waterfalls, river excursions
Interesting fact: The highest peak in the Blue Mountain Range is located in Portland at 7,402 feet

St Thomas

If you read Jamaican history books published before independence in 1962 you might read, as a passing reference to the parish of St Thomas, about a minor disturbance, or the disorderly conduct caused by a Baptist deacon named Paul Bogle. Modern history books paint a very different picture of Jamaica's National Hero, the Right Excellent Paul Bogle

Bogle was conferred this title in 1969 for leading a resistance effort to fight against poverty and injustice that ultimately shaped the course of history. St Thomas is memorialised as 'ground zero' for the 1865 Morant Bay Rebellion. Bogle joined hands with George William Gordon, a mulatto lawyer and assemblyman from the plantocracy, to lead a protest march at the main courthouse. Armed militia shot into the crowds, causing a riot that left nearly 500 people dead and the courthouse burned to the ground.

Bogle and Gordon, who is also a national hero, were eventually captured and hanged in the resultant reprisals, which saw the execution of hundreds of people and the burning down of thousands of houses. The reprisal was so ruthless that the British government intervened, impeaching Governor Edward Eyre and disbanding the House of Assembly, which had stood for over 200 years.

Jamaica marched on to independence 100 years later and St Thomas became a symbol of hope and strength. Today, the Morant Bay Courthouse is adorned with a towering statue of Paul Bogle, as a reminder of his courageous efforts. Behind the courthouse is Bogle's grave, alongside the Morant Bay Fort. ▷

Bath Botanical Gardens were first established in 1779 and are the second oldest in the Western Hemisphere. Photo: Jamaica Tourist Board

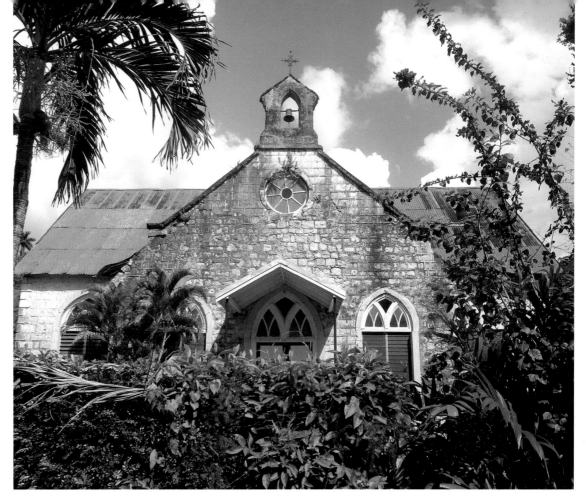

ABOVE: *Church in Bath.*

FACING PAGE: *Erected in 1841, Morant Point Lighthouse was the first to be built in Jamaica. Photos: Klaus Wolf*

Firmly rooted in its revolutionary past, St Thomas displays the wherewithal to court modernity with contemporary and unconventional attractions. The Sun Coast Adventure Park is one of the newest attractions in the parish, just twenty minutes away from the Norman Manley International Airport. This is Jamaica's first and largest paintball facility, fully equipped with hiking trails, tightrope walks, zip-lines, a fence maze and, of course, a paintball battlefield.

Some of the best surfing in the Caribbean is found in St Thomas. The Jamnesia Surf Club is fully staffed with internationally certified surfing instructors and competitors. The winter months provide the best waves, but surfing goes on for eight months of the year, with waves reaching ten feet in height. The annual Jamnesia Surf Camp attracts surf enthusiasts from around the world.

The Bath settlement and its featured botanical gardens and fountain were put on the map in the eighteenth century because the water in this area was found to have high mineral values, effective for treating skin diseases, rheumatic fever and gout. At one time, a hospital stood nearby the springs and the water, with its sulphur, magnesium, lime and other mineral content, was used for naturopathic treatments.

Over the years, St Thomas natives have dabbled in a lot of agricultural and manufacturing processes, from dairy production to cement production. Although the banana, sugar and coconut plantations of St Thomas are nowhere near the size they used to be in their heyday, they still make up a large part of the local economy, along with ground provisions that are widely grown.

OVERVIEW

Established: 1867 (St Thomas-in-the-East joined with St David to form St Thomas parish)
Name Origin: after Lord Thomas Hickman-Windsor, 1662 Governor of Jamaica
Land Area: 742.8 sq km (286.8 sq miles)
Capital: Morant Bay
Main Towns: Port Morant, Yallahs, Bath, Easington, Seaforth, Golden Grove
Commerce: Agriculture, Manufacturing
Places of Interest: Morant Bay Courthouse, Bath Botanical Gardens and Spa, Lyssons Beach
Popular activities: paintball, surfing, beach
Interesting Fact: Breadfruit was introduced to Jamaica in about 1792 from Tahiti by Captain William Bligh. The first plants were established in the Bath Botanical Gardens

St Catherine

When many people visit Jamaica they are looking for reggae music, Rastafari, the Blue Mountains and the excitement of the north coast. The parish of St Catherine, just a few miles outside of Kingston, is not on their minds, and when it is, they think of it as a thoroughfare to reach somewhere else.

Many overlook this parish because of the notorious reputation of Spanish Town, forgetting that this city, now St Catherine's capital, was for over 200 years during the colonial era, the nation's capital. It still contains the original buildings of the old colonial government, as well as modern parish council offices.

While there are ongoing efforts to reduce the level of poverty in Spanish Town's residential communities, the main Spanish Town Square, where Spanish señoritas once strutted down the streets and sandal-clad friars preached about salvation, maintains its original charm.

Hidden tunnels below the city, used by the Spanish to transport artillery, were sealed by the British when they snatched the city from the Spaniards in 1655 and changed the name from St Jago de la Vega. These tunnels are still largely unexplored. Because of its historical importance, Spanish Town is a national heritage district maintained by the Jamaica National Heritage Trust.

Spanish Town is the oldest continuously inhabited city in Jamaica. A short distance away is Portmore, the single largest residential community in the Caribbean. With an estimated

The Rodney Memorial dominates Parade Square in Spanish Town. Built in honour of Admiral George Rodney who, in 1782, defeated a combined French and Spanish invasion fleet at the Battle of the Saints. The monument depicts various battle scenes in sculpted panel reliefs and the statue itself is flanked by two brass cannons captured from the French flagship. Photo: Jamaica Tourist Board

250,000 people living on a plain of reclaimed swampland, Portmore is a coastal city with an intricate canal system to prevent flooding.

This rapidly growing community is barely known for its tourist attractions, although it contains two of the most popular beach hangouts and fishing communities on the outskirts of Kingston. Hellshire Hills and Fort Clarence Beach are best explored in the early mornings when the beaches are empty. Later in the day, many restaurants open their doors for a rustic, seafood dining experience. And for over eighty days a year, the Caymanas Park Race Track hosts equestrian activities that provide great family entertainment.

St Catherine is also the second largest industrial centre, next to Kingston, at one time having almost 100 manufacturing establishments. This is where Jamaica's sweet and creamy condiment – condensed milk – is produced in the only factory on the island,

ABOVE: The Old House of Assembly in Spanish Town Square was built in 1762. Photo: Brian Rosen

FACING PAGE: St James Cathedral. Photo: Jamaica Tourist Board

as well as the largest salt producing factory in the Caribbean. Cigarettes, batteries, plastic(s) and pharmaceuticals are all manufactured in the parish.

The fishing villages around St Catherine are numerous. In Spring Village there is a fish farm where visitors can stand on the edge of cultured ponds or sit in model fishing boats and catch their lunch. The Serenity Park Fishing and Wildlife Sanctuary also features nature trails and horseback riding activities.

OVERVIEW

Established: 1867
Name Origin: after Queen Catherine of Portugal
Land Area: 1,192.4 sq km (460.4 sq miles)
Capital: Spanish Town
Main Towns: Old Harbour, Portmore, Linstead, Bog Walk, Ewarton
Commerce: Manufacturing, Agriculture, Tourism
Places of Interest: Spanish Town Square, Port Henderson, Sligoville, Flat Bridge
Popular Activities: horseracing, nightlife, fishing, beaches
Interesting fact: the Jamaican Iguana is indigenous to St Catherine

The memorial statue of Admiral George Rodney, depicted as a Roman emperor, was created in 1801 by British sculptor John Bacon. Photo: Andrew P. Smith

St Mary

F ew people in the world would look at a 256-page avifauna book, featuring over 400 species of birds found in the Caribbean, and somehow correlate it to conspiracy theories, terrorists, secret agents and warfare.

In fairness to Ian Fleming, creator of the legendary James Bond character, it was probably more the way the author's name reverberated than the subject matter of the book that inspired him to name his licensed-to-kill spy James Bond. But, believe or not, 007 was named after James Bond, author of the book *Birds of the West Indies*, Fleming's birdwatching bible.

All of this happened while he sat at a desk on his beachfront island retreat in Oracabessa, St Mary, where the calm and charm of his private oasis inspired him. There, on his 15-acre estate called Goldeneye, he wrote fourteen of his James Bond novels, of which, five were set in Jamaica.

For the aspiring novelist or not, Goldeneye today is a highly cherished spot in Jamaica's north-eastern parish. The house is owned by Island Records music producer Chris Blackwell, but private tours can be arranged. A more wet and wild way to see the property is a jet-ski tour along the St Mary coast and up to Fleming Beach.

Bolt Estate House is a nearby ultra-luxurious five-bedroom cottage dating back to the Fleming era. The rich and famous from around the world were entertained at this estate house overlooking the Port Maria Harbour. With its modern renovations, renting this cottage will instantly transport you to another time and space.

St Mary has been an appealing settlement location for centuries. The Spanish created their second city at Port Maria – today, St Mary's capital. ▷

The statue of Noel Coward, at Firefly, overlooks Port Maria Bay. Photo: Jamaica Tourist Board

ABOVE: Ian Fleming's former home is a highly cherished spot in Jamaica's north-eastern parish. Photos: Klaus Wolf

MAIN PICTURE: St Mary's Church at Port Maria.

It was on the shores of the Rio Nuevo town in 1658 that English and Spanish soldiers shed their blood in the last definite stand-off between the two warring nations, before the Spanish retreated to Cuba. This battle ended 150 years of Spanish rule in Jamaica.

Just off shore, in 25-feet of water, is the Rio Nuevo wall dive, with resident barracudas, parrotfish, turtles and other tropical marine life. No one has yet found the spoils from the 1658 aquatic battlefield, but then again anything is possible.

Castleton Gardens is a picnic-lover's paradise. This botanical garden sits in a valley running alongside the Wag Water River. Many varieties of palms and trees provide ample shade in the grassy garden or along the riverside.

St Mary was once synonymous with bananas. Even though bananas stretch for acres and acres across Annotto Bay, today this is only a fraction of its former glory. Sugar, coconut, citrus, pimento, cocoa and several other crops are also cultivated in the area. Prospect Plantation and Brimmer Hall offer guided tours through two working plantations where visitors can experience an actual case study of farming the Jamaican way.

OVERVIEW

Established: 1867 (current demarcation)
Land Area: 610.5 sq km (235.7 sq miles)
Capital: Port Maria
Main Towns: Highgate, Oracabessa, Richmond, Annotto Bay
Commerce: Agriculture, Manufacturing
Places of Interest: Firefly, Goldeneye, Castleton Gardens, Rio Nuevo
Popular Activities: swimming, hiking
Interesting fact: Over the course of the nineteenth century, the number of sugar factories was reduced from 63 to three in the parish of St Mary

St Ann

T he one thing the world knows about Jamaica is the 'one love' reggae music of the Right Honourable Robert Nesta Marley, otherwise known as Bob Marley. Only one parish and one town can claim status as the place of his birth: Nine Mile, St Ann.

Bob Marley was as much influenced by rural community life in his remote hometown as he was by the harsh conditions of life in Downtown Kingston. Every February crowds flock to Nine Mile for the annual concert to celebrate Marley's birthday. But pilgrims year-round wind their way past the scenic settlements of Muir House and Brown's Town, deep into the Hills of St Ann, to tour Marley's homestead.

Visitors go to see where Marley said he would cook cornmeal porridge; to lie down on Marley's famous pillow made of rock, and stand on the spot, Mount Zion Rock, where he used to meditate on life. On this truly unique and inspirational tour, visitors can even say a prayer at the graveside, where Marley is laid to rest.

St Ann was also the parish to nurture Pan-Africanist Marcus Garvey, who galvanised the 'Back to Africa' movement in the United States. He grew up in St Ann's Bay, where he would sit by the Roaring River Falls, observe ships headed for Germany and America loaded with produce, and listen to the grand stories of seamen. He founded the Universal Negro Improvement Association in 1914 and became an inspirational figure for future civil rights activists throughout the world.

Between Bob Marley and Marcus Garvey, St Ann has contributed to widespread global consciousness about Jamaica and the struggle of all human beings for freedom, justice and peace. ▷

Dunn's River Falls. Photo: Jamaica Tourist Board

The parish has come a long way from being a mere pristine Horseshoe Bay, as Christopher Columbus called it when he first landed in Jamaica. It has come a long way from being the first colonial capital on a fifteen-acre settlement of land in Sevilla Nueva, now St Ann's Bay. It has come a long way from its days of nurturing Garvey and Marley.

St Ann is shaped by its rich heritage, and it is moved by modernity, serving as the second largest tourist centre in Jamaica. The town of Ocho Rios was in fact built specifically for the purpose of being a resort town: over 90 percent of the population is employed in tourism and tourism related industries.

The town centre mainly contains craft markets, shopping centres, arcades, banks, supermarkets and restaurants, like the Island Village Shopping Centre, where Jimmy Buffet's popular Margaritaville Bar and Grill is located and the interactive reggae music museum, Reggae Xplosion.

On the peripheries there is everything else: the 600-foot Dunn's River Falls, with semi-vertical climbs interspersed between small lagoons; an aquatic bay to swim and play with trained dolphins; the Green Grotto Caves; and the newest attraction, Mystic Mountain.

The mountain top park is perched 700 feet high at the peak of the actual Mystic Mountain. It is accessed by riding on a towering ski lift, or hiking up a nature trail. The reward is everything from bobsledding, roller coaster rides, waterslides, zipline canopy tours, birdwatching walks and more, over the 100-acre lot of land.

OVERVIEW

Name Origin: after Lady Anne Hyde the first wife of King James II of England
Land Area: 1212.6 sq km (468.2 sq miles)
Capital: St Ann's Bay
Main Towns: Ocho Rios, Browns Town, Runaway Bay, Claremont
Commerce: Tourism, Agriculture, Bauxite Mining, Manufacturing
Places of Interest: Ocho Rios, Discovery Bay, Seville, Moneague Lake, Dunn's River Falls, Fern Gully
Popular Activities: Ochos Rios Jazz Festival (June), golf, bob sledding, waterfall climbing, beaches, dining, dancing
Interesting fact: St Ann has 54 documented caves

Clarendon

There is no point further south in Jamaica than Portland Point, sitting at the tip of Clarendon's natural peninsula. This site is off the regular tourist path, but is of great significance, since it once served as the home of the Arawaks, prior to the arrival of Columbus.

Jackson's Bay Cave, one of more than 57 caves accessible in Clarendon, is also on the peninsula. This cave contained original petroglyphs created by the Arawaks; it has 12,000 feet of passageways with spectacular rock formations and underground lakes to explore. Through the Jamaican Caves Organisation there are organized expeditions for beginners and expert cavers alike.

Despite its extensive cave network, Clarendon is predominantly made up of flat lands, being surrounded by two mountain ranges, the Braziletto Mountains and the Carpenter Mountains. It is known as a dry parish and has, over the years, had to engineer special irrigation schemes to support agricultural production.

Challenges with rainfall did not prevent Clarendon from assuming the right to host the largest agricultural show in the Caribbean: Denbigh Agricultural Show. With a fifty-year history, Denbigh is now an official Jamaican independence activity, held every August to celebrate Jamaica's pride in domestic food production.

The three-day agriculture show welcomes 60,000 enthusiasts to view the biggest and best livestock, produce, agricultural technology and horticultural exhibitions from farmers across the island. The hallmark events are the National Champion Farmer, the National Young Farmer Competition and the Coronation of the National Farm Queen.

Not all Clarendonians get their hands dirty; many of them have a need for speed, and they indulge this craving at regular drag racing events.

Jamaica's first car-racing track was established just over sixty years ago on a United States army air force base. Vernam Air Force Base housed bomber squadrons during the Second World War that conducted antisubmarine patrols in the Northern Caribbean. It was later used as a weather reporting facility for the US military.

When it was finally closed in 1949, it became derelict for decades until the drag racers took over what was left of the original 6000-foot concrete runway and two shorter asphalt runways. Car racing is now popular across Jamaica, with dirt bike racing tracks and go-cart tracks in other parts of the island. In 2007, a local reality television show, Jamspeed Adrenaline Rush, was even developed as a spin-off from the sport's popularity.

Milk River Spa is a major natural mineral spring and heritage site, famous for its therapeutic waters. The level of radioactivity in this bath is nine times higher than the level of the most active bath in England and 54 times as active as the Baden Bath in Switzerland. The radioactive properties along with the mineral content is what makes Milk River valuable in treating ailments like gout, rheumatism, eczema, and kidney and liver troubles.

Influential Harlem Renaissance poet Claude McKay was a native of Clarendon. His liberating writings gave inspiration to a generation of civil rights activists.

OVERVIEW

Name Origin: in honour of the Lord Chancellor Sir Edward Hyde, Earl of Clarendon
Land Area: 1196 sq km (461.9 sq miles)
Capital: May Pen
Main Towns: Chapelton
Commerce: Agriculture, Bauxite Mining
Places of Interest: Milk River Bath, Rio Minho, Vernam Field, Halse Hall Great House
Popular Activities: Racecar driving, caving, beaches
Interesting Fact: The parish was formed from a combination of three parishes: St Dorothy's, Vere and the old parish of Clarendon. Before the merger, the capital was Chapelton

Stocking up on ice at Rocky Point. Photo: Klaus Wolf

Manchester

While the earth in Manchester may appear to be bleeding, it is only the aluminous rich reddish-brown bauxite characteristic of Jamaica's sedimentary rock core. Bauxite has been mined for commercial export in Jamaica since the 1950s; the industry is the largest commodity export sector in Jamaica.

Deposits of varying sizes exist across the island, from the north-east in Trelawny to the south-west in St Catherine. The largest deposits are in Manchester, and in some of the surrounding parishes like Trelawny and St Elizabeth. In most instances bauxite is unprocessed and exported to Europe and North America, but Manchester was first in the island with a processing plant to produce the refined derivative material alumina. While the industry has been eclipsed in importance by remittance revenues and the fast growing tourism industry, it remains an important sector for Jamaica.

Bauxite is usually found 1000 feet above sea level. Manchester is situated in a prime position with altitudes varying between 2000 and 3300 feet. These high altitudes also make Manchester ideal for coffee farming. Jamaica's most high profile brew is Blue Mountain Coffee, but Manchester coffee farmers situated in the Don Figueroa, May Day and Carpenter Mountains are also highly rated.

While the bauxite industry has had an impact on the availability of productive farmlands, agriculture and agro-business remain the largest employers of labour in the parish. Manchester leads the country in corn production and Irish potato cultivation; dairy farming exists along with farming of ground provisions, pimento and banana. ▷

Red mud lake. Photo: Klaus Wolf

Propagation of the famous orange and tangerine crossbreed, the ortanique, began in Manchester in 1920 thanks to the likes of farmer Charles Jackson. This hybrid fruit is a favourite of Jamaicans, often bought along the roadside in large bags when travelling through the country.

Manchester is not caffeine free, but it is the only parish in Jamaica that can boast of being sugar free. Sugarcane plantations never ventured into Manchester. Possibly because the hilly countryside that now constitutes the parish was once the wilderness area of three other parishes, including one of the sugar super states, St Elizabeth.

The capital Mandeville is in the centre of the parish. It is a wealthy city with modernised communications systems and pizzazz. Driving through the town is a tour in itself, with many mansions and manicured lawns to observe. Many colonialists would take holiday retreats in Mandeville and eventually settled there after emancipation. As the 'coldest' parish in Jamaica, the temperate climate suited them. Today, many Jamaicans live in Mandeville to savour the quality of life and commute 62 miles daily to Kingston.

A popular rest stop just outside of Mandeville is located at the top of Spur Tree Hill, the gateway to St Elizabeth, where a steep road switchbacks down the hillside. Many travellers stop to grab a pound of jerk chicken, pork or sausage, smoked on an open pit grill, before they descend into the plain.

FACING PAGE: Church in Mandeville.
ABOVE: Mandeville Courthouse. Photos: Klaus Wolf

OVERVIEW

Established: 1814
Land Area: 830.1 km (320.1 sq miles)
Name Origin: Duke of Manchester, then Governor of Jamaica for nineteen years, setting the record as the longest serving Governor of the island
Capital: Mandeville, laid out in 1816, and named after Viscount Mandeville, the eldest son of the Duke of Manchester
Main Towns: Christiana, Mile Gully, Newport, Porus, Williamsfield
Commerce: Tourism, Agriculture, Bauxite Mining, Manufacturing
Places of Interest: Kendal, Northern Caribbean University
Popular Activities: golfing, birdwatching, hiking
Interesting Fact: No rivers run through this parish. In 1865, the Manchester Horticultural Society was formed and is one of the oldest in the world. Manchester Golf Club was established in 1868 making it the first golf course in the Caribbean.

Trelawny

It seems like the twenty-first century is shaping up to be another era for once-in-a-lifetime leaders. From Barack Obama, the first African American president of the United States, to Usain Bolt, Jamaica's sprinting mastermind; the genius of fate producing both men has enabled them to realise feats unparalleled in history.

Usain Bolt, a country boy from Trelawny, rose to international stardom in 2008 when he became the first man since Carl Lewis in 1984 to win three sprinting events at a single Olympics. To top that achievement he also ran world record times in all three events, and later took the two top sprinting titles in the World Championships that season.

Long before the lights started flashing in Beijing, Usain Bolt was a household name in Jamaica, making his early mark at the Jamaica National Boys and Girls [High School] Championships ("Champs"). The phenomenon of Champs is largely credited as the reason why Jamaican athletes are so successful. The competitive climate at this athletics meet is even greater than that of senior national championships. The sponsorship dollars are arguably greater too.

With a 100 year history to boast of, Champs today features over 3,500 athletes from 150 schools, competing in front of 30,000 fanatical devotees at the National Stadium: that is more than seven times the size of England's national high school championship. Trelawny's brightest Bolt won his first Champs medal in 2001 when he took silver in the 200 metres. He broke both the 200-metre and 400-metre records in 2003, just before he launched his senior career.

Bolt might be an international megastar today, but his roots are in the north-western heart of rural Jamaica. Trelawny might not appear to be an ▷

Rafting on the Martha Brae River. Photo: Jamaica Tourist Board

Olympic gold factory, but look again; this parish also gave birth to Veronica Campbell-Brown, Merlene Frazer and Michael Green, all highly successful Jamaican Olympians.

What makes Trelawny so special to have produced Bolt and his band of lightening fast compatriots could be anyone's guess. Some say it is the Trelawny yam, but no one really knows the secret. Another unique feature of Trelawny is the great Cockpit Country; a 500 square mile wet limestone forest, with towering cliffs, underground rivers, caves and flowing waterfalls. This largely unpopulated area is a taste of prehistoric Jamaica, home to many species of indigenous birds, plants and reptiles. The area gets its name from an abundance of conical hills and deep sinkholes that undulate across the terrain.

Trelawny received great exposure in 2007 when its US $30 million Greenfield Stadium was inaugurated for the 2007 Cricket World Cup. The multi-purpose stadium, just 40 km east of Montego Bay, was constructed primarily to host the opening ceremony. It has a 25,000 seating capacity and is now used for other sports like football, rugby and American football.

Opening around the same time was the Outameni Experience, an interactive, multimedia cultural village. At each section of the guided village tour the stage is set in a different historical era: Taino, Spanish, African, English, Indian, Chinese and modern. Locals from each era re-enact various plots and schemes to give visitors a real taste of the many colours of Jamaica. The Georgian architecture from the old British era is so well preserved in the capital Falmouth that in 1996 the city was declared a national heritage site.

OVERVIEW

Established: 1770
Name Origin: after William Trelawny, former Governor of Jamaica
Land Area: 874.6 sq km (337.7 sq miles)
Capital: Falmouth
Main Towns: Clarks Town, Duncans, Wakefield, Wait-a-Bit, Albert Town
Commerce: Agriculture, Manufacturing
Places of Interest: Martha Brae River, Rio Bueno
Interesting fact: In its heyday there were more sugar estates in Trelawny than in any other parish

St Elizabeth

The only thing more spectacular than the athletic talent of Jamaican sprinters is the national pride of the Jamaica people. Even as the largest English-speaking island in the Caribbean Sea, Jamaica is only 146 miles long and 51 miles wide. In true opposition to the belief that size matters, Jamaicans would say: "we likkle, but we tallawah". Jamaica is small, but strong, powerful and not to be underestimated.

There is one source of national pride not often spoken about in public, particularly during the day in the company of ladies. But at night, when the city lights come on, the speaker boxes blaze up, and the rum bars across the island open their doors, the one thing on the minds of many Jamaicans is the selection of home-grown beers, wines and spirits on the drink menu. Red Stripe beer might be the most hip local brand, but Appleton Estate Jamaica Rum is the most cherished, with over 250 years of history.

The parish of St Elizabeth might as well be the rum capital of Jamaica: 11,000 acres of land inside the Siloah Valley of the Black River region are occupied by Jamaica's oldest sugar estate and distillery, Appleton Estates. The range of premium rums produced by the distillery, such as Appleton Estate 21 Year Old Jamaica Rum and Wray and Nephew White Overproof Rum, is available in 65 countries around the world. The Appleton Brand is a repeat gold title winner in the prestigious International Wine & Spirit Competition.

As the second largest parish in Jamaica, St Elizabeth has a lot of land to provide many opportunities, and not just in food and beverage. The Caribbean's premiere literary event, the lively three-day Calabash International Literary Festival, is hosted every May in Treasure Beach. The star- ▷

Treasure Beach. Photo: Jamaica Tourist Board

Fishing community at Alligator Pond Bay. Photo: Jamaica Tourist Board

studded line-up assembled every year for storytelling, poetry reading and music is enough to make festival-goers keep coming back. Treasure Beach is also home to Jamaica's longest running triathlon, the annual charity event, Jakes Off Road Triathlon.

In the area, there are many fine guesthouses serving as great hideaways for peaceful vacations, business retreats or special events. Taino Cove's meeting room and guest suites overlooking the mosaic tiled pool deck and beachfront have been the perfect host for off-site business meetings, photo shoots, wedding parties, wine tasting, family reunions and for getting away to relax.

For being the parish to bring Jamaica its first electricity, first imported motor car and first racehorse track, St Elizabeth is accustomed to being first. Another pioneering effort for the parish was wind power. Munro College is an all-boys boarding school which was established 150 years ago to provide education to boys in the poverty stricken region. The institution was the first in Jamaica to receive an independent power producer licence for renewable energy technology. Their 225-kilowatt turbine sits 3000 feet above sea level at the highest point of the Santa Cruz Mountain Range, one of three ranges in the parish, along with the Lacovia Mountains and the Nassau Mountains.

OVERVIEW

Created: 1814 (latest demarcation)
Name Origin: after the wife of Sir Thomas Modyford, the first English Governor of Jamaica
Land Area: 1212.4 sq km (468.1 sq miles)
Capital: Black River
Main Towns: Santa Cruz, Maggoty, Junction, Balaclava
Commerce: Tourism, Agriculture, Bauxite Mining, Sugar
Places of Interest: Y.S. Falls, Mexico cave, Peru Cave, Lovers Leap, Bamboo Avenue, Accompong

St James

Slave revolts played an important role in Jamaica's colonial history. The uprising that gave St James its notoriety occurred on the cusp of emancipation. While abolitionists were battling in England, Sam Sharpe, a Baptist preacher from St James, was mobilising a secret society of fellow Africans in the art of passive resistance.

Sharpe was one of the few literate slaves. In 1831, he became convinced slavery was abolished. He was just two years too soon. But he and his followers refused to work during the Christmas holidays unless they received due recognition from their estate owners.

As word spread of the civil disobedience, the colonial government mobilised their warships. Slaves set fire to a building on the Kensington Estate and a violent clash ensued, leaving many dead and much destroyed. The reprisal was swift and severe: Sharpe paid with his life. For six weeks following, there were daily hangings of slaves, two at a time, in the city centre. Sharpe was later named a Jamaican national hero, and Sam Sharpe Square, Montego Bay, became a memorial to the struggle.

As Jamaica's official second city, Montego Bay has all the facilities of a large urban centre and all of the allure of a most favoured tourist destination. The five-mile stretch of white sand known as Doctor's Cave Beach is one of the best on the island. Art galleries, craft markets and shopping centres abound.

Chukka Caribbean Adventures has 28 innovative and award winning tours, largely centred in Montego Bay and Ocho Rios. A dog-sled tour is the latest instalment to their line-up of river tubing, white-water rafting, zip-line canopy tours, all-terrain vehicle rides, kayaking and more. ▷

Rose Hall Great House. Photo: Jamaica Tourist Board

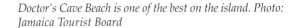
Doctor's Cave Beach is one of the best on the island. Photo: Jamaica Tourist Board

St James is also a magnet for investors. A steady stream of domestic and foreign direct investment has helped to develop the parish. The completion of the North Coast Highway connecting Montego Bay to Ocho Rios in St Ann was a major development, providing a central artery to increase accessibility and efficiency.

Since 2000, Spanish investors have put more than US $2 billion into tourism, transportation and telecommunications in Jamaica, including developments like the lush and lavish adults-only Iberostar Rose Hall Beach and Spa Resort. They compete with other international luxury resorts along the north coast highway like the new Palmyra Resort and Spa, the Ritz Carlton Golf and Spa Resort and Rose Hall Resort and Spa.

Chinese investors are also in the mix. Their bilateral cooperation with the Jamaican government was set up to fund the construction of a convention centre, providing 20,000 square meters of meeting rooms, exhibition halls and other event spaces.

Jamaican investors are keeping up. The largest shopping village on the island is wrapping up construction. The Whitter Village Centre is the largest mall in the Caribbean and is designed to emulate a traditional Jamaican town in four blocks of eight units with 32 skilfully designed offices. The Village will boast a bandstand area for live entertainment, a children's playpen, exhibition pavilion, landscaped gardens and outside dining areas.

The annual Jamaica Jazz and Blues Festival and the Reggae Sumfest festival provide an annual boost to the St James economy.

OVERVIEW

Created: 1665
Name Origin: named after Duke of York, who later became James II
Land Area: 549.9 sq km (212.3 sq miles)
Capital: Montego Bay
Main Towns: Adelphi, Cambridge, Montpelier, Catadupa, Fairfield, Somerton, Irwin, Dumfries
Commerce: Tourism, Agriculture, Manufacturing

Westmoreland

Jamaicans will often joke that, wherever in the world you go, Jamaicans "deh deh". In other words, from down under to the Far East, in desert storms or ice blizzards, you will always find a true Jamaican, or at least a wannabe.

There is no escaping Jamaica's reach abroad, but the joke plays the other way too. Jamaica's national motto, 'Out of Many, One People', is truly representative of the many cultural influences on the island: there are descendents of Amerindians, Africans, Europeans, Indians, Chinese, Jews, Syrians, Lebanese and more.

Travel through the west coast and you might find a group of dark-skinned Jamaicans with blue eyes and blond hair. These are the genetic remnants of the nineteenth-century Germans who once inhabited the hills of Westmoreland, at their primary settlement in Seaford Town. While there is little German retention, some names survived, such as Hacker, Eldemire and Schleifer. The largest impact was left on the religious life of the west, where the Moravian church thrives.

There are several value-added experiences to explore the hills of Westmoreland and rural Jamaica, in an increasing trend of community tourism. Countrystyle Jamaica is an award winning company that designs community tourism experiences, like village weddings, home stays and study tours. Their popular Beeston Spring Experience is a walking tour of a 140-year-old, award winning community, about 30 minutes uphill from the new Sandals Whitehouse European Village & Spa.

On the tour, there is a stop at the natural spring which gave the community its name; the New Hope Moravian Church built in the 1860s; and a send off party, featuring live traditional ▷

Negril is a favoured tourism destination. Photo: Jamaica Tourist Board

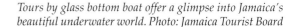
mento music, a precursor to ska, rocksteady and reggae.

Westmoreland's traditional sun, sand and sea offerings are not to be outdone. Negril is by far one of the best places in Jamaica to watch the sunset. The spectacular views are best enjoyed along the cliffy coast of Negril's west end. Several boutique resorts, like the Villas Sur Mer or Rockhouse Hotel, are chiselled into the cliffs. Most resorts have low platforms for cliff jumping, but the most famous is a 35-foot platform at Rick's Café restaurant and bar.

A seven-mile stretch of white sand beach can be found a few miles north of the cliffs, on the hip strip, with a row of small, medium and large hotels and restaurants. Some of the most popular spots include all-inclusive hotels like Sandals Negril, Poinciana Beach Resort, Grand Lido and Hedonism II.

Every December, thousands of people run through the streets of Negril, participating in Jamaica's premier international marathon event, The Reggae Marathon & Half Marathon. This road race is known for its creativity, with reggae music blasting along the race route at one-mile intervals to keep up the 'irie' mood.

One of the newest Negril attractions is the Kool Runnings Water Park: an enchanting place for splashing, sliding, swimming and floating about in one of ten super slides, and a lazy river. Cooling down in this water world might just be the perfect remedy for the natural high experienced when exploring the many facets of Westmoreland.

OVERVIEW

Established: 1703
Name Origin: because of its western location
Land Area: 807.0 km (311.6 sq miles)
Capital: Savanna-la-mar
Main Towns: Whitehouse, Bluefields, Little London, Negril, Frome, Seaford Town
Commerce: Tourism, Agriculture, Manufacturing
Places of Interest: Savanna-La-Mar Fort, Negril Point Lighthouse, Mannings High School
Popular Activities: water sports, cliff diving
Interesting Fact: The wetlands of Westmoreland, called the Great Morass, are home to Jamaica's crocodiles

Hanover

D rive north of the white sand beaches of Negril or west of the cruise ship capital Montego Bay and you will end up in the picturesque parish of Hanover, located at the most north-western tip of Jamaica. Many motorists zip past Hanover, manoeuvring through the busy streets of its capital, Lucea, and never stop to discover this historic town once inhabited by the indigenous Taino people of the Caribbean.

Hanover might be a rural farming parish, but locals know the mountainous terrain and picturesque coastline has much more to offer than meets the eye. The luxurious resorts offer their guests a level of privacy many crave. Top among them is the five-star Grand Palladium Jamaica Resort and Spa, with its five swimming pools, over ten restaurants, kids' club and soundproofed rooms.

The Tryall Club, often mistakenly identified as being in St James, is known for its glamorous weddings, where brides can choose from a number of locations across the sprawling plantation. From the Great House to the garden, or the beach to the pier, each venue is full of enchantment. They are almost as dazzling as the spectacular views on the 18-hole, 6,221-yard, par-72 championship golf course designed by Texas golf course architect Ralph Plummer.

Ask a Jamaican about Hanover and a well-known titbit you might hear is that the parish gave birth to Jamaica's first Prime Minister, Sir Alexander Bustamante. In the centre of Sir Alexander Bustamante Square sits a clock tower braced by Corinthian columns. This distinctive landmark was mistakenly sent to Hanover's capital, Lucea, in the early nineteenth century. It was, in fact, a gift from Germany for the people of the southern Caribbean island of St Lucia. ▷

Tryall Waterwheel. Photo: Jamaica Tourist Board

Bustamante was a pre-eminent agitator for Jamaican independence. While he is buried with his wife at Hero's Circle, a memorial for Jamaica's national heroes in Kingston, their three-acre residence in Hanover is a museum and heritage site.

One 'must-do' activity while in Hanover is to feast on the many varieties of yam cultivated on a large scale in the parish. Of the varieties like sweet yam, yellow yam and negro yam, Lucea yam is by far the most popular.

Hanover is one of the few parishes in Jamaica where you can still witness traditional African ancestral ceremonies being practised. The African retentions of the Ettu people in Hanover originate from the enslaved African labourers, who arrived in Jamaica from as early as the sixteenth century. As decedents of the Yoruba people of Nigeria, these Hanover natives perform special ceremonies on occasions like deaths and weddings. Other African retentions on the island include Revival and Kumina spiritual practices.

The perfect daytrip to Hanover might just involve comfortable walking shoes, a packed lunch and a short hike through the wooded hills to visit the Cousins Cove Cave. These caves served as a major archaeological site for researchers at the University of the West Indies, who discovered a burial ground and cave paintings from the era of the Tainos. Artefacts are now displayed inside the Hanover Museum.

OVERVIEW

Established: 1723
Name Origin: after the ruling British family at the time
Land Area: 450.4 sq km (173.9 sq miles)
Capital: Lucea
Main Towns: Sandy Bay, Hopwell, Chester Castle, Riverside, Green Island
Commerce: Tourism, Agriculture, Manufacturing
Places of Interest: Fort Charlotte, Lucea Harbour, Kenilworth, Tryall Waterwheel, Clifton Cave and Cousins Cove Cave, Riley River Rafting
Popular Activities: golfing, caving, swimming, heritage tours
Interesting Fact: Animal Hill was so named because the hog, deer and lamb families lived there.

Food for the heart and soul

SHARON ATKIN-O'BRIEN

The cuisine of Jamaica is a synthesis of many cultures, races and religions that have migrated to the island since the sixteenth century, following the arrival of Christopher Columbus.

Since the times of the original Taino inhabitants, cassava, corn, guavas, roasted fish and crabs have been an integral part of the cuisine.

Once the Spanish arrived in large numbers during the sixteenth century they introduced not only flora, fauna and a variety of livestock to the island but also different methods of cooking and preparing food. Limes, lemons, Seville oranges, sugar cane, plantains and bananas, naseberries, guinep, coconut, ginger and tamarinds were widely used. Pigs, goats and cattle not only provided the Spanish with more variety of meals but also with cooking fat – as lard – in the absence of olive oil.

When the British finally occupied the island, they replaced the workforce with enslaved Africans, largely from West Africa. The influx of both Africans and British coincided with more fruit and vegetables being introduced both to feed the slaves and settlers and to develop for export.

The infamous Captain Bligh of 'The Bounty' was responsible for the introduction of ackee and breadfruit, whilst the Africans brought coffee, okra, cocoa and calabash.

Spices were an important commodity both for home use and export. Food given to slaves was often poor in quality, so the spices and peppers not only enhanced the flavour but also disguised the rancid meat and dried fish that the slave masters provided. Allspice, nutmeg and Scotch bonnet peppers were used to enhance various dishes.

Sephardic Jews had originally settled in Jamaica when the Spanish controlled the island but chose to remain after the British took control, and from that community the egg plant, also known as aubergine, was brought into the island and is still widely grown and used today. It is also thought that the Jews also brought sesame seeds, which they used in the early years to make cakes and sweetmeats.

Another significant group was drawn from the system of indentured workers, which the British brought to Jamaica following the abolition of slavery. Irish, Chinese and Indians all settled and with them came their cuisine. Today, the potato is still called Irish potato in order to differentiate between sweet potato and yams.

The East Indians were responsible for the enduring and immensely popular curry goat and many other curried dishes such as lobster and chicken. Chinese cuisine has remained very popular ▷

FACING PAGE: Jerk chicken is an almost essential ingredient to any Jamaican celebration or gathering. Photo: Josh Hunter

BELOW: Ackee and saltfish is the national dish. Photo: Brian Rosen

in Jamaica and can be found in many restaurants around the island.

On the east coast of the island, where many of the British settlers were Scottish, their culinary legacy is typified by porridge, although it is true that the Tainos also made a similar dish from maize.

The British also introduced Christmas pudding and Christmas cakes, which nowadays have been adapted by Jamaican cooks to make the most fabulous cakes heavily laced with Jamaican rum.

The last significant group of settlers to Jamaica were Arabs. Their style of cooking has largely been incorporated into mainstream Jamaican cuisine – such as pulses and flatbread, which are still associated with this community.

The Maroons maintained their traditional methods of cooking, especially in the settlements at Accompong, Moores Town and Charles Town. The famous jerk pork, which was prepared almost exclusively in the Parish of Portland, emanates from the Maroons in that district. Today, it is widely available throughout Jamaica but many still claim that the best jerk is from Portland.

One-pot cooking, in the form of stews and soups, dates back to the days of slavery when fuel was in short supply, labour was hard and the cuts of meat needed long, slow cooking.

Pulses in the form of red peas and gungo peas, which have given us rice and peas, has now spread around the world especially when so many Jamaicans migrated to Britain, Canada and the USA.

Ackee and saltfish is wholly associated with Jamaica. Originally cooked as a breakfast dish, it is now often served at any time. Outside of Jamaica, ackee is only available in tins but salt fish can be found in many countries, especially in Britain, France, Spain and Portugal.

Another famous food of Jamaica is the patty. Thought to have originated in Haiti, it is now very much associated with Jamaican cuisine. Patties, which were traditionally made with spiced beef in a pastry case and sold as snacks, are now made with a variety of fillings including saltfish, vegetarian, curried goat and chicken.

Over the years, Jamaican coffee has come to be regarded as the best in the world. Grown in the famous Blue Mountains, it has a depth of flavour but is never bitter and remains the most sought after coffee worldwide.

Like coffee, Jamaican rum and more recently Jamaican beer enjoys popularity around the world.

The huge variety of fruits such as guavas, oranges, Seville oranges, grapefruit, shaddock and the home-developed ortanique are invaluable sources of vitamin C and also provide the basis for many juices, marmalades and preserves. Jamaican honey is another important food source, which today is recognised as having excellent properties that heal, nourish and boost the immune system.

The diversity of Jamaican cuisine must also include the Rastafarian element to cooking and preparing food, and the aspect of the nation's approach to healthy eating. Rastafarians refrain from eating pork and many do not eat meat or poultry; some eat fish while others are either strict vegetarians or vegans but all believe in eating low salt diets and cooking in an 'Ital' way. Rastafarian cooking is similar to the Mediterranean diet, which has been hailed by the medical profession in recent years as extremely healthy and well balanced.

The food of Jamaica owes much to the creativity and ingenuity of the host of diverse settlers and the indigenous people. The climate, rich soil, tropical waters and the range of available fruit, fish, vegetables and livestock has resulted in a remarkable cuisine which is healthy, nutritious, varied and full of flavour. Like reggae music, Blue Mountain Coffee and Usain Bolt, Jamaican cuisine is now available throughout the globe … and to critical acclaim! ∎

FACING PAGE: One-pot cooking dates back to the days of slavery. Photo: Josh Hunter

Jamaica's heritage in music and dance

Jamaica's rich tradition of music and dance, which resulted from the European and African influence in the country's history, has transitioned into truly indigenous artistic creations.

The traditional dances emerged as African slaves mixed movements specific to their native tribes with those of the Europeans. Dances such as the 'dinki minnie', 'ettu', 'quadrille', 'maypole' and 'goombeh' were developed, and are still practised today.

Dances like 'jonkunnu' (called John Canoe by the British) took on increasing significance in slave society when the European masters began to encourage festivities among the slaves on their plantations. Jonkunnu is a band of masqueraders who would perform at Christmas in villages and towns. The characters, such as 'King', 'Queen', 'Devil', 'Pitchy Patchy' and 'Belly Woman', were frightening to onlookers.

A new dance, 'bruckins', was performed in celebration of the Emancipation from slavery. It was an amalgam of European and African elements and participants wore elaborate costumes which depicted the extravagance of the Royal Court. The main movement was a dip or 'kotch' of the body as dancers moved their arms across their chests in an upward movement.

Since the post-Emancipation era, several popular and distinctly Jamaican dance moves have emerged, and continue to receive local and international attention for their vibrance and dexterity. The traditional and modern dances have kept pace to match with the rapid and ongoing evolution of Jamaica's music forms, beginning with mento in the mid 1900s – a fusion of African and British music.

Traditional dances continue to receive local and international attention. Photo: Jamaica Tourist Board

ABOVE: Maroon drummers during Nanny Day celebrations. Photo: Josh Hunter

Blending the rhythms of mento with the melodies and themes of North American rhythm and blues, Jamaica produced ska in the early 1960s and this ushered in the era of sound systems and nightly dance sessions. Ska began to decline in the late 1960s and transitioned into rocksteady, whose lyrics reflected the social, political and economic conditions in the society. Rocksteady incorporated electronic sounds and instruments to create more complex melodies and heavier bass lines.

By the end of the early 1970s, rocksteady gave way to reggae. Characterised by heavy, melodic bass and complex instrumentals, reggae's popularity has grown on the local and international stages. Credit for its popularisation worldwide is given to talented performers such as Bob Marley, Dennis Brown and the group Black Uhuru.

While reggae's popularity has not waned, it laid the foundation for 'deejay' and 'dancehall', which originated as artistes began to speak rhythmically over reggae beats. These music forms and their accompanying dances have acquired a significant number of fans internationally.

While it is a phenomenon of the Eastern Caribbean, calypso has steadily gained popularity in Jamaica, and several Jamaican groups have gained international fame for association with calypso. Local groups such as Fab Five, Byron Lee and the Dragonnaires, and the Bare Essentials, have placed Jamaica among the top calypso groups from the Caribbean.

Also of note are ballet, Rastafarian music, gospel, jazz and classical music, which have an important place in the rich tapestry of Jamaican music and dance.

Music and dance continue to be an outlet for creative expression, and play an integral role in uniting Jamaicans at home and abroad. ∎

Adapted from 'Rhythms: Jamaica's Heritage in Music and Dance', published by the Jamaica Information Service

The musical styles of Jamaica

HERBIE MILLER

Jamaica is, perhaps, best recognised for its music. So popular is the island's reggae beat that it has become a generic term representing all popular Jamaican music including mento, ska, rock steady, roots reggae and the current fad, dancehall. Like the rest of the Caribbean, Jamaica's folk, play and ritual music has strong ties to Africa and the 'middle passage'. It is also influenced by European musical traditions. So too has the island's popular music been a reflection of this experience. Jamaican musical heritage is therefore symbolic of what cultural scholar Professor Rex Nettleford calls "the rhythm of Africa meeting the melody of Europe".

QUADRILLE

Quadrille was the preferred music and dance of the British plantocracy during the 19th century. It has a number of variations and is still performed at special cultural events and festivals across the island. Utilising guitars, banjo and fife, it at times, when available, also adds bass fiddle or rumba box. Black musicians, who added a break or fifth figure that gave birth to mento, performed quadrille at colonial balls during the plantation period.

MENTO

Mento is a 19th century musical form that has its roots in both European and African antecedents. To entertain their masters, slaves performed this blend of quadrille and Afro-Jamaican rhythms. A typical band was five musicians performing on fiddle or violin, banjo, fife, shakers and a vocalist who doubled on guitar or one of the earlier mentioned instruments. By the early 1900s, the rumba box was introduced by Jamaican workers returning from reaping sugar cane on Cuban plantations.

Mento reached its highest popularity in the 1950s with stars like Harold Richardson and the Ticklers, Lord Fly, Count Lasher, and Lord Flea, its biggest star. One such star was Sugar Belly a unique musician playing a homemade bamboo saxophone who lasted well into the seventies doing studio recordings and performing in stage shows and festivals.

Mento's earliest stars found work in hotels entertaining tourists on Jamaicans north coast. Mento bands are sometimes required to supply the music for floorshow acts like limbo dancers and stilt walkers and usually relieve pop music bands in tourist resorts. Many, especially in rural areas, also performed in communities where bands played at wakes and nine nights for the bereaved family and friends of their recently deceased loved ones. This light-hearted Jamaican music re-emerged within the last few years as an addition to Jamaica's musical export. Current bands are the Jolly Boys, the Lititz Mento Band, the Blue Glaze Band and the late Stanley Beckford. Often confused with, and referred to as, calypso, mento continues to be popular among eclectic music connoisseurs and foreigners, especially Europeans, for its humour, social commentary and suggestiveness.

JAZZ

Though never attracting a major following, jazz in Jamaica had a loyal audience. The big band tradition was picked up and carried on by leading orchestras on the island during the 1940s through the early 1950s. Bands like Redver Cook, Milton McPherson, Roy Coburn and the legendary Eric Deans Orchestras sharpened the talents of musicians that would later make names for themselves on both sides of the Atlantic. Saxophonists Wilton Gaynair, Harold "Little G' McNair, and Joe Harriott; trumpeters Dizzy Reece and Sonny Gray, and pianist Monty Alexander are among the many that established themselves internationally. A second generation remained at ▷

Joe Harriott made his name on both sides of the Atlantic

home and became the innovators of ska, which would become the next phase in the evolution of popular Jamaican music.

Jazz continues to be of relatively minor interest in Jamaica and for its fans it is kept alive by the veteran trumpeter and bandleader Sonny Bradshaw – whose sixty-year involvement in local music ended with his death in 2009. His big band consists of young and veteran musicians willing to support Bradshaw in his willingness to educate and entertain using jazz or as he calls it "Black classical music". Bradshaw also produced the annual Ocho Rios Jazz Festival, which celebrated its twentieth anniversary in 2010. He presented jazz in its purest form bringing to Jamaica authentic practitioners of the genre presenting them with the best of the local players. Over the years they have included James Moody, Jimmy Smith, Herbie Mann and Huston Person. The Jamaica Jazz and Blues Festival is another musical event held annually in Montego Bay. It is a more commercial music festival that is light on jazz and blues and heavy on vintage R&B, contemporary soul, pop, reggae and country and western music, which have proven to be a huge success with locals. Live smooth jazz can be heard at clubs across Kingston and in hotel taverns.

NIABINGHI

Prior to 1959, popular Jamaican music was mento, which was also the music of Rastafarians. Mystic Revelation of Rastafari, lead by master drummer Count Ossie, was first known as Count Ossie and the African Drums. Their achievements are many and important beyond measure. It was not until Count drew on references from both Kumina and Burru, both traditional drumming forms, that Rastafarians codified a unique musical identity. And by attracting the best jazz horn players to Wareaka Hills for jam sessions called 'grounations' these Rastafarian drummers played a seminal role in the development of popular Jamaican music. "Oh! Carolina," being the touchstone of musical innovation and excellence, became the template for what would become ska and its later derivatives. It was the drums of Rastafari that made it a hit and provided Count Ossie and his drummers their breakthrough recording. Modern Jamaican music has continued to evolve over that fifty-year period. Indeed, it was the dynamic rhythm of "Oh! Carolina" that catapulted DJ superstar Shaggy to occupy the number one spot on both sides of the Atlantic in 1993. The seniors among the Mystic Revelation of Rastafari have lived the span that reflects the totality of our popular musical evolution and Niabinghi music has become a genre that is at once ritual and commercial.

SKA

By 1959, there were two distinct musical streams established by local musicians. On one hand there was a main stream played by older and more sociably established musicians led by Carlos Malcolm and Sonny Bradshaw that included Bertie King, Taddy Mowatt, Baba Motta and others. On the other hand, a group of younger socially radicalised musicians aligned with Rastafari drummer, Count Ossie, comprised the latter. It included among its leading figures, trombonists Don Drummond and Rico Rodriquez, trumpeter Johnny "Dizzy" Moore, trap drummer Lloyd Knibb, and tenor saxophonists Tommy McCook and Roland Alphonso. The first group of musicians relied on traditional jazz sensibility merging it with Jamaican folk and mento music in an effort to remain current, if not to search for an elusive 'riddim'. The younger set represented the ongoing reality that jazz is forever avant-garde, fluid and daring. By applying bebop approaches they embraced Rastafari riddims, largely unexposed to the mainstream audience. They drew on traditional and diverse sources such as mento, Afro-Cuban jazz and American rhythm and blues superimposing on them hot bebop solos to innovate and introduce the new musical expression called ska.

During the sixties, as ska reached an international audience, the Skatalites were the most authentic ska band. Half of its members were graduates of the famous Alpha Boys School in Kingston. They were, however, all outstanding musicians giving the band an all-star personnel. Ska had a fast paced rhythm over which the horn players soloed in the jazz tradition. Some of the Skatalites' members, such as Don Drummond, Tommy McCook, Roland Alphonso and pianist/organist Jackie Mittoo, became household names because of the lead role they played as soloists and as individual recording artists. Songs like "Eastern Standard Time," "Freedom Sounds," and "Tear Up," have become standards and have provided a point of departure for many contemporary music arrangements.

During the 1960s, the Skatalites were also the pre-eminent studio band backing early artists like Prince Buster, Derrick Morgan, the Wailers, Alton Ellis, Jimmy Cliff, Justin Hines and the Dominoes, Toots and the Maytals and many others. Additional bands playing ska were Carlos Malcolm's Afro-Jamaican rhythm, Byron Lee and the Dragonaires and the Vikings, though, none with the authenticity, authority, or conviction of the Skatalites. Ska waned by 1965 giving way to its offspring, rocksteady. Today, ska can be heard as part of the repertoire of most bands and remains popular with older fans and younger revellers.

Bob Marley, left, was reggae's pre-eminent personality, but others such as Jimmy Cliff are also renowned across the globe.

ROCKSTEADY

With the decline of ska came the emergence of rocksteady. This musical style was much slower than ska and with it more singers emerged. Among the first songs to become popular in this new style were Hopeton Lewis's "Take It Easy," Roy Shirley's "Hold Them", and Alton Ellis's "Girl I've Got A Date". Rock Steady also switched from the predominant horns associated with ska and placed emphasis on solid melodic bass lines instead of the 4/4 lines that pulsated ska. Dancing was also less energetic and partygoers were able to occupy the dance floor for longer periods of time. Among the stars of the rocksteady period are the Paragons, Heptones, Wailers – popular through all styles of Jamaican popular music – Ken Boothe, Bob Andy and the late Alton Ellis who was considered the godfather of rocksteady. Like its predecessor, ska, rocksteady only lasted a relatively short time and by 1968 reggae was the new rhythm that Jamaicans were dancing to.

REGGAE

It is generally accepted that Toots Hibbert was the one to coin the term 'reggae'. The label on Toots's recording was, however, a different spelling. His song was called "Do The Reggay". Today, reggae music is accepted internationally as Jamaica's musical identity and as music with appeal to a vast and diverse set of artists. Reggae's emergence began around the early part of 1970 and with few variations continues in its classic form to the present. Its first major exponents to gain international following were Jimmy Cliff, and Toots and the Maytals, primarily through their appearance in the movie The Harder They Come. However, its most impressive breakthrough was the Wailers whose 1971 album "Catch A Fire" was hailed as a seminal moment in international popular music. The group's members, Bob Marley, Peter Tosh and Bunny Livingston, exemplified the very ethos of the creative genius of the Jamaican marginalized citizen. It was also the beginning of the Rastafari influence that would become synonymous with reggae. In a way, reggae encapsulates all that went before – mento, ska and rocksteady and it also incorporated social and political sensibilities for the sum of its parts. Musically, reggae introduced a hypnotic beat that seemed to draw in listeners as if intoxicated or overcome by spiritual powers.

Bob Marley is reggae's pre-eminent personality, but others such as Peter Tosh, Toots Hibbert, Third World, Bunny Wailer, Black Uhuru, Jimmy Cliff and musicians Sly and Robbie are major international stars as well.

A variant of reggae is the roots style popularised by Burning Spear and boasting among its best artists the late Joseph Hill of the Group Culture, Wailing Souls, Big Youth, Abyssinians, and the Congos.

Gregory Isaacs, Maxi Priest, Sugar Minot and the late Dennis Brown, are best recognised in the Lovers Rock category of reggae that is as popular as any of the other styles. Currently the classic reggae style is kept vibrant by the likes of Beres Hammond, Freddie McGregor, Luciano and Marcia Griffith, while Tarus Riley, Etana and Queen Ifraca represent a youthful group that favours the traditional form of reggae music over its most modern incarnation, Dancehall.

DANCEHALL

The new era of reggae is championed by DJs and a few singers or, as they are called in Jamaica, 'singjays'. While the next musical development after ska, rocksteady gave more room to singers who would totally represent reggae's ascendancy to international recognition, singers have now been forced to settle behind young, rapid-talking artists of the dancehall genre.

Popular agreement is that dancehall started when veteran producer King Jammy used a toy Casio keyboard to make a rhythm on which Wayne Smith recorded his biggest hit "(Under Me) Sleng Teng". So popular was this sparse jaunty rhythm that literally hundreds of versions were made by others and a new era of Jamaican music resulted. This new phenomenon also rocketed producers to top importance, some even more important than artists. This is so because the 'riddims' that drive the hits in a style of music where artists popularity turnover is rapid, singers and DJs are anxious to sample hot new grooves to keep them current and relevant in front of a youthful audience as impatient for newness as are the artists themselves.

Other important DJs are Bounty Killer and Ninjaman, but by far the most popular is Beenie Man, whose ability to swing with the groove and constantly reinvent his image has kept him valid longer than most. ∎

Ocho Rios
Jazz Festival

SONNY BRADSHAW AND MYRNA HAGUE BRADSHAW

With the success of the first presentation of the Ocho Rios Jazz Festival on Fathers Day, June 7th, 1991, the producers, Sonny Bradshaw and Myrna Hague declared, "June is Jazz Month". The festival, which is the first jazz festival in the Caribbean, celebrated its 20th anniversary in 2010.

Launched in the sleepy town of Ocho Rios, St Anne, the annual International Ocho Rios Jazz Festival is now a week-long event regarded as the Caribbean's complete jazz vacation and can be experienced in all major tourist areas of Jamaica. Many visitors now plan their vacation for June in order to experience this unique concentration of

FACING PAGE & BELOW: Myrna Hague and the late Sonny Bradshaw performing at the Ocho Rios Jazz Festival. Photos: Earle Robinson

jazz. To date, it has featured stars like B3 organists Jimmy Smith, Jimmy McGriff and Charles Earland, great guitarists Charlie Byrd, Mundel Lowe and Herb Ellis, trumpeters Arturo Sandoval and Clark Terry, shell and trombone player Steve Turre, vibraharpist Milt Jackson, percussionist Ray Baretto, singer Etta Jones, saxophonist Jame Moody, and flautist Herbie Mann.

The festival has also been the platform for many young stars such as Eric Alexander, Rudi Mahanthappa, Ken Yamazaki, Jon Williams, Yolanda Brown (UK MOBO Jazz winner), and violinist Nadje Leslie, who have made their names both in Jamaica and overseas.

Many of the features of the Jazz Festival have been copied by other jazz festivals in the Caribbean including the free public concerts during Jazz Week, with both visiting and local musical combinations participating.

The music education aspect of the festival is also of major importance attracting visits from North American schools such as the Duke Ellington School of the Performing Arts, the Detroit Young Lions, the Antelope Valley Big Band and local schools such as the Herbert Morrison High School, the Browns Town High School and the Alpha Boys' School Band, all former winners of the School Jazz programme.

The Friends of Jazz (FOJ), which includes local and overseas jazz supporters, was formed to assist in the preservation and promotion of this Black classical music in the Caribbean. They can be seen at many jazz events wearing their FOJ button and willing to engage with every and anyone about their musical subject. ■

"Disguise up de English language"

Louise Bennett and the politics of identity in Jamaica

CAROLYN COOPER

Jamaican poet, folklorist, actress and cultural critic Louise Bennett, popularly known by her stage name, "Miss Lou," employs the image of trickery to describe the evolution of Creole languages in the Caribbean: "But we African ancestors dem pop we English forefahders dem. Yes! Pop dem an disguise up de English Language fi projec fi-dem African Language" [Our African ancestors tricked our English forefathers. Yes! Tricked them and disguised the English language in order to project their own African languages].[1]

This disguise motif highlights the way in which meaning can be concealed from outsiders who are not competent in Caribbean Creoles. Many Jamaican Creole words are of English origin and their meaning often seems transparent to non-native listeners. But the grammar and syntax of the language are not English so confusion often results. For example, many non-Jamaican reggae fans initially thought Bob Marley's line "no, woman, no cry" meant that if you didn't have a woman then you wouldn't cry.

The words "no," "woman" and "cry" seemed unmistakably English and the syntax and grammar appeared to be uncomplicated. But the meaning that was commonly heard was certainly not what the singer intended: quite the opposite. Marley's comfortingly nostalgic song evokes domestic intimacy and the shared rituals of community: "I remember when we used to sit inna govament yard in Trench Town." An accurate English translation of the line is "no, woman, don't cry." Misinterpreted, the song becomes a misogynist rejection of the company of women.

Incomprehension was reinforced by the faulty punctuation of the line on the original *Natty Dread* album jacket. The comma after the first "no" was omitted so that the singer's address to the woman was inaudible. Instead, a perfectly parallel structure of negation was scripted: "no woman, no cry." But the meaning of the two "no's" is not at all identical; nor is their pronunciation, a fact that is obvious to the insider. The first "no" is an interjection, as in English, signalling a negative. Its intensity is enunciated in the elongation of the vowel. The much shorter, sharper second "no" is the negative Creole particle that modifies the verb "cry."[2] This example draws attention to the importance of establishing an appropriate writing system for Caribbean Creoles. These languages must be taken seriously.

In several of her poems and dramatic monologues Louise Bennett explicitly addresses the divisive issue of language politics in Jamaica. As an aspiring poet in the 1930s, she first attempted to "express [her] thought /And whims in dulcet poetry."[3] But, responsive to the explosive sounds around her, Bennett abandoned "dulcet" poetry for "dialect" poetry. She claimed her mother tongue as the language of literary expression. Mervyn Morris, painstaking editor of Bennett's *Selected Poems*, describes the genesis of her first "dialect" poem in this way:

One day she set out, a young teenager all dressed up, for a matinee film show in Cross Roads. On the electric tramcars which were then the basis of public transportation in Kingston, people travelling with baskets were required to sit at the back, and they were sometimes resentful of other people who, when the tram was full, tried to join them there. As Louise was boarding the tram she heard a country woman say: 'Pread out yuhself, one dress-oman a come.' That vivid remark made a great impression on her, and on returning home she wrote her first dialect poem, "On a Tramcar," which began:

Pread out yuhself deh Liza, one
Dress-oman dah look like seh
She see di li space side-a we
And waan foce harself een deh (iv-v)

ENGLISH
Spread out, Liza
That woman who is all dressed up
Seems to have noticed the little bit of space between us
And wants to force herself into it.

This English translation does not adequately convey the meaning of spreading out the body that is such a powerful symbol of the irrepressible survival instincts of Jamaica's dispossessed who refuse to be squeezed out of existence.

Bennett's struggle, in the first instance, was to achieve "dialect" status and respectability for her mother tongue, as expressed in her satirical poem "Bans o' Killing:"

JAMAICAN
Meck me get it straight, Mas Charlie,
For me no quite understan –
Yuh gwine kill all English dialec
Or jus Jamaica one?

Ef yuh dah-equal up wid English
Language, den wha meck
Yuh gwine go feel inferior, when
It come to dialec?

Ef yuh cyaan sing 'Linstead Market'
An 'Wata come a me yeye'
Yuh wi haffi tap sing 'Auld lang syne'
An 'Comin through de rye'.

Dah language weh yuh proud a,
Weh yu honour and respec –
Po Mas Charlie, yuh no know seh
Dat it spring from dialec! (218-219).

Bob Marley's (right) line "no, woman, no cry" was misinterpreted by many non-Jamaican fans as a rejection of the company of women rather than its comfortingly nostalgic evocation of domestic intimacy. Photo: Adrian Boot

ENGLISH
Let me get it straight, Mr Charlie,
For I don't quite understand –
Are you going to get rid of all dialects of English
Or only Jamaica's?

If you want to measure up to English
Then just tell me
Why are you going to feel inferior,
When it comes to this business of dialect?

If you can't sing 'Linstead Market'
And 'Water come a me yeye'
You'll have to stop singing 'Auld lang syne'
And 'Coming through the rye'.

That language which you're so proud of,
Which you honour and respect.
Poor Mr Charlie! Don't you know
That it sprang from a dialect!

Bennett's persuasive argument was that English-speaking communities in Britain had regional dialects. The fact that Jamaica also had a regional dialect of English should be acknowledged without embarrassment.

Later, Louise Bennett would move beyond the limiting conception of the local language as a dialect of English. Indeed, she vigorously contested the popular view of Jamaican as a "corruption" of English. For example, in the dramatic monologue "Jamaica Language" she argues humorously, through the character Aunty Roachy, that just as the pedigree of respectable languages like English is never in question, Jamaican should be recognised as a legitimate language:

Like my Aunty Roachy seh, she vex anytime she hear people a come style fi wi Jamaican language as "corruption" a di English language. Yu ever hear anyting go so? Aunty Roachy seh she no know weh mek dem no call di English language "corruption" a di Norman French an di Greek an di Latin weh dem seh English "derived from." Unu hear di wud? English "derive" but Jamaica "corrupt." No massa, noting no go so. We not "corrupt," an dem "derive." We derive to. Jamaica derive.[4]

ENGLISH
As my Aunty Roachy says, she gets vexed whenever she hears anyone classifying our Jamaican language as a "corruption" of the English language. Can you imagine? Aunty Roachy says she doesn't understand why they don't describe English as a "corruption" of the Norman French and the Greek and the Latin that they say English is "derived from." Do you see the word they use? English is "derived" but Jamaican is "corrupted." Not at all; I simply don't accept that. We are not "corrupted," and they are "derived." We are derived, too. Jamaican is derived.

In addition, Bennett now gives a more complicated genealogy for Jamaican that extends the origins of the language beyond the dialect-of-English genesis. The African linguistic heritage is acknowledged and its subversive ethos is celebrated. The emergence of Jamaican Creole is now conceived as the end result of a radical political process. The new language is a cunning, revolutionary assertion of African verbal creativity and cultural autonomy. But Bennett's inclusion of "we English forefahders" in the Creole family history craftily acknowledges the English elements in Jamaican Creole and simultaneously underscores the "mus-an-boun" [must-and-bound] constriction that is an essential element of the enslavement process.

Bennett also derides the presumed limitations of the English colonisers who could not master the African languages:

For Jamaican Dialec did start when we English forefahders did start mus-an-boun we African ancestors fi stop talk fi-dem African language altogedder an learn fi talk so-so English, because we English forefahders couldn understan what we African ancestors-dem wasa seh to dem one anodder when dem wasa talk eena dem African language to dem one annodder![5]

ENGLISH
For the Jamaican dialect developed when our English forefathers began to compel our African ancestors to stop speaking their own African languages altogether and learn to speak only English, because our English forefathers could not understand what our African ancestors were saying to each other when they spoke in their various African Languages!

Having creatively demonstrated the authority of her mother tongue, Louise Bennett has inspired generations of younger writers to experiment with the language. ▷

Notable among them are Joan Andrea Hutchinson and Amina Blackwood Meeks. Dub poets, reggae singers and dancehall DJs also acknowledge her influence. For example, DJ Anthony B pays respect to Louise Bennett in this way: "Talk like Miss Lou, mi no talk like foreigner"[6] [I talk like Miss Lou, I don't talk like a foreigner]. The DJ here explicitly makes the connection between language and national identity.

Similarly, Oku Onuora defines 'dub poetry' in such a way as to suggest its distance from the conventions of English metrics:

> It's dubbing out the little penta-metre and the little highfalutin business and dubbing in the rootsical, yard, basic rhythm that I-an-I know. Using the language, using the body. It also mean to dub out the isms and schisms and to dub consciousness into the people-dem head. That's dub poetry.[7]

Barbadian historian and poet Kamau Brathwaite in his book *History of the Voice* makes the most precise connection between language and national identity in his coinage of the term "nation language" to define indigenous Caribbean languages such as Jamaican Creole. He argues, somewhat metaphorically like Onuora, that "[w]hat English has given us as a model for poetry, and to a lesser extent prose (but poetry is the basic tool here), is the pentameter ... There have, of course, been attempts to break it."[8] He continues: "It is nation language in the Caribbean that, in fact, largely ignores the pentameter."[9]

The increased use of the Jamaican mother tongue in a variety of creative forms marks an important stage in the development of a mass-based nationalist consciousness among Jamaicans at home and, equally importantly, in communities of migrants the world over. Part of the legitimising process has been the writing down of the language. Bennett, herself, insists that she is a writer: "From the beginning, nobody ever recognised me as a writer. 'Well, she is 'doing' dialect'; it wasn't even writing you know. Up to now a lot of people don't even think I write."[10]

Like many other literate Jamaicans, Bennett employed the notoriously inconsistent conventions of the English writing system to represent Jamaican, a language which had a sound system quite distinct from that of English. The choice of an inappropriate writing system had an important psychological effect. Many persons who were literate in English and also spoke Jamaican Creole could claim with some justification that Jamaican Creole material was difficult to read. Such claims emphasised the superiority of the standard 'language,' English, relative to its non-standard 'dialect', Jamaican Creole.

An important solution to the writing system dilemma became available in 1961 with the publication of *Jamaica Talk* written by the linguist Frederic Cassidy. Like the lay-person, Bennett, the linguist Cassidy, to some degree, represented Jamaican as a 'dialect' of English, as evidenced in the subtitle of the book: "Three Hundred Years of the English Language in Jamaica." In the appendix to *Jamaica Talk* Cassidy presented a consistent, phonemically based writing system for Jamaican Creole.[11]

This was further discussed and illustrated in the introduction to the *Dictionary of Jamaican English*, the name of the later book itself confirming the popular view that Jamaican was not an independent language but one inseparably linked to English.[12] Indeed, the Cassidy writing system had the important advantage of not employing any symbols not used in the orthography of English.

In spite of Cassidy's concession to the English writing system, the majority of literate Jamaicans saw no reason over the years to go to the trouble of learning a new writing system for a set of language varieties which were not 'a language' proper. Mervyn Morris gives the common-sense rationale for the writer's choice of an English-looking orthography for Jamaican:

> But, anxious not to be rejected unread, most of us have chosen compromise. The most common (if inconsistent) approach is to write the vernacular for the eye accustomed to standard English, but with various alterations signalling creole.[13]

Over time, with the strengthening of a mass-based nationalism, alternative views have appeared. Under the leadership of the linguist Hubert Devonish, the Jamaican Language Unit at the University of the West Indies, Mona, Jamaica has published a book and compact disc, *Writing Jamaican the Jamaican Way / Ou fi Rait Jamiekan*, designed to popularise the specialist writing system for the Jamaican language.[14] The Cassidy/JLU system makes Jamaican 'look' on the page like a language totally distinct from English. Indeed, the strangeness of the orthography restores to Jamaican its integrity. It gives the language and its speakers presence and makes a persuasive political statement. ∎

FACING PAGE: In several of her poems and dramatic monologues Louise Bennett, above, explicitly addresses the divisive issue of language politics in Jamaica.

NOTES & REFERENCES

1. Mervyn Morris, ed. Louise Bennett, *Aunty Roachy Seh*, Kingston: Sangster's, 1993, 2.

2. For a lucid account of the structure of the Jamaican language, see Pauline Christie's *Language in Jamaica*, Kingston: Arawak Publications, 2003. See, also, Velma Pollard, *From Jamaican Creole to Standard English: A Handbook for Teachers*, 1993; rpt. Barbados: Jamaica: Trinidad and Tobago, The University of the West Indies Press, 2000.

3. Louise Bennett, quoted in Mervyn Morris' "Introduction" to Louise Bennett's *Selected Poems*, Kingston: Sangster's, 1882; rpt. 1996, iv. Subsequent references cited in text.

4. Louise Bennett, "Jamaica Language," Track 3, *Yes M'Dear*, Sonic Sounds Miami, SONCD-0079, n.d. This dramatic monologue is published in Mervyn Morris, ed. Louise Bennett, *Aunty Roachy Seh*, Kingston: Sangster's, 1993, 1-3.

5. *Ibid*, 1-2.

6. Anthony B, "Nah Vote Again," Track 7, *Universal Struggle*, VP Records, VPCD 1510 2, 1997.

7. Statement made at a seminar on "Dub Poetry," Jamaica School of Drama, January 17, 1986. Transcript of excerpts done by Mervyn Morris.

8. Kamau Brathwaite, *History of the Voice* (London: New Beacon Books, 1984) 9.

9. *Ibid.*, 13.

10. "Bennett on Bennett," Louise Bennett interviewed by Dennis Scott, *Caribbean Quarterly* 14 .1-2 (1968) : 98.

11. Frederic Cassidy, *Jamaica Talk*, London: Macmillan & Kingston: Institute of Jamaica Publications, 1961, 433.

12. Cassidy & LePage, *Dictionary of Jamaican English*, 1967, 1980, pp. xxxvii-lxiv.

13. Mervyn Morris, "Printing the Performance," *Jamaica Journal* 23.1 (1990) : 22.

14. The Jamaican Language Unit/Di Jamiekan Langwij Yuunit, *Writing Jamaican the Jamaican Way/ Ou fi Rait Jamiekan*, Kingston: Arawak Publishers, 2009.

The Jamaican woman: spirit of the nation

JOANNE SIMPSON

In the short space of one generation, Jamaica has seen a new cadre of female leaders with influence and powerful positions, creating a 'Jamaican woman' of a new style, capable of unusual levels of achievement.

From a complex and difficult beginning the typical Jamaican woman has evolved to demonstrate a strength of character and determination that have produced the role models and pioneers in both the public and private sectors.

The struggles of the women of Jamaica to overcome the historical barriers inherent in the patriarchal system, is merely a unique chapter in the global struggle to recognise women's rights as human rights.

Driven by a passion to overcome shackles of inferiority, domination and unfair advantage imposed by a history that was not particularly kind to their gender, Jamaican women, by and large, learnt important lessons from their marginalised positions of low paid workers, heads of households, migrant workers, higglers, traders, school teachers, nurses, mothers and grandmothers.

They provoked radical change. Some were vociferous in their manner, some quiet and shrewd, but all possessing a common denominator in all their lives – determination, love of humanity, hard work and steadfast focus on their goals.

Driven by their assertiveness, natural capability, talent, passion, caring, pig-headedness even, and a willingness to take a stand, our women have displayed tremendous courage and fortitude – qualities that have made them beacons to other women of other cultures across the world.

Some were privileged, but many escaped poverty to ensure a better life not only for their families but also for the society as a whole. Overcoming notions of women being the weaker sex, our women have become the driving force in this nation, rising from the ashes of obscurity to emerge as a group to be reckoned with.

When we examine the contribution of the Jamaica woman at home and overseas, we can feel nothing less than pride and gratitude in their accomplishments. Several have assumed political leadership, are heading large and complex corporations, and are making an indelible mark in many of their activities, claiming their rights under a patriarchal system.

The reality, demonstrated by the statistical data, is that females in Jamaican society have higher literacy rates than the males. The latest statistics reveal that seventy percent of the students in the faculties of law and medicine at the University of the West Indies are female. These numbers are an indication of the reality that the emphasis of the women's movement on the need for women to be educated, has been gaining currency in Jamaica.

What is also significant is not that Jamaican women are more literate than the men; it is that in spite of her literacy the female unemployment rates in 2007 have been twice that of males. This trend has not shown any indication of change and women continue to struggle to gain equitable access to the job pool in the labour force. Yet, it is reported that the progress made by the Jamaican woman in bridging the income gap surpasses the progress made by her counterparts in the industrialised countries.

The story of individual Jamaican women breaking through barriers to become high achievers and exemplary citizens in commerce, entertainment, the professions (traditional and non-traditional), sports and culture are documented in many historical and popular media.

We admire the contribution of the following women who have become visible 'movers and shakers' but the unsung heroines continue to toil against great odds to hold together the fragmented and often contentious Jamaican society.

In the area of politics, in spite of entrenched attitudes and hostile conditions, a Jamaican woman has had the distinction of joining one other Caribbean woman to become the Prime Minister of her country. We speak of none other than Portia Simpson Miller.

Another area that continues to be challenging to the status of the Jamaican woman is her under representation at the highest levels of decision making.

According to the latest tally by the Electoral Office of Jamaica, while there have been women at different times occupying the position of Prime Minister, Minister of Justice, Attorney General, and President of the Senate, it is obvious that women "remain peripheral in the major political,

LEFT TO RIGHT: Current Prime Minister Portia Simpson Miller, Audrey Marks, Angela Whitter and Louise 'Miss Lou' Bennett.

economic and social decision making levels of the society." Currently, the exception to this trend is seen in the justice system where women occupy strategic positions as Attorney General (Dorothy Lightbourne), Chief Justice (Zaila McCalla) and Director of Public Prosecution (Paula Llewellyn).

Our women have also taken that drive and spirit of determination to foster change on the international scene. We commend the efforts of the late Dr Lucille Mair, one of our most distinguished ambassadors who made an exemplary contribution at the United Nations and especially through her work on the question of Palestine. We note also the work of the late Angela King and her work in relation to the cause of the advancement of women and her contribution to the transition from apartheid to democracy in South Africa. Also a significant figure in international politics is Jamaican Diane Abbott who became the first black female elected to British Parliament in 1987, representing the Labour Party in the Hackney North and Stoke Newington districts.

Outstanding women in business include Lois Sherwood of Burger King, Audrey Marks of Paymaster, Jamaica, top banker Minna Israel of RBTT, real estate developer Angela Whitter, stockbroker Rita Humphries Lewin and restaurateur Thalia Lyn, all of whom are highly regarded in business circles.

A lot is owed to the pioneering spirit of the late Una Marson, Amy Bailey, Amy Jacques Garvey, Amy Ashwood Garvey and the late Lady Gladys Bustamante, whose relentless efforts in the late 19th and early 20th century steered Jamaica away from racist and female oppression without fear of ostracism in a male dominated and racist society.

Our foremost cultural icon is Louise 'Miss Lou' Bennett (who died in 2006), who is credited for skilfully engineering acceptance of our dialect and our local culture. We cannot overlook the contribution of our women in the entertainment arena. Millie Small gave us our first taste of international recognition with her popular song, 'My Boy Lollipop'; the I-Threes comprising Rita Marley, Judy Mowatt, and Marcia Griffiths performed as backup for Bob Marley, and who now still commandeer the stage as solo artistes. We note the contribution of the late Madge Sinclair, Sheryl Lee Ralph, the National Dance Theatre Company. We stand in awe of the contribution of scientists like Professor Pam Rodgers-Johnson, our athletes, the most current, our Olympians Veronica Campbell, Shelly-Ann Fraser, Sherone Simpson, Melaine Walker, Aleen Bailey, Kerron Stewart, and the former champions who have placed Jamaica on the track and field map; Merlene Ottey, Deon Hemmings, Grace Jackson and Marlene Cuthbert. Of note also are equestrian Samantha Albert and Olympic swimmers Janelle Atkinson-Wignall and Alia Atkinson.

Jamaica's women have also featured prominently on the international beauty arena and the modelling stage. Classic beauties such as Carol Joan Crawford, Cindy Breakespeare and Lisa Hannah captured the Miss World crown in 1963, 1976 and 1993 respectively. Jamaica has also produced top runway models who have graced international runways and magazine covers.

The splendour and mystique of our women, their beauty, their high intellect, varied charms, diverse capabilities, 'salt of the earth' characters, are now eroding what took centuries to cultivate – 'women's place in society'. Hardly easy to contain, the Jamaican woman's assertiveness, with a surety, has been threatening the status quo, creating serious dilemmas in the way women are perceived and the role they now play in modern society.

But while stories persist of the remarkable achievements of individual Jamaican women, the bigger picture of the search for gender equality and the empowerment of the majority of Jamaican women remains a story worth redefining. ■

The Jamaican Diaspora – strengthening the links

DELANO FRANKLYN

It is estimated that there are 2.7 million Jamaicans living in Jamaica; it is also estimated that the same number of Jamaicans live outside of Jamaica. This external population is largely referred to as the Jamaican Diaspora. In fact, hundreds of thousands of Jamaicans are part of the transnational families, living and contributing in two countries, two economies and two cultures at the same time.

Diaspora is a word of Greek origin meaning, 'to sow over or scatter'. Until recently the term conjured in one's mind the narrow definition of persons whom, for one reason or another, lived outside of their homeland.

In the last fifteen to twenty years, however, the word diaspora, has become a term of self identification among varied groups who migrated or whose forbearers migrated from one place to another. Jamaica therefore, can no longer be classically defined by its traditional geographical space, but by its demographic space, resulting in Jamaicans living outside of Jamaica being regarded as an extension of the island state.

INFLUENCE OF JAMAICANS

Jamaicans have been migrating, settling, revisiting and resettling in other countries for decades now.

They have in their host countries built and operated transportation and communications infrastructure such as canals, railways and highways; operated social infrastructure and services, education and health being just two examples; developed and sustained major areas of economies such as sugar, bananas, tobacco and orange plantations, mines and factories, and built social organisations such as trade unions and political parties. Jamaicans have also risen to the highest levels of business, professions, research and academic institutions and of policy and decision-making in their host countries.

The influence of Jamaicans has been very strong in developed countries such as the United Kingdom, the United States of America and Canada where the vast majority of Jamaicans in the Diaspora are to be found. However, Jamaicans, and by extension the influence of Jamaicans can also be found in countries and regions such as Cuba, Panama, Nicaragua, Costa Rica, Colombia and other countries in Central America, Caribbean islands and sections of Africa.

MAINTAINED LINKS

Jamaicans living abroad have maintained, through various means, strong links with Jamaica:

- Through its Ambassadors, High Commissioners, Consuls General and Honorary Consuls.
- Through the growing number of parish based home coming associations formed in different parishes.
- Through the vast array of alumni associations that maintain very strong links with their alma mater in Jamaica.
- Through the overwhelming support given to the country's footballers, netballers, athletes, musicians and artistic performers when they display their talents in places such as New York, Miami, Toronto, London or Birmingham.
- Through the number of Jamaicans who return home for vacation especially during the summer and at Christmas.
- Through returning residents who have formed themselves into very formidable local organisations in Jamaica and who have maintained personal links with friends and family in the diasporic communities.
- By way of business connections. Jamaican manufacturers producing such items as beer, rum, coffee, reggae music, processed foods have found markets in the overseas community and in some areas have spread out in mainstream markets. By extension, commercial linkages have expanded with a growing number of individuals in the business community in the Diaspora identifying and developing out of their small export and import business, opportunities for joint ventures or investments.

Jamaicans in the Diaspora have also consistently contributed to the development and growth of schools, hospitals, churches, communities and

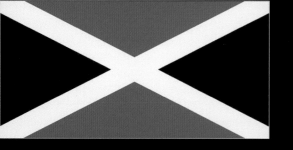

charities in Jamaica. This is manifestly so in times of crisis, especially after the island has been affected by hurricanes.

There is also the contribution to family and friends in the forms of remittances, which have significantly increased in the last few years. From US $164.2 million in 1990, remittances reached a record high of nearly US $2 billion in 2008, surpassing gross earnings from tourism and the bauxite sector.

INCREASED LINKS

In recognition of the ever-increasing importance of the Jamaica Diaspora a number of initiatives have been recently undertaken at the national level to deepen and strengthen the organisational linkages between Jamaica and the Diaspora. These include:

- The organisation of a biennial conference, which allows Jamaicans from the diasporic communities to come together, discuss and put forward workable proposals on matters of concern.
- The establishment of a Jamaica Diaspora Board, where persons in the Diaspora can elect their representatives to interface with representatives of Government.
- The proclamation of June 16, as Jamaica Diaspora Day.
- The establishment of Trade Councils. This is in order to assist the process of encouraging Jamaican entrepreneurs to develop joint venture business prospects between Jamaica and the Diaspora.

The establishment of a Jamaica Diaspora Foundation of which the principal goals are:

- To strengthen the links and support systems between Jamaicans residing abroad and those at home, and to deepen the collaboration and cooperation between the stakeholder groups that serve them.
- To facilitate and increase the scope of the impact of the contributions of the Diaspora to the development of Jamaica.

JAMAICA DIASPORA FOUNDATION

The Jamaica Diaspora Foundation is a limited liability non-profit organisation led by a Board of Directors comprised of well-placed Jamaicans at home and abroad. Among the functions of the Foundation are the following:

- Serving as a liaison between Jamaica Diaspora Communities and the government, the private sector, academic institutions and community based organisations in Jamaica.
- Conducting research and serving as a central repository and clearing house for research and data relating to the Jamaican and Caribbean Diaspora.
- Organising and hosting conferences, symposiums and roundtables on topics of relevance to the Diaspora.
- Promoting and supporting the formation of strong, active and responsive lobby groups in the Diaspora to protect the interest of Jamaicans at home and abroad.
- Promoting educational, sporting, musical and cultural exchange programmes between Jamaica and its Diaspora.
- Facilitating projects inside and outside of the Diaspora, which are targeted at serving the needs of the Diaspora and projects in which members of the Diaspora can invest.
- Providing independent views and recommendations for government policies related to the Diaspora.
- Fundraising activities to advance the work and objectives of the Foundation.

BORDERLESS CONNECTION

The implementation of these new organisational linkages aimed at fostering a greater relationship between Jamaica and the Diaspora has been made much easier by new communication technologies resulting in an almost borderless connection between Jamaicans at home and abroad.

This has increased the ability of Jamaicans in the Diaspora to retain their emotional, cultural, familial and spiritual links with the country of their origin, and in turn, has led to a greater appreciation by Jamaicans at home of those Jamaicans living in the Diaspora. ∎

The Rastafarians of Jamaica

BARBARA MAKEDA BLAKE HANNAH

The Rastafari movement was born one hundred years after the abolition of slavery, out of the darkest depression that the descendants of Africans enslaved in Jamaica have ever endured. The growth of the Rastafari philosophy in the 1930s was a revolution, not of bullets and bloodshed, but of thinking, as out of the hearts and minds of the poorest descendants of slaves arose a sentiment so pure, so without anger, so full of love: the 'peace and love' philosophy of the Rastafari believers.

The early beginnings of the Rastafari movement manifested in the 1930s when island-wide labour unrests were stirring up Jamaican workers to militancy. The teachings of the Jamaican prophet and philosopher Marcus Mosiah Garvey, who urged Black people to study and love their African history and roots, had a profound effect on thinkers in his home Jamaica, inspiring them to study and love African history and culture and to see their indivisible connection with the Motherland. Study of Garvey's philosophy and his founding of the Universal Negro Improvement Association, caused the spiritual adventurers of this former slave colony to focus their attention on the continent from which their ancestors had been taken.

Some Afrocentric mystics began a physical and intellectual withdrawal from society to become hermits, drawing a few close followers around them in 'camps' to study their bibles and reason on life from a Garveyite perspective. The coronation in 1930 of the Ethiopian Emperor Haile Selassie I as "King of Kings, Lord of Lords, Conquering Lion of the Tribe of Judah and Defender of the Faith," seemed to them fulfilment of the biblical psalm: "Ethiopia shall soon stretch out her hands unto God."

This caused some men of African descent both in Jamaica and New York to study their bibles and the prophecies of Garvey more closely. They had accepted his statement that people of African descent should "see God with African spectacles"

and, most of all, they remembered his prediction of a Messiah to come, "Look to Africa where a Black King will be crowned". In studying the history of Emperor Haile Selassie, the lineage from which he was descended and the devoutness of his Christian faith, these men became convinced that the Emperor fulfilled this promise.

Prominent among the Jamaicans discussing these events were Leonard Howell, Joseph Hibbert, Archibald Dunkley, Paul Earlington, Vernal Davis, and Ferdinand Ricketts. These Jamaicans became the pillars of the Rastafarian movement, while their counterparts in New York City became the founders of the Ethiopian World Federation.

These early Rastafari saw themselves as different from and at odds with established society, which they felt epitomised the Biblical domain of 'Babylon' and which they therefore shunned. Seeing the effects of slavery and colonialism in their economically deprived lives, and the ways in which established society had failed to be a model of the Christianity it claimed to be based on, they also shunned organised religion. Instead, they began to openly discuss a view of society that would manifest a Biblical perspective and interpretations, and especially a better spiritual pathway that implemented basic Biblical teachings. Most controversial of all, they proclaimed that it was the life and teachings of Emperor Selassie that had inspired them to stretch forth their hands and hearts unto God, whom they called by the biblical name, Jah. (Psalm 68. V.4)

At the same time Rastafari began an on-going demand for descendants of African slavery to be returned to the African continent from which their ancestors had been taken, with the cost of such repatriation to be paid out of reparations from Europe for slavery's labour and human crimes. With a philosophy so diametrically different from the ruling status quo, Rastafarians soon came into conflict with society who used the Police to conduct raids on Rasta camps and to arrest and imprison followers for their only crime: the use of marijuana as a sacrament in their religious and daily activities.

With the assumption that every Rasta was a ganja smoker, many early Rastafari endured the brutality of police beatings because of their visible profession of faith in dreadlocks, beards, sandals and clothing embellished by red, gold and green colours and portraits of Selassie. Many suffered in larger atrocities such as the Coral Gardens massacre, when the then-Prime Minister ordered a raid on the Rasta community with the instructions that if there were not enough jails to hold them, there were enough cemeteries. Later came the destruction of Pinnacle, the first Rasta village established by 'the first Rasta' Leonard Howell in St. Catherine where Rastafari grew vegetables and

Ethiopian Emperor Haile Selassie I. Photo courtesy African-Caribbean Institute of Jamaica / Jamaica memory Bank

produced furniture, tools and craft items which were sold to pay for their living expenses.

As the objects of oppression, scorn and condemnation, Rastas were seen as a militant movement waiting to launch a violent revolution. Yet, the feared-for Rastafari uprising against 'Babylon' never materialised. Instead, Rastafari 'turned the other cheek' by packing up its message and presenting it to the world in an interesting and appealing format: a new music. Reggae's unusual new beat had evolved directly from the religious ceremonies of Rastafari's Nyabinghi. At these ceremonies the ancestral links to Africa manifested in the drums that beat without ceasing throughout the night's continuous praises to the Creator. The collection of drums at such an event comprised the large bass funde drum that maintained the heartbeat thud, the smaller kette drums on which the drummers galloped their individual rhythms and over which the singers harmonised their voices in the unique Nyabinghi hymns. These evolved into the now-famous One Drop rhythm.

To the drumbeats, Rasta singers added lyrical verses of new social and spiritual commentary that told a Third World story of suffering, confrontation, hope and love and which captivated listeners in Jamaica, and then around the world, becoming anthems for oppressed people and hymns of praise celebrating and advertising a new vision of God. As Jamaican music evolved from the Rasta camps into the jukeboxes and sound systems of the dance halls, Rastafari exploded its message through its music to the world.

Reggae's greatest messengers, Bob Marley & the Wailers achieved the widest message spread, with album after album of truly wonderful music, revolutionary anthems like "Get Up, Stand Up For Your Rights", human rights statements like "One Love" and Rasta revolutionary chants like "Exodus". The list of Rastafari singers and players

of instruments is endless: Peter Tosh, Bunny Wailer, Jacob Miller, I-JahMan Levi, Burning Spear, Joe 'Culture' Hill, Bunny Wailer, Dennis Brown, and many more. The list of reggae music stars that began in the 1970s continues non-stop to this day.

Beneath the red, gold and green exterior of Rastafari lays a complex religious philosophy inspired by the greatness of the life of Emperor Haile Selassie I and the rich Christian history of Ethiopia. Rooted in Biblical Christianity, the philosophy encompasses Afrocentric and Pan-African philosophy expressed by such thinkers as Franz Fanon, George Padmore, Walter Rodney, Eric Williams, Angela Davis and a host of contemporary Caribbean intellectuals, and it has caused people of all races in all countries of the world to adopt Rastafari as their spiritual pathway, and to wear the locks and colours of the faith despite the parental and social ostracism they often face for their choice.

Rasta practices include a vegetarian diet, love of nature, non-material lifestyle and great emphasis on family and traditional values. Women dress modestly without makeup and cover their heads in keeping with traditional African female practices. Male Rastas are often self-employed cultural artisans who provide good role models for their children as well as young adults in their communities.

Though the image of the Rastafari movement is sometimes limited only to reggae music, dreadlocks, red, gold and green colours, and ganja, in what is now the third generation of the movement, there are Rasta lawyers, doctors, engineers, MBAs, PhDs, university lecturers, authors, film makers, IT consultants, gourmet chefs and bankers. Rasta colours have become Dior fashions; Rasta's 'ital' diet is adopted by vegetarians, books about and by Rastas fill libraries around the world. Rastas have served in the Parliaments of Jamaica, Trinidad and New Zealand, where the Rastafari population numbers more than 200,000.

Rastafari envisage the creation of a 'new heaven on earth' in Ethiopia, Africa, where they will build a new civilisation based on a strong spiritual and Afrocentric foundation. That this objective has not yet been achieved is not for lack of effort and a new generation of Rastafari is aware of the destiny it has inherited. As the movement continues its growth, philosophically as well as geographically, the Jamaica nation has finally accepted with pride the blessings Rastafari has bestowed upon its country of origin.

The Rastafari culture has made Jamaica famous and its icons of Red, Gold and Green colours, dreadlocks hairstyle and the reggae music of Bob Marley have given Jamaica a unique international identity that sets it apart from other Caribbean nations and brings thousands of visitors annually to enjoy the island's beauty and culture. ∎

The Maroons

The Maroons of Jamaica date back to 1517 when the Spaniards, who were the first Europeans to colonise the island, imported enslaved Africans as cheap labour after having caused the near extinction of the native Taino Arawaks from overwork and European diseases. However, in 1655 when the English invaded the island, many Spaniards fled to Cuba, releasing their slaves as they fled.

The freed Africans sought refuge in the mountainous regions of the country and became known as 'Maroons' – a derivative of the Spanish word 'cimarron', meaning 'wild' or 'untamed'. Those who settled in villages in the north-eastern section of the island – Moore (Nanny) Town, Charles Town and Scots Hall – were called the 'Windward Maroons'. And, those who settled in the south and north-westerly parishes – Trelawny Town in St James, and Accompong in St Elizabeth – were called the 'Leeward Maroons'.

The Maroons would frequently invade the British plantations in search of ammunition, food, and cattle, and also to free other slaves. This resulted in ongoing tension between the groups, which escalated into the First Maroon War in about 1734. The British retaliated by sending troops across the island to capture the Maroons. Despite being fewer in number, the Maroons, under the leadership of Nanny, Cudjoe and Quao, were able to maintain an advantage in war through their superior knowledge of the terrain, and the use of camouflage and guerrilla warfare.

The British army, led by Colonel Guthrie, went to Trelawny Town to negotiate with Cudjoe, and in 1739, a peace treaty was signed. Three months ▷

Descendants of the Maroons celebrate Nanny Day in honour of Jamaica's national hero, Nanny of the Maroons. Photo: Andrew P. Smith

later, the Windward Maroons, under Quao, signed a separate peace treaty. A peace treaty was signed with Nanny about one year later. These treaties guaranteed land to the Maroons and freedom from taxation. In return, the Maroons agreed to end their attacks on the plantations and to assist in the capture and return of runaway slaves.

Peace lasted until 1795, when a Maroon, who allegedly was caught stealing, was whipped by a slave. A Maroon delegation was sent to discuss the growing tension between the Maroons and the British settlers in an effort to prevent confrontation. The delegation was arrested and placed in irons. The Maroons declared war against the British in what became known as the 'Second Maroon War'. On 3 August 1796, the then Governor, the Earl of Balcarres, was given the powers of Martial Law. The colonial troops sought out and destroyed Maroon provisions in the hope that they would surrender. But the Maroons remained resolute.

Faced with heavy losses of life and funds, the British asked the Maroons to turn themselves over to the authorities. However, after the last Trelawny Maroon surrendered, they were all captured and

ABOVE: Traditional Kramanti dancing accompanies the 'possession' ritual, where ancestral Maroon spirits are 'cleansed' from the body by religious leaders (pictured in red dresses). Photos: Andrew P. Smith

FACING PAGE: Drumming, dance and white rum are among the key ingredients for celebrating Nanny Day.

transported to Nova Scotia in Canada. Other Maroons were returned to Sierra Leone in Africa on their request in July 1798, when the Jamaican Assembly voted to cease supporting the Maroons.

Those who remained in Jamaica soon intermarried with non-Maroons, and others continued to live within the many Maroon villages in the island. To this day, the Maroons remain true to their traditional customs and beliefs – singing their traditional songs and telling stories of their ancestors, ensuring that the heritage of this proud and powerful people is never forgotten. ∎

Adapted from 'The Maroons of Jamaica: A glance at their history', published by the Jamaica Information Service (2006)

143

Exploring the interior

ANDREW P. SMITH

Jamaica possesses a wealth and diversity of natural attractions that belie its small size. A two-hour drive will take you from the rainforests, majestic peaks, coffee farms, flowing rivers and powerful waterfalls of the Blue Mountains in the east to the arid scrublands of the Hellshire Hills of southern Jamaica, home of the Jamaican iguana. To the west, you can hike the Dolphin Head Mountain in Hanover, discover Negril's Great Morass, go birdwatching in Bluefields, become personally acquainted with the many crocodiles on the Black River or explore the wonders of the Cockpit Country – both above and below ground.

Jamaica's natural beauty and variety is due to a combination of its geography and geology. Born under the Caribbean Sea 120 million years ago, remnants of its volcanic past are found in the Blue Mountains, which boast Jamaica's highest point, Blue Mountain Peak, at 2,256 metres above sea level. However, most of the island is covered by limestone, a result of the island being re-submerged under the sea. This has resulted in inland hills and uplands such as the Hellshire Hills, John Crow Mountains and the world famous Cockpit Country.

Due to Jamaica's isolation, upon these rocks and soil grew forests, which became home to species of flora and fauna, many of which are found nowhere else in the world. Of Jamaica's over 3,000 flowering plant species, at least 780 are endemic, mostly found in the Blue Mountains and the Cockpit Country. Endemic animals include the Jamaican iguana, the Jamaican boa and the second largest butterfly in the world, the giant swallow-tailed butterfly which has a wing-span of 15 centimetres. There are over 25 species of endemic ▷

The Blue Mountains are home to Jamaica's highest peak and an abundance of natural wonders. Photo: Andrew P. Smith

birds, including the yellow-billed and black-billed parrots. All of these elements caused Christopher Columbus in 1494 to describe Jamaica as "the fairest isle that eyes have beheld, mountains and sky, all full of valleys and fields and plains".

HIKING IN THE BLUE AND JOHN CROW MOUNTAINS NATIONAL PARK

Jamaica's first terrestrial national park, the Blue and John Crow Mountains National Park (BJCMNP) was established in 1993 and covers 76,000 hectares in eastern Jamaica. Over 30 per cent of the flowering plants found here are found nowhere else in the world. Its forests provided refuge for Jamaica's first inhabitants, the Tainos, as well as escaped West African slaves known as Maroons who successfully waged guerrilla warfare against Spanish and British colonisers. Maroon villages still exist in the Blue Mountains at Charles Town and Moore Town, It is because of this rich natural and cultural history that the park was nominated as a UNESCO World Heritage Site in 2009.

For hikers, the main attraction is hiking to the Blue Mountain Peak. Most hikers start their journey from Mavis Bank, from where they either hike to the lodges at Penlyne Castle or charter transportation from one of the lodges or tour companies to drive from Mavis Bank to Penlyne Castle. Once you arrive at Penlyne Castle, be prepared for between three to six hours (depending on your fitness level) of one of the most exhilarating, awe-inspiring and strenuous hikes that you will experience in Jamaica.

Many hikers opt to start at midnight in order to get to the Peak for sunrise, which is an unforgettable experience – if the peak is not immersed in cloud cover! If this option is done, flashlights and an experienced guide are mandatory. In addition, never forget the number one rule of hiking to the Peak: There are no shortcuts! Many are the hikers who ignored this rule at their peril and have ended up lost, discovering why the natural vegetation is known as 'rainforest'. But if you stick to the trail, dress appropriately and carry enough food and water, you will experience the true wild side of Jamaica, seeing plants and animals found nowhere else in the world. These include the rufous-throated ▷

ABOVE RIGHT: Cascade Waterfall.

RIGHT: Blue Mountain Bicycle Tour.

FACING PAGE: Sambo Hill is a hiking trail in the Buff Bay valley of Portland. It was used by the Maroons during their guerilla war with the British. Photos: Andrew P. Smith

solitaire, whose piercing whistling can be mistaken for communication between groups of hikers.

Apart from the hike to the Peak, there are two other regions of the BJCMNP that hikers can enjoy. Hollywell Recreational Park and the Buff Bay Valley are found to the west of the park, while the Rio Grande Valley is found east of the Park.

Hollywell is accessed by driving from Papine in east rural St Andrew, driving through Irish Town, through Redlight and the JDF camp at Newcastle. At the border of St Andrew and Portland you will find Hollywell. Cabins and tent sites can be rented, and many people get their first taste of the Blue Mountains on Hollywell's hiking trails. Continuing on the road past Hollywell to Section, then taking a left turn, takes you to the Buff Bay River Valley, which starts at 4,000 feet above sea level. Here is the site of the Blue Mountain Bicycle Tour, as well as the Charles Town Maroons. Other attractions, including an 18th century coffee plantation and several hiking trails and caves have been uncovered in 2009 under an agro-tourism project sponsored by the Inter-American Institute for Cooperation in Agriculture (IICA).

The Rio Grande Valley in west Portland is one of the most inaccessible regions of Jamaica, due to the one road from Port Antonio. Once you have entered the valley, you are struck by the scenery found in between the Blue Mountains on your right and the John Crow Mountains on the left. Once in the upper Rio Grande Valley near Millbank and Bowden Pen, local guides will lead you in search of dozens of hidden waterfalls. They will also take you along historical Maroon trials such as the Cuna Cuna Pass, which leads into Bath in St Thomas. You may also spy the endemic giant swallow-tailed butterfly, the second largest butterfly in the world and the largest in the western hemisphere, which is found only in the Rio Grande Valley and the Cockpit Country. Also be on the lookout for wild hogs, tusked descendants of pigs which escaped from Spanish colonisers in the 15th and 16th centuries and are hunted locally for their lean and tasty flesh. ▷

ABOVE RIGHT: Many visitors get their first taste of the Blue Mountains on Hollywell's hiking trails.

RIGHT: Established in 1841 in the grounds of a former coffee estate, Newcastle, in St Andrew, is home to the Jamaica Defence Force training camp.

FACING PAGE: Crystal-clear rivers snake their way through the mountains.

OVERLEAF: The Cockpit Country covers an area of more than 500 square kilometres. Photos: Andrew P. Smith

THE COCKPIT COUNTRY

The Cockpit Country owes it unique topography to its karst (limestone) geology. Layers of white and yellow limestone have been eroded by rain for millions of years, resulting in a landscape of alternating circular hills and valleys which resembles egg-cartons. The resemblance to cock-fighting pits gave this region of west-central Jamaica its name, which covers over 500 square kilometres. Maroons found the region ideal to wage guerrilla warfare against the British, and their decendants still live in villages at Accompong and Maroon Town. Another legacy from this time are place names such as "The Land of Look Behind", "Me No Send, You No Come" and "Rest and Be Thankful."

Exploration of the Cockpit Country can be done in a variety of ways. There is one road that traverses the region, from Clarks Town in the north to Albert Town in the south. There are various hiking trails starting at both the north and south of the area which will immerse you in a forest that is home to the Jamaican boa, dozens of endemic birds, frogs, reptiles and insects. There are over 150 species of vascular plants, of which 100 are found nowhere else in the world. The biodiversity of the region is so rich that some plant species are restricted to a sole hilltop. The ultimate hike is from Troy in the south to Windsor in the north. This will take all day and is a long and sometimes tiring journey.

Beneath the surface are sinkholes, caves and underground rivers which provide 59 per cent of Jamaica's fresh water and must be explored with experienced cavers and local guides. Ropes, helmets and flashlights are basic necessities for caving, as well as not being claustrophobic or afraid of the dark. Among the well-known caves are Quashie's River Sink in the south and Windsor Cave in the north. The latter possesses thousands of bats, stalactites and stalagmites within massive caverns with names such as Big Room, Royal Flat and Squeeze Up.

Exploring Jamaica's interior is an exhilarating experience. Whether climbing to the Blue Mountain Peak or exploring the subterranean depths of the Cockpit Country, visitors will discover many wonders and gain a greater appreciation of a country which possesses so much in such a small area. ■

Discovering Jamaica's undersea treasures

STEVEN K. WIDENER

Scuba Diving in Jamaica has always been slightly ignored by the diving community at large since there is not much support given to the industry by the government tourist entities. It has never been exploited and considered a dive destination and perhaps that is what makes diving in Jamaica so unique and virginal. One only has to realise that the same Cayman Trench and currents that run by the Cayman Islands, Cuba, and on through the Bahamas is the same that passes only five miles to the north of the northern coastline of Jamaica. The coral and reef growth and fish population are the same. Granted, due to the lack of strong enforcement on fishing regulations, the fish population is lacking in some areas of the diving sites of Jamaica. But as the saying goes, "there are no fences in the ocean," so one can see many varieties of the large fish on occasion such as hammerhead sharks, bull sharks, nurse sharks, turtles, sting rays, spotted eagle rays, dolphins, manatees, sturgeon, grouper and snapper.

Perhaps it is the micro view that the slow methodical diver or photographer takes that gives the most enjoyable viewing of the underwater life around the coastline of Jamaica. The coral and reef makeup also varies greatly around the island giving a diver the variety of seeing many different underwater seascapes.

The various corals and reefs and formations found around Jamaica are all basically the same. At any given site, one will most likely see brain coral, stag horn, plates and plenty of barrel sponge. Research has been conducted along the coastline testing the barrel sponge for its special properties that might be a breakthrough to cancer treatment.

Beginning in Negril, the western most tourist area of Jamaica, aside from the wonderful ▷

RIGHT: The reefs around Jamaica are teeming with life.
Photo: Steven K. Widener

ABOVE & FACING PAGE: Scuba diving in Jamaica provides the doorway to an undersea world of marine wonders and spectacular colours. Photos: Steven K. Widener

amenities found on land, the scuba diving off the coast of Negril is basically flat terrain with a lot of white sandy bottoms, not many ledges or ridges, but a good collection of beautifully coloured coral. The dive sites are relatively close to the dive facility and the currents are minimal. The diving is generally in the 40-60 foot range.

In Montego Bay the diving is varied and enjoyable. There are several drop-offs and walls to dive on and the colour and variety of fish life is more abundant here than anywhere else around the island.

The government established a Marine Park several years ago and, although it is not enforced as it should be, the abundance of the larger and more scenic fish can be seen here. There is one dive site called Widow Maker, the name more ominous than the actual dive, which the diver descends down a wall to about 100 feet and enters a cave of a pretty good size. You travel for approximately twenty feet and then you follow a chimney up to an opening at about 50 feet. There is no real danger and a novice diver, with a good dive master present, would have no trouble making the dive. Natural lighting prevents it from getting too dark inside the tunnels.

Most of the dive sites around Montego Bay are within a short boat trip and the currents are usually nominal and the depths can be from 50 feet to 100 feet or more.

Ocho Rios has been able to sink several wrecks at their dive sites and there any number to choose from. They have created some good home reefs for several fish groups. The current is stronger at the dive sites in Ocho Rios but usually not of any consequence. Sites are a little longer to get to and the depths can be 50 feet to 100 feet.

Port Antonio on the far eastern side of the island has the most virginal diving of all. Surrounded by semi rain forest settings, the dive operator has over a dozen well-established dive sites which are beautiful and enjoyable to tour. At no more than fifteen minutes by boat from the dive facility, the sites vary in depth from 40 feet and comprise walls, ledges, swim-through caves, reef outcroppings and plenty of drop-offs. Turtles, nurse and hammerhead sharks, rays, dolphins and manatees can often be spotted.

Kingston does have diving facilities and only local boat operators are available to take divers out. This is not recommended for inexperienced divers. The sites are quite far off the coast and are beyond a second reef, but once there, the sites are enjoyable and include a couple of old wrecks.

Treasure Beach has a few dive facilities and the sites are quite nice, although they are further out and the currents and surface action are a little stronger.

Enthusiasts should always use a reputable dive operator and ensure that it is accredited to one of the world recognised dive organisations such as PADI, NAUI or CMAS. It is also advisable to use a licensed dive operator that is registered and monitored by the Jamaica Tourist Board. ∎

Birdwatching in Jamaica

JOHN FLETCHER

Jamaica has long been famous for its sand, sea and sun – but there is much more to this tropical Caribbean island of towering mountains, lush forests, rolling plains and fascinating wetlands.

For birdwatchers, Jamaica is a particularly attractive location with more than three hundred species recorded, of which about one hundred are permanent nesting residents. But the greatest avian attractions are the twenty-eight endemics to be found nowhere else, and the seventeen Caribbean endemics shared with one or more other nations. These are the main targets of serious birdwatchers, but in the cooler months (October to April) they will also find a wide variety of North American migrants sitting out the northern winter in tropical comfort.

Finding the endemics can be easy (the streamertail hummingbird is present in almost every flower-filled garden) to very difficult (the Jamaican blackbird feeds mostly on the small creatures living in bromeliads which grow on large old trees in the deep forests). But with reasonable luck all can be seen in a week, visiting a few accessible sites within eighty kilometres of the capital.

Two of the country's most spectacular endemics are the tiny emerald green Jamaican tody (a flying green leaf until it turns and flashes its bright red gorget) and the reclusive crested quail dove flaunting its haute couture colours along mountain pathways where its melancholy call has earned it the local name of 'mountain witch'.

The Caribbean endemics include some beauties, outstanding among them being the rufous-throated solitaire, and for the birder willing to add an extra day to visit their limited ranges, ▷

Jamaica has been recognised as an attractive location for birdwatchers for more than forty years. Photo: Jamaica Tourist Board

the Bahama mockingbird and West Indian whistling duck are important additions to anyone's list.

For visitors with limited time it is recommended that they fly into Kingston and concentrate on the Blue and John Crow Mountains in the eastern part of the island where all the endemics and many of the Caribbean endemics can be found. Two or three days in the Blue Mountains and the same in or near the John Crow Mountains will provide ample opportunity to find the birds and to be enthralled by the spectacular mountain scenery.

A more extensive trip would start in Montego Bay and take in the Negril Royal Palm Reserve, Cockpit Country (a 100 sq. km trackless tropical forest that provides an important refuge for many species including the endangered yellow-billed and black-billed Amazon parrots), Treasure Beach, the Black River wetlands, Portland Ridge and then the Blue and John Crow Mountains. This could be covered comfortably in nine or ten days, using four overnight stops in convenient locations.

Jamaica has been recognised as an attractive location for birding for more than forty years mainly by North American groups and, more recently, by British groups, so there is an active network of small hotels, experienced guides and transport facilities from rental cars to 20-seater buses, available from Montego Bay or Kingston.

Breathtaking scenery, splendid food and comfortable accommodation provide an ideal platform for the visitor to use and enjoy while satisfying his or her love of wildlife and the outdoors; and other facets of the country's fascinating history and geography can be added, such as rafting on the Rio Grande following the route once used to transport bananas to Port Antonio.

Distances are manageable, but the mountain roads will challenge any driver so it is recommended to use a local driver and guide (both of which are readily available and can usually be arranged by your hotel) and to book early to have the best choice.

FORRES PARK BIRDING TOURS

Forres Park is a small, intimate fourteen-room hotel snuggled in the foothills of the Grand Ridge of the Blue Mountains. The serene ambience is broken only by the singing of birds and the rustling of leaves. Here you can engage in guided bird watching of the 28 exotic endemic species and other resident and migrant species found in Jamaica. Frequently seen birds include the Jamaican owl, Jamaican tody, woodpecker, red-billed streamertail, mango hummingbird and migrant species, the Jamaican parakeet and the common barn owl.

FORRES PARK TO HARDWARE GAP

Hollywell Park is the watershed between the northern and southern parts of the island and home of many of the Jamaican endemic birds. Species commonly seen here include the Jamaican and Blue Mountain vireos, arrowhead warbler and Jamaican blackbird.

FORRES PARK TO ST THOMAS

This eastern Jamaican parish is an exciting place for birding due to its varied relief and subsequent varied rainfall patterns and vegetation types. Sites such as the Ramble Estate and the Yallahs Salt Pond are common dwellings for native and migratory birds which include the Jamaican woodpecker, Caribbean dove, peregrine falcon, white-chinned thrush and black-billed streamertail.

ABBEY GREEN BIRDING

Ascend into the Blue Mountains by four-wheel drive vehicle to Abbey Green. You are likely to see the elusive crested quail-dove and white-eyed thrush and the always difficult to spot Jamaican blackbird. North American winter and migrant wood warblers include the prairie and northern parula, and the American redstart may also be seen here.

FORRES PARK TO ECCLESTOWN (PORTLAND)

This wet limestone forest is located on the eastern fringe of the John Crow Mountains. Ecclestown and the adjoining areas are the only areas in eastern Jamaica where the threatened Jamaican black-billed parrot (*Amazona agilis*) occurs. This is also a likely area to find the yellow-shouldered grassquit, chestnut-bellied cuckoo, Jamaican tody, blackbird and crested quail-dove.

For birdwatchers, Jamaica is a particularly attractive location with more than three hundred species recorded, of which about one hundred are permanent nesting residents. Photos: Andrew P. Smith

Geological wonders lie waiting to be discovered

KLAUS WOLF

When Christopher Columbus returned to Spain after 'discovering' Jamaica, he was asked by Queen Isabella to describe the island. It is alleged that he crumpled a sheet of paper in his hands and simply pointed to it. His actions, whether true or false, confirmed the rugged nature of the terrain.

Jamaica has a complicated geological history that involved major tectonic shifts. The oldest parts are of volcanic origin and were situated in the early Cretaceous period (140 million years ago) between the North and South American plates. About 70 to 45 million yeas ago, the landmass containing Jamaica collided with the Yucatan Peninsula, which was attached to the North American plate. This plate movement resulted in the creation of an extensive mountain range, which remained connected to the North American plate.

The terrestrial fauna in the days when Jamaica was still connected to the North American plate include the world's most primitive manatee or sea cow (*pezosiren portelli*). A fossilised skeleton was discovered by a research group from Howard University, the Florida Museum of Natural History and the University of the West Indies. A model of the two-metre long skeleton is on display in the Geological Museum of the Department of Geography and Geology at the University of the West Indies, Mona. In contrast to present day sea cows, *pezosiren portelli* can be described as amphibious in that it had conventional legs and could walk on land.

Over the next million years the landmass was eroded and developed into a series of very low lying islands where coral reefs formed. Only minor

The Cockpit Country is a hilly and largely inaccessible region in the west of Jamaica noted for its distinctive land formation and wet limestone forest. Photo: Klaus Wolf

ABOVE: *The fossilised skeleton of the world's most primitive manatee was discovered in Jamaica and dates back to when the island was still part of the North American mainland. This model is on display in the Geological Museum of the Department of Geography and Geology at the University of the West Indies, Mona.*

MAIN PICTURE: *Jamaica's Blue Mountains are the result of tectonic events which took place about fourteen million years ago. Photos: Klaus Wolf*

areas may have stayed dry during this period, which was characterised by the deposition of a limestone layer in places more than a kilometre thick. Renewed tectonic events about fourteen million years ago raised the Jamaican landmass to its current location in the Caribbean Sea. The limestone has eroded in many places exposing sedimentary and the older volcanic rocks in areas such as the Blue Mountains which rise up to 2,256 meters (Blue Mountain Peak).

Where the limestone has been only partially dissolved by slightly acidic rain, a rugged landscape known as karst has formed. The hilly and largely inaccessible Cockpit Country in the west of Jamaica is an example of a karstic region and is covered by wet limestone forest. The karstic dome and ridge-shaped Hellshire Hills and Portland Ridge on the south coast, have dry limestone forest.

Cave systems are common in karst terrain. Indeed, Jamaica has a large number of caves which have been more or less carefully mapped. Up to 1977, a total of 1200 sites have been described. The largest among them are the coastal caves in the Portland Ridge (Jackson Bay) and the Windsor Cave in the Northern Cockpit Country. In the former cave, Amerindian pottery and bones have been found suggesting its use as a burial site or shelter. The smaller "Nonsuch Caves" near Port Antonio and the "Green Grotto Caves", located between the resort centres of Ocho Rios and Montego Bay on the North Coast, are show caves where guided tours are offered to visitors.

Despite the considerable thickness of the limestone layers in Jamaica, the deepest cave found so far – Morgan's Pond Hole in the parish Manchester – was a mere 200 metres deep. Geologists, however, expect that deeper caves will be discovered in the largely inaccessible and poorly-studied John Crow Mountains, a ridge running parallel to the east coast of the island. Additionally, there are blue holes, also known as

submarine caves or sinkholes, in Jamaica. Perhaps the most notable is the Blue Hole east of Port Antonio, which served as the backdrop for the 1980 movie, The Blue Lagoon.

Jamaica has a relatively short history of land areas and was largely colonised by plants and small animals arriving on floating plant material over the water, possibly driven by hurricanes. The arrival of larger animals, in particular mammals, was much more limited and explains the country's relatively poor mammalian fauna.

Overlying the limestone in karst depressions, there are an estimated 1100 million metric tons of high-grade bauxite. This mineral is mined in western and central Jamaica for the production of alumina. The bauxite is chemically separated from iron oxides which are discarded in so-called red mud lakes in the mining areas or are thickened and discharged onto carefully graded slopes.

Until the global recession in 2008/2009, Jamaica was a leading exporter of bauxite. Government revenues fell from about US $900 million in 2003 to less than US $40 million in 2009, resulting in the closure of several bauxite plants. ∎

More than just "the sprint capital of the world"

ALDRICK ALLIE MCNAB

Like the legendary Bob Marley of reggae music fame, Usain "Lightening" Bolt, the world's fastest man has transformed how Jamaica and Jamaicans are viewed across the globe.

Welcome to the "Land of Wood and Water", beautiful white-sand beaches, reggae music, jerk chicken (Bolt's favourite), jerk pork, ackee and saltfish, and of course some of the most beautiful women in the world (Jamaica having produced three Miss World winners).

Back to sports, there is a question out there: "Why do Jamaicans run so fast?" Is it in the food we eat? Yam is currently under the microscope. Investigative teams from around the world have, over the years, descended on the island studying the early lifestyle and diet of the great Merlene Ottey, the most successful female sprinter – in terms of medals won, with eight Olympic and fourteen World Championship medals; Donald "Don" Quarrie, was the 1976 Montreal Games 200 metre Gold Medallist and 100 metre Silver Medallist.

In most recent times, in the search for the "Elixir of Youth", the 'Investigators' hoping to find the "Elixir of Speed" have travelled to the Birthplace and communities of Veronica Campbell, the 100 metres and 200 metres champion, whilst also searching out Asafa Powell, one of only two men to clock under 10 seconds for the 100 metres over fifty times (America's Maurice Green being the other; 52 times). The big difference is that Asafa is still active. And also with Usain Bolt's Olympic exploits, new found "searchers" are holed-up in Trelawney – Bolt's home parish eating as much yam as possible, claiming there is

FACING PAGE: Usain Bolt celebrates his 100m world record at the 2008 Beijing Olympics. Photo: Pniesen/Dreamstime.com

something in it. Where can the answer be found? Why do Jamaicans run so fast with so many, over the years, soaring to world class athletic fame?

The inspiration actually began many years ago at the 1948 and 1952 Olympics, when four audacious Jamaicans; Herb McKinley, Arthur Wint, Lest Lang and George Rhoden, first paraded their talent in England, then reintroduced themselves to the world stage at the Helsinki Olympics winning gold in the 4x400 metres in a world record time. Herb McKinley, who went on to gain legendary status, not only as an athlete but also as a coach, barely missing out on the Gold Medal in the 100 metres where not even the photo finish could separate him and American "winner" Lindy Remegino. Then there was the magnificent 100 metre specialist Lennox 'Billy" Miller who sped to historical glory, becoming the first man in history to win multiple "medals" in this special event at the Mexico Olympics of 1968 where he won Silver, while at the 1972 Games in Munich copped a bronze medal.

The basis of the achievements of Jamaicans is quite simple, right in your face, if you know what to look for. It is no secret really, you see, Jamaica has over the years honed and toned, fine-tuned if you will, our high school track and field system. Our educational system is structured on British standards (Prior to 1962 we were a British colony).

However, in spite of the rich track and field history of Jamaica and even the success of "Bolt & Co" at the Beijing Olympics and the betterment of the performances in terms of medals won at the Berlin World Championships, it is football that is the most popular sport in Jamaica. The country's love affair with football, and in particular the Brazilian way of playing the "Beautiful Game", brought the island to a virtual standstill in 1998 when we qualified for the FIFA World Cup finals in France.

Like Usain Bolt's Beijing exploits, the "Road to France" campaign, as the qualifiers were called, invigorated the country in spite of severe economic hardships. The process, which started two years prior, saw the coming together of the Jamaican people, a fusion from all walks-of- life sharing a common dream; especially so at our National Stadium dubbed "The Office" where the true spirit of our motto "Out of many one people", was personified in supporting their team. The hopes of 2.7 million people (Jamaica's population) rested on the team's shoulders and they delivered, becoming the first English-speaking Caribbean team to qualify for football's biggest arena, the World Cup in 1998. Not only did the Captain Horace Burrell (JFF's President) led, and Rene Simoes (Brazilian) coached, "Reggae Boys" bring joy to Jamaica and the region, but unified a nation

and inspired our Caribbean neighbours, Trinidad and Tobago, to qualify for the "Big Show" in 2006.

However, despite the proverbial 'beating of the chest' and 'macho' behaviour of our males, Jamaica's best and by far world-ranking in team sports, rests with the ladies of netball. It's the "Sunshine Girls" who hold pride of place. These darlings of the courts have, over the years, been consistently ranked in the world's top four behind New Zealand, Australia – inter changing the third spot with England from time to time.

In 2003, the island played host to over thirty countries who took part in the World Championship in Kingston, and although not winning the tournament, were brilliant in finishing third. The Sunshine Girls, playing in the inaugural "Fast net" Championship, in October 2009, and en-route to the Silver Medal, beating power house teams England and Australia and narrowly losing out to the "Silver Ferns", New Zealand. Jamaica also has the distinction of providing the world's governing body, IFNA with their current leader, in the person of President, Molly Rhone, who is into her second term in office.

Jamaica's performance in the sport of netball has also opened up opportunities for some of our top girls who are plying their trade professionally in Australia and New Zealand.

The sport of cricket, another of our inheritances from our colonial forefathers, has over the years, seen Jamaicans making their mark internationally. To name a few; the great George 'Atlas' Headley, the little genius whose exploits as a batsman caused the cricketing world to dub him the "Black

ABOVE: In 1998, Jamaica's Reggae Boys became the first English-speaking Caribbean football team to qualify for the World Cup finals.

FACING PAGE: Jamaica's Chris Gayle is a powerful opening batsman for the West Indies. Photos: Jamaica Information Service

Bradman" drawing comparisons to the legendary Australian, Don Bradman, who ended his test career with an unbelievable 99.94 running average.

Headley, who played from 1930 to 1954, ended his career with a batting average of 60.83, the best by any West Indian batsman to date including Gary Sobers, the world's greatest all-rounder, and Brian Lara, arguably the world's greatest batsman.

Two Jamaicans are among a select band of test batsmen who have carried their bat for a "triple century"; in 1974, Lawrence "Yagga" Rowe, that batting stylist, enriched the Oval in Barbados, with a stroke-filled 302; in 2005, the hard-hitting opener, Chris Gayle, pulverised the visitors' bowling, for a merciless 317 runs versus South Africa – in the end, it was mixed emotions of thankfulness and sorrow, for the South Africans.

When a batsman's stumps are shattered, especially by a fast bowler, it makes the game that more thrilling and exciting. Well, Jamaica gave to the world a fast bowler of phenomenal speed and accuracy in the form of Michael Holding. His slender gait punctuated by his gazelle-style run up to the wicket was poetry in motion; but Holding ▷

was deadly accurate and just as ruthless. In my opinion, there were two extraordinary performances by this man they called "whispering death". In 1976, at the Oval in England on a feather-bed wicket, Holding dug deep and arched his back for fourteen wickets versus England, taking 8 for 92 in the first innings and six more wickets in the second innings. A few years later in the Caribbean, again versus England and bowling to the master of defence, opener Geoff Boycott, Holding hurtled down, possibly the best 6 balls ever bowled in an over, finally destroying the wicket of Boycott with the last ball.

It was a chess-game with a boxing knockout, Boycott was set up then finished off, and as one commentator said, "We have just witnessed the best ever Over bowled in test cricket.

Holding ended his career with 249 test wickets and whilst Holding was ending his career another Jamaican was beginning to make his mark ... fast bowler, Courtney "Cuddy" Walsh. This 6 feet 5 inches speedster not known for devastating speed, but for his workman like approach, went on to develop into one of the world's top performers in the art of fast bowling.

Walsh formed a destructive partnership with Antiguan Curtly Ambrose, whose 6 feet 7 inches frame allowed him to deliver balls from a trajectory few batsmen could negotiate. Walsh, though, was his partner in crime and by the time the Jamaican's career came to an end he had become the first fast bowler to take over 500 wickets in test cricket, ending his career with 519 test wickets and achieving the feat in his homeland Jamaica at the famous Sabina Park Grounds, a feat that was marked with widespread celebrations throughout the island and indeed the Caribbean. Incidentally, in spite of his magnificent bowling exploits, where his best figures are 7 for 37 and in the one-day games, 5 wickets for 1 run, Walsh also holds the dubious distinction of scoring most 'ducks' (zeros) as a batsman. "Cuddy" is, however, loved by one and all, and never seemed to let this or anything else bother him.

You would want to think Jamaicans only participate in athletics, football, cricket and netball; let me assure you Jamaica's interest in other sports is wide and varied. Take boxing, we have had a World Champion or two; the "body snatcher", Mike McCallum, who held world titles in three different weight division is now a boxing hall of famer. The late Trevor Burbick, who is more famous for his defeat at the hands of Mike Tyson, making Tyson the youngest heavyweight champion of all time. But Burbick was and is Jamaica's only heavyweight champion. Jamaica has had other World Champions in Lloyd Honeygan, Simon Brown, Keith Mullings, Uriah

Grant, O'Neil Bell and Glen "The Road Warrior" Johnson. Jamaica would also like to claim as its own, heavyweight legend Lennox Lewis. You see, both of Lewis's parents are Jamaicans and he has always been a regular visitor to his homeland. In fact, since his retirement, the hard-hitting boxer has lived in Montego Bay. You will also notice that in the latter part of his career Lewis reclaimed his heritage by sporting "dreadlocks" which is definitely Jamaican; even his accent is Jamaican. Can we claim him? Yes we can!

Other popular local sports include volleyball, badminton, table tennis and lawn tennis is played quite a bit in Jamaica, especially in the hotels, which attract overseas visitors. Jamaica's most notable performance on the court came many years ago when two local lads, Richard Russell and Lance Lomsdon stunned the Americans in Davis Cup action in Kingston. Russell and Lomsdon stung the vaulted paring of Arthur Ashe and Charlie Pasarell in the doubles. Sadly, though we lost the tie.

The name Samantha Albert won't conjure up any autograph-seeking youngsters, but she sealed her place in history when she qualified for the equestrian event at the Beijing Olympics. She created history when she participated in the cross-country, dressage and eventing disciplines and dignified the colours of Jamaica in the three-day event.

Samantha made her mark in announcing her skills at the Pan American Games. No doubt she has and will inspire future show-jumpers.

Never tell a Jamaican he can't do anything, especially when it comes to a sport. We don't have snow in Jamaica; the temperature ranges between 80 and 90 degrees for most of the year. Even during the rainy season in October, the raindrops are sweaty from the heat! The movie 'Cool Runnings' was based on the true story of Jamaica's first bobsled team trying to qualify for the Winter Olympics. But, in reality, the original quartet are four individuals that embodied the saying, "what your mind conceives a Jamaican can achieve". Chris Stokes, Dudley Stokes, Winston Watt and Wayne Thomas decided to take-up bobsledding. Only one of them had a visa to leave the island, so why would they let a little thing like no snow stop them from taking part in the 1988 Winter Olympics in Canada. The rest, as they say, is history. By 1994, in Lillehammer, Norway, Jamaica shocked the world and, in particular, one of the world's super powers of the four-man event, by finishing 14th overall and thereby relegating the USA to 15th position.

The sons and daughters of Jamaica continue to chart new frontiers in non-traditional sports across the world; we also have participants in

Courtney Walsh was one of the world's top fast-bowlers.
Photo: Jamaica Information Service

medals in swimming; 3 Bronze medals in the Shot-Putt discipline; and captured 6 of his 18 Gold medals in one calendar year at the 1970 Olympics held in Scotland. Now with a name like Octavius Morgan can you expect anything but Gold?

Jamaica also plays its part in other 'challenged' sporting disciplines and is the leading Caribbean country in the Special Olympics events. The organisation, Special Olympics Jamaica (SOJ) was formed in 1978 and since then has continued to make great strides, both in the international and local arena.

The SOJ now has over 3000 registered athletes and has introduced the Young Athletes Programme which comprises children aged from three to seven with intellectual disabilities. Jamaica is one of only nine countries in the world catering to this age group.

After suffering numerous defeats at the World Winter Games, the Special Olympics Jamaica athletes were involved in a nail-biting victory over Special Olympics Canada at floor hockey at the 2009 World Winter Games in Idaho, capturing Gold for the first time in this sport. The roller-skaters continue to capture gold ... skating on ice? Think about it! Jamaica plus snow and ice ... it doesn't add up! But, I guess we're talking about Jamaicans aren't we? "No problem mon!"

Returning to cricket, Jamaica gave the sport one of, if not the, most revered umpires of the game in the form of Steve Bucknor. A member of the International Cricket Conference (ICC) Elite Panel, Bucknor, who began his international career in 1989, stopped officiating in 2009. During that time he had taken part in 181 one-day matches and 128 test matches, a world record at the time. Steve Bucknor was a well-regarded umpire and in 2005/2006 his umpiring accuracy was 96 per cent as compared to 94.8 for his counterparts.

Speaking of statistics and coincidences, did you know that Usain Bolt's record breaking performance at the Beijing Olympics where he clocked 9.69 for the 100 metres and 19.3 for the 200 metres, saw him breaking the records at the Berlin World Games exactly one year to the day for the 100 metres 9.58 and one year to the date 19.19 for the 200 metres.

Did you know also that at the Beijing Olympics, when the Jamaican quartet of Michael Frater, Marvin Anderson, Usain Bolt and Asafa Powell, clocked a world record for the 4x100 metres relay in 39.10, Powell's final leg was timed at 8.7 seconds, the fastest split for a relay leg ever recorded.

Indeed, we are more than the "Sprint Capital of the World". Bob Marley sung "One Love" and Bolt capped it off with his trademark display of arms ... "Jamaica to the world". ∎

triathlon and dominoes ... another of the country's most popular sports.

You may well be still basking in the awe and wonder of Jamaica's performance at the Beijing Olympics and Berlin World Championships, but in terms of consistency, and gold medals won, there is one son of the soil even Bolt has to take a back seat to. I speak of Para Olympian extraordinaire, Octavius Morgan... who has also proven that one should not place limits on a Jamaican. Morgan, as we have heard it told, is a direct descendant of Sir Henry Morgan, pirate and Governor of Jamaica in the 1600s. He represented his country from 1966 to 1981. During this period, he made a magnificent haul of 26 championship medals, which comprised 18 Gold and 5 Silver

The sport of kings reigns supreme in Jamaica

AINSLEY WALTERS

Horseracing may be known as the sport of kings, but in Jamaica, much like the island's cultural mix, it is a diverse melting pot.

Jamaican horseracing enthusiasts and professionals continue to command the respect and admiration of other jurisdictions worldwide. Jockeys such as Richard Depass, George HoSang, Eclipse Award winner, Shaun Bridgmohan and current superstar, Rajiv Maragh are as well known in North America as they are to fans who cram into Caymanas Park most Wednesdays, every Saturday and on all but two of Jamaica's public holidays.

Overseas visitors to Caymanas Park, the island's only racetrack, which celebrated its 50th anniversary in 2009, continue to marvel at the passion shown by fans – said to be among the world's most knowledgeable. As such, various tourism-related organisations, especially the Jamaica Hotel and Tourist Association, now recognise Caymanas Park as a tourist destination. This has been achieved mainly through the efforts of people such as Millicent Lynch who, during her ten-year stint as executive marketing manager at Caymanas Track, worked tirelessly to have the venue listed among the island's many attractions.

A sprawling 196-acre property located in St Catherine, the island's biggest parish, Caymanas Park, upon completion in 1959, was rated as the best racetrack in the Caribbean. However, Jamaica's love affair with horses started long before Caymanas Park became the island's racing Mecca.

Horses were introduced into Jamaica in the early 1500s. By 1655, when the English invaded the island, wild horses were in abundance. By ▷

RIGHT: *Jamaican jockeys are as well known in North America as they are to fans who cram into Caymanas Park. Photo: Klaus Wolf*

1777, horses were being imported from England for racing in Jamaica. However, the island's favourable weather, lush pastures and quality water sources soon led to Jamaica being renowned for producing thoroughbreds, which were being exported to Central America and even back to England. The popularity of the sport was clearly evident in the mid-1800s when almost every parish had its own racetrack.

Horseracing is further cemented in Jamaican folklore by song. In the late 1960s, The Pioneers recorded two smash hits about a horse named Long Shot. The first song, 'Long Shot', was about the popular horse losing a race and leaving The Pioneers without bus fare to get back home from Caymanas Park. In 1969, another hit, 'Long Shot Kick De Bucket', reflected on the demise of Long Shot who fell and died during a first-race spill. It was also a big success in Europe, further emphasising the fusion of Jamaican music and the popularity of horseracing.

Long Shot might have been made famous in song but other Jamaican thoroughbreds let their performances speak for themselves. Legendary horses include Rameses, Legal Light, Royal Dad, The Viceroy, Eros, Miracle Man and None Such, after whom the Jamaican racing industry's annual

ABOVE & RIGHT: Hailed as the "Home of the Caribbean's #1 Derby, Caymanas Park is Jamaica's only racetrack. This popular venue marked its 50th anniversary in 2009. Photos: Klaus Wolf

awards ceremony is named. Miracle Man, owned by Joseph Duany and trained by Hall of Famer Allan E. 'Billy' Williams, gave Jamaica its finest hour in international racing by closing out an unbeaten year – 2006 – with victory in the Confraternity Classic in Puerto Rico.

Jamaican horses have also dominated regional events, winning the Trinidad and Tobago Derby on four occasions from as early as 1950. Frank Watson's Footmark, trained by Leo V. Williams and ridden by Lester Newman, won the 1950 Trinidadian Derby. The following year, the filly Embers, which had previously won the Jamaica Oaks and Jamaica Derby, won the Trinidadian version. Mr Lover Lover, with Simon Husbands aboard, underlined the dominance of Jamaican horses with an impressive victory in 1997. Terremoto did the same in 1998 with Charles Hussey astride.

In July 2009, Bruceontheloose travelled to win the twin-island republic's Midsummer Classic, the second leg of the Trinidadian Triple Crown Series, beating six other Jamaican-bred horses. Bruceontheloose, winner of the 2009 Jamaica 2000 Guineas and St Leger, and a narrow Derby loser, did so under the care of Philip Feanny, the most accomplished trainer in the history of Jamaican racing. Feanny, a fourteen-time champion trainer, has thirteen Derby wins to his credit, teaming up on eight occasions with jockey Winston Griffiths.

Griffiths and Feanny's Derby winners include Prince Consort (1986), Liu Chie Poo (1988), The Viceroy (1989), Milligram (1992), Simply Magic (2002), I'm Satisfied (2000), A King Is Born (2003) and Distinctly Native (2004). Feanny achieved two more Derby victories without Griffiths – Hello Poochie Liu with Neville Anderson aboard in 1983 and Wells Fargo ridden by Charles Hussey in 1994.

Winston Griffiths has not only ridden more winners than any other jockey at Caymanas Park, but he has also ridden more winners than any other jockey in the English-speaking Caribbean. In a career spanning 34 years, he has won an unprecedented five jockeys' championships, established a world record eight consecutive classic wins including all five in 1992 (Triple Crown winner, on Milligram, as well as Guineas and Oaks winner, on Clasique) and has booted home a record 44 classic winners (among them eleven Derby champions). He was also the first jockey to attain a thousand winners, riding Eros to victory in the Red Stripe Caribbean Sprint on 13 November 1993. For his outstanding contribution to the sport, Griffiths was conferred with the National Honour, the Order of Distinction (O.D.) on Heroes Day, 1999. He is also the recipient of the coveted None Such Award for lifetime achievement. ■

The politics of then and now

Paul Bogle, left, and Marcus Garvey were instrumental in the creation of Jamaica's political landscape.

DELANO FRANKLYN

Jamaica, with a current population of nearly 2.7 million, like most of the other countries of the English-speaking Caribbean community, had the historical misfortune of being subject to colonial rule. The island was first claimed by the Spanish and then captured by the British. In the process, the indigenous occupants of the land were completely annihilated. Slaves from Africa and indentured labourers mostly from India, brought in by the British to work on sugar cane plantations, which at the time constituted the economic backbone of the country, replaced them.

The inhumane conditions brought about by slavery fuelled numerous slave revolts culminating in the abolition of slavery in 1834. Thereafter, the former slaves, now landless peasants, faced increased exploitation and social degradation, creating the basis for the Morant Bay rebellion, which took place in 1865. This rebellion was led by arguably the most influential peasant leader of the time, Paul Bogle, who is now one of Jamaica's national heroes.

The response to the Morant Bay rebellion by the planter class led by the colonial Governor was brutal and draconian. More than 354 people were executed, 1,000 homes burnt, 600 people flogged and Paul Bogle hanged. The structure of government was also changed. The existing Assembly was dissolved and replaced by crown colony government which established the authority of the Governor to make laws with the consent of a legislative council elected under a very restrictive franchise based on the ownership of land and payment of taxes.

The introduction of crown colony government led to increased agitation among the leadership of the expanding peasantry, the emerging nationalistic middle class and the growing intelligentsia, particularly among the teachers, who were not prepared to be ignored by the colonial masters.

The activities of influential and widely respected leaders among the masses such as Charles Campbell in the 1870s and 1880s and Robert Love in the 1890s; the formation of the Jamaica Agricultural Society in 1895, which is still the main organisation for farmers in Jamaica today, and the Jamaica Union of Teachers, the forerunner to the Jamaica Teachers Association in 1894 which, up until today, remains the foremost organisation for teachers in Jamaica; the militancy of the deeply religious and influential urban leader Alexander Bedward from 1891 to 1921; the work of lawyer and legislator J.A.G. Smith, and the political mobilisation of the internationally renowned Jamaican inspirational leader Marcus Garvey through his People's Political Party, formed in 1929, clearly demonstrated that the leaders of the broad masses of the Jamaican people were not prepared to sit still and be excluded from the structures of government.

This increased agitation by the representatives of the former slaves and their followers gained further traction as a result of the deepened social and economic hardship brought on by the First World War and the international economic depression of the early 1930s, culminating in an all-island labour rebellion in 1938. This national uprising by the people pushed lawyer extraordinaire Norman Manley and the flamboyant labour leader Alexander Bustamante to the forefront of Jamaica's national politics.

In 1938, Norman Manley became the leader of the newly formed People's National Party (PNP) and Alexander Bustamante formed the Bustamante Industrial Trade Union (BITU), followed by the Jamaica Labour Party (JLP) in 1943. The PNP, formed on the basis of a democratic socialist philosophy, and the JLP with its conservative ideological platform, have since then been the two primary political parties in Jamaica. This is so despite the fact that from 1944 to the present more than thirty other political parties have been formed, the vast majority of which are no longer in existence.

The national movement led by the PNP between 1938 and 1942 until it began its keen

Alexander Bustamante, left, and Norman Manley led the campaign for Jamaica's independence which was granted in August 1962.

rivalry with the JLP in 1943 forced the British to grant universal adult suffrage in 1944. For the first time, Jamaicans were given the opportunity to vote without conditions. Since then, the country has had sixteen general elections of which the PNP has won nine and the JLP seven.

Norman Manley and Alexander Bustamante, who became the two dominant political figures between 1938 and the 1960s, and whom have both been conferred with national hero status were followed by seven other leaders who went on to become Prime Ministers. These include Donald Sangster (1967), Hugh Shearer (1967 – 1972), Edward Seaga (1980 – 1989) and Bruce Golding (2007 – 2011) of the JLP, and Michael Manley (1972 – 1980 and again from 1989 to 1992); Percival James Patterson (1992 – 2006) and Portia Simpson Miller (2006 – 2007 and again from 2012) of the PNP.

Following a referendum of 1961, in which the people voted against Jamaica continuing as a member of the short-lived federation of British West Indian territories, Bustamante and Manley led the campaign for the country's independence which was granted in August 1962.

The 1962 constitution provided for the election of between 45 and 60 members from single-member constituencies to a House of Representatives, and the appointment of 21 senators – 13 nominated by the Prime Minister and 8 by the Leader of the Opposition, and that national elections be held on or before the expiry of every five years. The head of state remained the British sovereign, whose representative, the Governor General, has ceremonial powers, while the Prime Minister and his Cabinet exercise executive authority.

Although the Constitution does not make any provision for the existence of parish councils, the enactment of other laws provides for the election of parish councillors, thus making local government a component of the structure of government with the holding of elections every three years.

Against the backdrop of this evolving party political landscape, the country can boast an enviable parliamentary democratic record for being able to reject and elect the political party of

Portia Simpson Miller is Jamaica's current Prime Minister. Photo: Jamaica Information Service

its choice on sixteen consecutive occasions, without the country falling prey to the hazard of a military or one-party dictatorship, a coup or civil war. Apart from the long tradition of a stable two-party democracy with extraordinary freedom of expression, as well as an independent judiciary, Jamaica is privileged to have a vast array of natural assets, outstanding scenic beauty, high levels of bio-diversity, the world's richest flora, a range of premium agricultural commodities, and one of the most advanced telecommunication infrastructures in the world, and is world-renowned for its creativity in the areas of music, other performing arts, visual arts and athletic prowess.

Despite these positive attributes, the country continues to grapple with very serious social and economic issues – unemployment, political tribalism, increased crime, a heavy debt burden and low economic growth. These issues present the political leadership of the country with a formidable challenge. The challenges are further compounded by the global recession, which is having a significant impact on small island developing states such as Jamaica.

However, Jamaica can take pride in the fact that it is inhabited by resilient people, whose propensity to rebound has been demonstrated by their being able to overcome the twin plagues of slavery and colonialism. Also, the Jamaican people, despite the odds, were able to push for and successfully achieve universal adult suffrage and independence. The next step is destined to be sustained economic and social development which will result in significant and qualitative improvement in the lives of all Jamaicans. ∎

Government

Jamaica is a parliamentary democracy based on a system of representative government. The Constitution of Jamaica (1962) is primarily based on British socio-political culture and is modelled on the Westminster-Whitehall system of government.

The British monarch is the titular Head of State and is represented by a Governor-General. The Governor-General has limited powers granted by the Constitution of Jamaica. The incumbent plays an important role in the appointment of significant national figures including the Prime Minister, Leader of the Opposition and the Chief Justice. Plans are being considered for Jamaica to become a Republic within the Commonwealth and to replace the Queen as Head of State with a President.

Citizens vote for their representatives in general elections and are subject to the "rule of law". They have the right to privacy of home and property; the right to secure the protection of the law; and, protection from discrimination on the grounds of race, religion, politics, colour, sex, creed, beliefs, and place of origin.

The State has three arms whose functions remain separate in keeping with the Constitution – the Legislature, the Executive and the Judiciary.

THE LEGISLATURE

Legislative responsibilities rest with the elected representatives of Government, which is headed by the Prime Minister.

Parliament consists of two Houses – The House of Representatives/Lower House and The Senate/Upper House. The former comprises 60 members, who are elected by the people, and, whose consent is required on all legislative matters.

The Senate consists of 21 members who are appointed by the Governor-General on the advice of the Prime Minister and the Leader of the Opposition – thirteen and eight members, respectively. The Senate primarily reviews bills passed by the Lower House. It may also initiate bills, except financial bills.

The life of Parliament spans five years, at which time it is dissolved, and a general election held. However, the Prime Minister may advise the Governor-General to dissolve Parliament at anytime. Parliament must also be dissolved and a general election held, if a majority of the members of the Lower House support a no-confidence motion against the Government.

THE EXECUTIVE

The Prime Minister presides over the Cabinet, which initiates policies and programmes, and controls the general direction of Government. It must consist of the Prime Minister and no fewer than eleven other ministers, only four of whom may be appointed from the Senate.

The business of Government is conducted by a number of ministries, each headed by a Cabinet Minister, who may be assisted by State Ministers and Parliamentary Secretaries.

THE JUDICIARY

Jamaica's Judiciary is based on English common-law and practice. The administration of justice is vested in the courts, namely, the Judicial Committee of the Privy Council, Court of Appeal, Supreme Court, Gun Court, Family Court, Traffic Court, Resident Magistrate's Courts, Revenue Court, and Petty Sessions Courts.

CHECKS AND BALANCES

Checks and balances have been established by the Constitution to limit the power of the Executive. These include the offices of the Leader of the Opposition, Auditor General, Director of Public Prosecution, and the three services commissions. The Prime Minister must consult the Leader of the Opposition on some matters, such as the appointments of the Chief Justice, President of the Court of Appeal and members of the services commissions.

LOCAL GOVERNMENT

Parochial affairs are administered by Parish Councils which are chaired by Mayors. Membership of the Councils varies between thirteen and twenty-one elected representatives.

Adapted from: "The Government of Jamaica" Published by the Jamaica Information Service

RIGHT: Prime Minister's official residence. Photo: Brian Rosen

Prime Ministers of Jamaica

PREPARED BY THE JAMAICA INFORMATION SERVICE

SIR ALEXANDER BUSTAMANTE

National Hero, the Right Excellent Sir William Alexander Bustamante (below, left), rose to national prominence during the early 1930s when he protested the harsh social conditions facing the poor, at public gatherings and in the local press.

In agitating for the rights of the workers on the waterfront, Sir Alexander was charged with sedition and detained for four days in 1938. His arrest resulted in widespread unrest among low income workers, who refused to resume work until he was released. That same year, he formed the Bustamante Industrial Trades Union (BITU) in order to intensify his advocacy on behalf of the workers. Two years later, he was once again detained for 17 months, following a series of BITU-led strikes.

In 1943, he formed the Jamaica Labour Party (JLP), creating a two-party political system in Jamaica. Under his leadership, the JLP was victorious in the first general election under Universal Adult Suffrage in 1944, and again in the 1949 polls. He became Jamaica's first Chief Minister and Head of the Council of Ministers when, changes were made to the constitution in 1953.

The JLP was victorious in the 1962 polls, and when Jamaica secured full Independence from Britain on 6th August that year, Sir Alexander became Jamaica's first Prime Minister. He served up to his retirement in 1967, though he suffered a stroke in 1964.

Some of Bustamante's major achievements include industrialisation through the Pioneer Industries Law of 1947; the introduction of the bauxite and alumina industries; and the expansion of the seasonal Farm Work programme to the United States.

He was declared a National Hero in 1969, and to this day, is the only person to receive that award while alive. Sir Alexander passed away peacefully on 6th August 1977. He was 93 years old.

SIR DONALD SANGSTER

The first indication that Donald Burns Sangster (below, right) would become a leading public figure was in 1933 when, at 21, he became Jamaica's youngest elected representative, after winning a seat on the St Elizabeth Parochial Board.

In 1949, he joined the Jamaica Labour Party (JLP) and won the South St Elizabeth seat in the general election that year. He was appointed Minister for Social Welfare and First Deputy to the JLP's Majority Leader, the Rt. Excellent Sir Alexander Bustamante. He later served as Leader of the House and Minister of Finance, and had oversight responsibility for Jamaica's entry into various international organisations and associations. He also sought to encourage greater integration between Jamaica and other Caribbean territories.

When the Prime Minister, Sir Alexander Bustamante, fell ill in 1964, and up to the time of his retirement in 1967, Sir Donald was called upon to carry out the duties of the office.

He was named leader of the JLP after Sir Alexander's retirement and led the party to victory in that year's general election. He was sworn in as Prime Minister on 22nd February 1967. His tenure as Prime Minister was short lived, as he suffered a brain haemorrhage on 18th March 1967, and died less than a month later on 11th April 1967.

Hallmarks of his career in the public service included the development of the Donald Sangster International Airport in Montego Bay, St James; improvements in the agricultural sector that produced record sugar and banana exports in 1966; and, he also positioned Jamaica as a leader in the Caribbean and among the nations of the Commonwealth.

HUGH SHEARER

Hugh Lawson Shearer (above, left) began his distinguished career of service to the nation at the age of 17, when he joined the staff of *The Jamaica Worker* newspaper, which was the official newspaper of the Bustamante Industrial Trade Union (BITU).

In 1942, Sir Alexander Bustamante made Hugh Shearer his protégé, and he steadily rose through the ranks of the Jamaica Labour Party (JLP) and the BITU, eventually assuming the post of President-General of the BITU. As he gained prominence among his colleagues, he developed a reputation for being affable and a good orator.

He entered representational politics in 1947, and was elected Municipal Councillor for the Central St Andrew Constituency. He was elected to the House of Representatives in 1955 for the Western Kingston Constituency and, in 1959, he was appointed to the Legislative Council. He was appointed to Jamaica's first Senate in 1962. In 1967, Hugh Shearer replaced Sir Alexander Bustamante as Member of Parliament for the South Clarendon Constituency, and successfully occupied that seat until his retirement from politics in 1993.

Following the death of Prime Minister Donald Sangster in 1967, Shearer was selected to become Jamaica's third Prime Minister, and served in this capacity until 1972. He retired from public office in 1993, and led a quiet life until his death on 4th July 2004.

His most notable accomplishments included the development of a system of major highways and bypass routes across the island, and steering the construction of over 150 primary and junior secondary schools.

MICHAEL MANLEY

A talented and multi-faceted individual, the political life of Michael Norman Manley (above, right) began in 1952 when he was elected to the National Executive Council of the People's National Party (PNP). In that year he also joined the PNP affiliated National Workers Union and, within three years, he rose to the position of First Vice President.

Manley was elected to Jamaica's first Senate in 1962, and five years later, he entered representational politics. He won the Central Kingston seat in the 1967 general election, and represented the Constituency up to his retirement from politics in 1992.

In 1969, he succeeded his father, Norman Manley, as leader of the PNP. Under Michael Manley's stewardship the PNP was victorious in the 1972 general election and he was sworn in as Jamaica's fourth Prime Minister. He led the party to victory again in the 1976 general election.

Under Manley's leadership, the National Housing Trust was established to provide

affordable housing solutions for citizens; paid maternity leave for women was enacted into law; free education was offered to Jamaican citizens; and legal recognition was granted to children born out of wedlock.

After a nine-year hiatus, the PNP, under Manley's leadership, won the 1989 general election, and he was sworn in for the third time as Prime Minister. His third term, though short, focused on the liberalisation of the economy through the passage of supporting legislation.

In 1992, after three years in office, he resigned from the positions of both Prime Minister and Leader of the PNP due to declining health. He died five years later, on 6th March 1997.

EDWARD SEAGA

Highly regarded among Jamaica's well respected pubic servants, Edward Phillip George Seaga (above, left) entered public service in 1959, when he was elected to the Legislative Council. A supporter of the Independence movement, Seaga was also a member of the committee that drafted Jamaica's Independence Constitution.

He entered the House of Representatives in 1962, representing the Kingston Western Constituency, which he successfully held until 2005, when he retired from active politics.

He was Minister of Development and Welfare from 1962–1967. Between 1967 and 1972 he served as Minister of Finance, and during this time he encouraged the establishment of local businesses and industries under the 'Jamaicanisation' programme. He also oversaw the establishment of the National Development Bank, the Urban Development Corporation and the Student Loan Bureau.

Edward Seaga was elected leader of the JLP in 1974, and was sworn in as Jamaica's fifth Prime

Minister after the party's victory in the 1980 general election. He served as Prime Minister until 1989. As Prime Minister, he led several national projects that further promoted the development of industry and the manufacturing sector, such as opening several garment factories, and establishing Jamaica International Promotions (now Jamaica Trade and Invest).

He served as Leader of the Opposition from 1989 – 2005 when he retired. He now serves as Distinguished Fellow at the University of the West Indies, and Pro-Chancellor at the University of the Technology.

PERCIVAL JAMES (P.J.) PATTERSON

Percival Noel James Patterson (above, right) was appointed Jamaica's sixth Prime Minister in 1992.

P.J. Patterson was appointed Opposition Senator for the People's National Party (PNP) in 1967, and two years later, he was elected to the post of Vice-President of the party. He was elected Member of Parliament for the South East Westmoreland Constituency in 1970. Following the PNP's victory in the 1972 general election, he was appointed Minister of Industry and Tourism. In 1976, he was given portfolio responsibility for the Ministry of Foreign Affairs and was named Deputy Prime Minister.

In 1989, following the PNP's victory at the polls, P.J. Patterson was appointed Deputy Prime Minister and Minister of Development, Planning and Production. Finance was added to his portfolio in 1990. As Finance Minister, he sought to expedite the liberalisation of the Jamaican economy by introducing new financial laws, including the Banking Act, Financial Institutions Act, and the Bank of Jamaica Act.

In 1992, after the retirement of the then Prime Minister, Michael Manley, he was elected leader

of the PNP, and subsequently sworn in as Prime Minister on 30th March 1992. He led the PNP to victory in the three subsequent general elections.

As Prime Minister, he implemented several policy initiatives, including the creation of the Jamaica Social Investment Fund, the Jamaica Drug for the Elderly Programme, and Government Executive Agencies.

He retired from his position as Prime Minister and from active politics on 30th March 2006.

BRUCE GOLDING

Orette Bruce Golding (above, left) took office as Jamaica's eighth Prime Minister on 11 September 2007 and served until 23 October 2011. His general election victory as leader of the Jamaica Labour Party (JLP), was the successful culmination of a 38-year career in representational politics.

In 1969, Bruce Golding was selected and successfully ran as the JLP candidate for West St Catherine for the 1972 general election. And between 1976 and 1980, he was an Opposition Senator as well as General Secretary of the JLP.

When the JLP won the 1980 elections, Mr Golding was re-appointed to the Senate and appointed Minister of Construction. He successfully represented the Central St Catherine Constituency in the 1983 general election, and occupied that seat until 1997.

In 1995, he resigned from the JLP, and was one of the founders of the National Democratic Movement, serving as its first President (1995-2001). In 2002, he rejoined the JLP and in November 2003 was again elected Chairman of the Party. Following the 2002 general election, he was re-appointed to the Senate. In 2005, he was elected leader of the JLP and Member of Parliament for the West Kingston Constituency.

PORTIA SIMPSON MILLER

Portia Lucretia Simpson Miller (above, right) became the first female Prime Minister of Jamaica on 30 March 2006 when she was sworn into office following the retirement of former leader of the PNP and Prime Minister, P.J. Patterson. She served until 11 September 2007.

On 5 January 2012, Mrs Simpson Miller was again sworn in as Prime Minister, succeeding Bruce Golding.

Prior to her first appointment as Prime Minister, Mrs Simpson Miller had served for 17 years as a Cabinet Minister with portfolio responsibility for Labour and Social Security, Tourism and Local Government, Community Development and Sport. She was conferred with the Order of the Nation in May 2006.

Mrs Simpson Miller has been an active and leading member of the PNP for many years. In 1974, she was elected Councillor for the Kingston and St Andrew Corporation as a PNP candidate, and has served as Member of Parliament for the South Western St Andrew Constituency since 1976.

In Government, she has occupied the positions of Parliamentary Secretary in the Ministry of Local Government and Office of the Prime Minister; Minister of Labour, Welfare and Sport; Minister of Labour, Social Security and Sport; Minister of Tourism and Sport; and, Minister of Local Government, Community Development and Sport. She also has a distinguished record of service at the international levels.

The leading architect of Jamaica's Master Plan for Sustainable Tourism Development, Mrs Simpson Miller has been tireless in promoting and strengthening urban renewal and community development, leading to fundamental reforms in local government. ∎

Governors-General of Jamaica

PREPARED BY THE JAMAICA INFORMATION SERVICE

SIR KENNETH BLACKBURNE, GBE, KCMG

Sir Kenneth Blackburne, Jamaica's first and only non-Jamaican Governor-General, began his tenure on 6th August 1962, transitioning into the post after serving as Jamaica's last British Governor.

Prior to assuming the position of colonial Governor in Jamaica, he served in the British Colonial Administrative Service, with assignments in Nigeria, Palestine and Galilee.

In 1941, he was appointed Colonial Secretary of The Gambia, and from 1943 to 1947 he was the Administrative Secretary to the Comptroller for Development and Welfare in the West Indies. He was promoted Governor of the Leeward Islands in 1950, and eventually retired from that position six years later.

One year later, Sir Kenneth was appointed colonial Governor of Jamaica and served until 6th August 1962, when Jamaica became an independent nation. At that time, he was invited to serve as Jamaica's first Governor-General, a duty he performed up to 30th November 1962, ending a five-year sojourn in Jamaica.

Sir Kenneth is credited with advocating better understanding between the British and Jamaican citizens, and also, the island's peaceful transition from a British colony into an Independent nation.

SIR CLIFFORD CAMPBELL, ON, GCMG, GCVO

The Most Honourable Sir Clifford Clarence Campbell is the first Jamaican to have been appointed Governor-General. He was sworn in on 1st December 1962, following distinguished careers in education and representational politics.

Sir Clifford was born in 1901 in the community of Petersfield in the parish of Westmoreland. After completing elementary education, he enrolled in the Mico Teachers' College in 1912. After graduation in 1915, he became an outstanding educator in his home parish, serving at Fullersfield Government School (1915 – 1918), Friendship Elementary School (1918 – 1928) and Grange Hill Elementary School.

In 1944, Sir Clifford successfully ran for the Westmoreland Western seat as a member of the Jamaica Labour Party (JLP) in the first general election under Universal Adult Suffrage, and represented this constituency until 1955. While he was a Member of Parliament he was elected Chairman of the House Committee on Education, Vice-President of the Elected Members Association, and Speaker of the House in 1950. In May 1962, he was elected President of the Legislative Council, and following Jamaica's Independence, he was appointed President of the Senate.

Sir Clifford served as Jamaica's Governor-General up to 1st March 1973 when he retired from office. He passed away on 28th September 1991, a few months short of his centenary.

SIR FLORIZEL GLASSPOLE, ON, GCMG, CD

The Most Honourable Sir Florizel Augustus Glasspole is the longest serving Governor-General of Jamaica, having served for a period of 18 years (1973 – 1991). He succeeded Sir Clifford Campbell.

Left to Right:Sir Kenneth Blackburne welcomes Princess Margaret to Jamaica in 1962 to participate in the country's Independence celebrations; Sir Clifford Campbell was the first Jamaican to have been appointed as Governor-General; Sir Florizel Glasspole served as Governor-General for an impressive 18 years.

Left to Right: Sir Howard Cooke rose from humble circumstances to become one of Jamaica's best loved public figures; Sir Kenneth Hall's tenure as Governor-General was characterised by a keen focus on promoting excellence among Jamaica's youth.

Considered one of the country's most distinguished patriots and founding fathers, his life and careers in trade unionism and politics reflected a deep commitment to helping Jamaica's poorest citizens.

Sir Florizel was born on 25th September 1909 in Kingston. While attending Wolmer's Boys School, he represented the school in athletics, and also played cricket and football. As a young man in the early 1930s, he worked at the Serge Island Sugar Estate in St Thomas, where he witnessed first-hand the plight of the working class. Inspired to create change, Sir Florizel became affiliated with the trade union movement representing low income workers. He would later help to form the People's National Party (PNP) in 1938.

In the 1944 general election, the first under Universal Adult Suffrage, he was one of four PNP candidates to win seats in the House of Representatives. He retained his seat – East Kingston and Port Royal constituency – until 1973, when he assumed duties as Governor-General.

During his 18 years as Governor-General, Sir Florizel was highly regarded for his objectivity and his continued activism for the working class. He retired from this office on 31st March 1991 and led a relatively quiet life until the time of his passing in September 1991.

SIR HOWARD COOKE, ON, GCMG, GCVO, CD

The Most Honourable Sir Howard Felix Hanlan Cooke, rose from humble circumstances to become one of Jamaica's best loved public figures, and Jamaica's Governor-General from August 1991 – February 2006.

Sir Howard, or 'Teacher' as he is affectionately called, was born in Goodwill, St James in 1915.

Teacher Cooke studied at the Mico Teachers' College and embarked on his first teaching assignment at the Mico Practising School in 1933. He subsequently served as headmaster at the Belle Castle elementary School in Portland and at the Montego Bay Boys' School in his home parish.

Sir Howard is a founding member of the People's National Party and started his career in representational politics in 1958, when he was elected to the West Indies Federal Parliament as the representative for St James. He served as Opposition Senator from 1962 to 1967. From 1967 to 1980, he was a member of the House of Representatives and a Minister of Government with portfolio responsibilities for Education, Pensions and Social Security, and Labour and the Public Service.

He was conferred the National Honour, Commander of the Order of Distinction in 1978 and in 1980, he was awarded by the Commonwealth Parliamentary Council for distinguished service.

He was President of the Senate from 1989 to 1991, when he resigned to assume the position of Governor-General. His tenure as Governor-General was marked by dedicated service, dignity, impartiality and decorum.

PROF. SIR KENNETH HALL, ON, GCMG, OJ

One of Jamaica's most distinguished academics and educators, the Most Honourable Professor Sir Kenneth Octavius Hall, became Governor-General on 16th February 2006, after ending a ten-year period as Principal and Pro-Vice Chancellor of the University of the West Indies (UWI).

Born in 1941 in Lucea in the parish of Hanover, Sir Kenneth received his secondary level education at Rusea's High School, and then moved on to the University of the West Indies, where he earned a Bachelor of Arts Degree in History in 1966. In the following year, 1967, he earned a post-graduate diploma in International Relations at the UWI St Augustine campus in Trinidad.

▷

LEFT: Sir Patrick Allen is Jamaica's present Governor-Genera

He subsequently taught for two years a Rusea's High School, and then moved on to the Queens University in Canada to pursue Master' and Doctor of Philosophy Degrees in History.

His career in academia in Jamaica and overseas culminated with his appointment as Pro-Vice Chancellor and Principal of the University of the West Indies in 1996. Sir Kenneth is committed to the Caribbean integration movement and paused from academic pursuits to serve at the CARICOM Secretariat in Guyana on two separate occasions. He has also published several books, articles and reviews on CARICOM issues.

Sir Kenneth served as Governor-General fo three years (February 2006 to February 2009). His tenure was characterised by a keen focus on promoting excellence within the productive secto and among Jamaica's youth.

SIR PATRICK ALLEN, ON, GCMG, CD, PHD

His Excellency the Most Honourable Sir Patrick Linton Allen was born in 1951 in Fruitful Vale Portland. He attended Fruitful Vale All-Age School and, after completing his GCE examinations in 1968, joined the school's staff as a pre-trained teacher.

Two years later, he enrolled at the Moneague Teachers' College and taught at Water Valley All-Age School in the parish of St Mary after graduating. He worked in St Mary for a number of years serving as principal of Robin's Bay Primary School (1976) and Hillside Primary School (1979 – 1981).

Sir Patrick is a devout Seventh-Day Adventist who went into full-time ministry in 1980. In 1983 he attended the Seminary at St Andrews University in Michigan in the United States, where he earned a Bachelor's degree in History and Religion, and later, a Master's degree in Systematic Theology.

He returned to Jamaica in 1986 and was ordained as a pastor in 1989. In 1993, he returned to Andrews University where earned his PhD in Educational Administration and Supervision in 1998. After returning to Jamaica, he was elected President of the Central Jamaica Conference o Seventh-Day Adventists. In 2000, he was elected President of the West Indies Union Conference o Seventh-Day Adventists with responsibility for Seventh-Day Adventist Churches and organisations in Jamaica, the Bahamas, Turks and Caicos, and the Cayman Islands.

In 2009, he retired from this post to become Jamaica's Governor-General, and was installed on 26th February 2009. ■

Foreign investors sharpen their focus on Jamaica

MARK THOMPSON

B rand Jamaica is internationally associated with quality, excellence and success in many fields, and big business is no exception as smart and serious global investors are increasingly embracing Jamaica as a prime destination for investment.

In the 2008/2009 financial year, capital expenditure from investment projects facilitated by Jamaica Trade and Invest (JTI) – the national investment and trade promotion agency – totalled JA $34.1 billion (US $383.4 million) across the tourism, agriculture, manufacturing, mining and energy, information and communication technology (ICT) and creative sectors. This figure represents a 40 per cent increase over the JA $24.3 billion (US $273.5 million) recorded in 2007/2008. Over the five-year period from 2003 to 2007, total Foreign Direct Investment (FDI) inflows into the island averaged US $733 million, peaking at US $882 million in 2006.

There are several factors that contribute to Jamaica's ability to attract substantial foreign investment. The country boasts an open and diverse economy with encouraging prospects and a strong international profile. This is supported by a sturdy political commitment to free enterprise, distinct brand identity and the expansion of benefits with no restrictions on the movement of capital, profits, and dividends. Additionally, there are virtually no exchange controls and no approval is required for repatriation of profits and dividends.

Jamaica's position as an ideal investment destination is further strengthened by its warm climate, large and friendly English-speaking population, competitively priced and diverse labour force and strategic location for trading with the rest of the Western Hemisphere. The island's other noted advantages are its proximity to both the United States and the Panama Canal, and its historic and emerging relationship with the Latin American bloc. Jamaica is also served by world-class port facilities, two modern international airports, well-developed infrastructure and an abundance of natural resources.

According to the World Bank Doing Business 2009 report, Jamaica's scores are on the same level as the advanced member nations of the Organisation for Economic Co-operation and Development (OECD) in areas such as business start-ups, dealing with licences, registering property, flexibility of labour market, protecting investors and enforcing contracts.

In addition to the policies and attributes that help to shape Jamaica's enabling business environment, the implementation of more focused and targeted national investment attraction strategies has played a critical role in the attainment of increased investment flows during the current decade.

SECTOR OPPORTUNITIES

TOURISM

Tourism clearly dominates Jamaica's economy, with over three million visitors flocking to the country's shores every year. In 2008/2009, JTI facilitated JA $13.4 billion (US $150.5 million) in capital expenditure in tourism investments, which accounted for almost 40 per cent of the total capital expenditure facilitated by JTI over the period. Significant FDI has flowed into Jamaica through the accommodations sub-sector in the last five years. Some of the top investment opportunities in this sector include the development of attractions, boutique hotels and facilities for health and eco-tourism.

INFORMATION & COMMUNICATION TECHNOLOGY

In today's world of fast and borderless communications, Jamaica is on the right side of the digital divide. A deliberate government ICT development strategy initiated in 2001 has ignited tremendous growth in the telecoms sector, which has benefited from nearly US $1 billion in investment over the last ten years. The most dynamic and fastest growing area within telecoms has been mobile telephony.

Major providers of high-quality services have made significant strides in developing Jamaica's

FACING PAGE: Welcome to Jamaica. Investment opportunities in the tourism sector include the development of attractions, boutique hotels and facilities for health and eco-tourism. Photo: Jamaica Trade & Investment

n today's world of fast and borderless communications, amaica is on the right side of the digital divide. Photo: amaica Trade & Investment

fibre optic/broadband connectivity and the sector's focus is now on telecommunications, software development and enabled/share services, which includes contact centres and Business Process Outsourcing (BPOs). Jamaica is presently ranked among the top international locations for offshore outsourcing.

AGRICULTURE

Jamaica has sought to diversify its agricultural base and improve its efficiency through the use of modern technology. While Blue Mountain coffee continues to sell at a premium on the world market, other traditional exports (sugar, bananas, etc) are undergoing significant diversification through the application of technology. The use of biotechnology and irrigation techniques has given rise to investment opportunities in non-traditional areas such as aquaculture, the cultivation of fruit trees, indigenous plants and herbal product.

MANUFACTURING

There is real diversity in Jamaica's manufacturing industry, which is a likely factor that contributes to the very strong year-on-year growth. In 2008/ 2009, JTI facilitated JA $5 billion (US $56.6 million) in capital expenditure in the sector. Companies involved in manufacturing range from the small to the very large; those that produce canned foods to those that deal with the extraction and processing of natural resources and chemicals.

While Blue Mountain coffee (left) continues to sell at a premium on the world market, other traditional exports, such as fruit and spices, are undergoing significant diversification through the application of technology.

Companies involved in manufacturing range from the small to the very large, such as cement manufacturing (bottom). Photos: Jamaica Trade & Investment

MINING AND ENERGY

Bauxite has for a long time been the most mined mineral in Jamaica, but other profitable minerals exist, such as limestone, marble, gravel, sand, gypsum, marl, dolomite, clay, whiting, silica, sand and lime. On the renewable energy side, investment opportunities are available in ethanol, wind energy and hydropower.

CREATIVE INDUSTRIES

Jamaica's reputation as the cultural Mecca of the Caribbean has positioned its creative industries as a key revenue generator for the local economy. The music and film sectors, two of the many areas in the creative industries with scope for increased investment in support services and infrastructure, generate US $250 million and US $1 billion respectively every year.

Bauxite has for a long time been the most mined mineral in Jamaica. Photo: Jamaica Information Service

READY FOR BUSINESS

In spite of the turbulence caused by the current global economic storm, Jamaica has managed to weather the situation quite well and remains on the radar of discerning investors. To facilitate all aspects of new business ventures, Jamaica has tailored a wide range of incentives, which include newly-tabled laws and agreements, as well as sector-specific concessions and incentives.

For more information contact Jamaica Trade & Investment (JTI) in Kingston or London.

18 Trafalgar Road, Kingston 10. Tel: (876) 978 7755 Toll free: +1 877 INVEST JA (468-4352). Email: info@jti.org.jm. www.jamaicatradeandinvest.org ∎

Spanish investors lead the way in hotel investment

Since 2001, Jamaica has experienced renewed linkage with Spain, a country with which it has a long history dating back some 500 years, but this time these links are being led by the private sector.

An unprecedented level of investment by Spanish hotel groups is helping to encourage a rapid process of expansion and transformation of the island's tourism industry. The process has been welcomed and encouraged by the Jamaican Government and a nation appreciative of foreign direct investments as a vital tool for job creation and economic prosperity.

Within the last few years, Spanish investment has become an important contributor to the economic development of Jamaica, having already reached, in 2006, one of the leading positions on the list of foreign investors in the island. All together, planned investments average some US $1,500 million with construction in the tourism industry of over 10,000 rooms. Spanish investments will represent a 50 per cent increase in Jamaica's room capacity over the next ten years.

The ambitious venture by Spanish investors is expected to have a significant impact on the future prosperity of the Jamaican economy, with resulting deep social consequences. The increased investments are expected to result in the creation of approximately 12,000 direct jobs and a further 30,000 indirect jobs.

These figures do not only imply benefits for both the Jamaican economy and the investors but also signify a challenge, as the country will have to upgrade its skills in education, housing, training of tourism workers and community development. In addition, Jamaica will be called upon to encourage the development of small and medium enterprises in fields such as craftsmanship, tourism activities and entertainment, retail shopping or agriculture.

The Spanish companies which have current investments in Jamaica, as a way of emphasising their commitment to the Jamaican society and the future, established the Spanish-Jamaican Foundation in 2006 which funds projects and activities in various areas – education, tourism training, teaching of foreign languages, social projects and community development. The Foundation's strong mandate is to contribute to improved social welfare and the fight against poverty, through social and educational priorities. The Foundation is governed by an Executive Board headed by the Ambassador of Spain to Jamaica as the Honorary President and comprises the Spanish Groups with investments in the country, which include the hotel groups – Iberostar, Bahia Principe Hotels, Seawind Key-Fuerte Hotel Group, Fiesta Hotel Group, Excellence Group, RIU, among other non-hotel investors.

The Executive Board relies on the experience and well-earned reputation of a number of leading personalities in the Jamaica society who form the Foundation's Advisory Board, for advice and guidance in the selection of the projects and priorities undertaken by the Foundation.

The **Gran Bahia Principe Hotel** is located in Runaway Bay on the north coast of Jamaica. This 5-star hotel consists of 680 junior suites offering a variety of services and facilities under the All Inclusive formula. It is part of the Grupo Piñero with hotels in Spain, Mexico and the Dominican Republic.

RIU Hotels and Resorts was the first Spanish hotel chain to invest in Jamaica. There are currently four RIU hotels operating on the island, the first opened in 2001 in Negril and the last in August 2008 in Montego Bay. RIU has built all of its hotels in Jamaica with an investment of over 300 million dollars, more than 2,400 rooms and has more than 2,000 employees.

The 4-star **Grand Palladium Jamaica Resort and Spa** and the **Lady Hamilton Resort and Spa** are located in Lucea, 20 minutes from Montego Bay and have 340 rooms.

Located in Montego Bay, **Iberostar Rose Hall Beach** laps the shores of Rose Hall Beach, the most exclusive beach in the area and is just 20 minutes from the Montego Bay Airport.

The tourism industry is the fastest growing sector and the brightest of all for future prospects and it has been doing better thanks to the massive investment which came at the right time just before the current global economic crisis began. ∎

Real estate in Jamaica: An investor's paradise

LASCELLES J. POYSER

O ne of the most positive sources of investment over the years is real estate. Compared to many parts of the world, Jamaica has one of the lowest habitations per acre. Therefore, investing in Jamaican real estate offers one of the best returns compared to other countries.

This jewel in the Caribbean is the historical and contemporary home to the rich and famous. They come for the sun, sea and sand, golf, fishing, carnival and reggae.

Jamaica's real estate is a pivotal point in the wealth creation for investors. Over the last few years the worth of real estate has risen to astronomical heights. Lands around the island that were once ignored or partially used, have now become boom areas. This trend is set to continue as the population grows.

At present, there is a shortage of over four hundred thousand living units, especially in the areas where new hotels are being built.

There is a vast amount of available land for sale throughout Jamaica in plots from five acres to ten thousand acres. Some have rivers flowing through them; there are beachfront sites; flat lands and hilltop farming locations.

In addition to the salubrious housing developments all over the island, there are luxurious condos such as the Palmyra in Montego Bay – one of the most glamorous in the Caribbean. Then there are superb shopping centres, including the 200,000 sq. ft. Whitter Shopping Complex in Montego Bay, which is one of the best in the Caribbean.

Jamaica's two major airports in Montego Bay and Kingston deal with millions of visitors every year and new seaports are being built to

CLOCKWISE FROM ABOVE: Jamaica has some of the finest real estate in the Caribbean; the Whitter Shopping Complex; residential housing; new apartments.

PHOTO: BRIAN ROSEN

PHOTO: TONY MATTHEWS

accommodate the mega cruise liners. The rise in tourist numbers, returning Jamaicans and new investors will serve to make Jamaica a real estate investor's paradise.

In recent years, Spanish investors have rediscovered Jamaica and they are now investing in major hotels. They are followed by the Chinese, Indians and Africans. Jamaicans who lived abroad are now returning to live their golden years in homes that rival those in Costa Rica and Florida. Their children, who were born abroad, but have legal status, are now investing and working in Jamaica.

The wide variety of available land and real estate includes small hotels, commercial complexes, residential resorts, tourist related properties and investment properties for renting to the tourist trade, or expatriates working in Jamaica.

Along with the traditional tourists, Jamaicans and their friends are increasingly visiting the island for vacations, weddings, family occasions, sports events, and music and cultural festivals. And they all need somewhere to stay!

With no special sales or purchase taxes for non-nationals, real estate investment in Jamaica is free to anyone.

For more information, contact the Real Estate Board, 1 Surbiton Road, Kingston 10. Tel. 1876-920-2950 /3789. Email info@reb.gov.jm ■

Agriculture, Fisheries and Forestry

STACY ROSE

Agriculture in Jamaica had its genesis in the Amerindian society where crops and livestock were mainly produced for food and fibre. The later conquest and colonisation of Jamaica in the late 15th and mid 17th centuries by the Spanish and British, respectively, saw the transition from a domestic sector providing for household needs, to one which was export led and dominated by sugar cane production.

Jamaica's conquest by the Spanish in the late 15th century saw the introduction of pigs, goats, cattle, sugar cane, banana, plantain, varieties of citrus, among other fruit trees and agricultural crops. The English also brought the world renowned coffee, ackee, mango, breadfruit, otahetie apple and jackfruit, among other crops to the island.

The rise of sugar as the main export commodity was during British occupation and led to the development of the plantation system where English planters owned and operated large sugar plantations on the plains in various parts of the island. Imported labour from West Africa was forced to work on these plantations in the capacity of slaves and eventually outnumbered the Caucasian population. The best portion of lands was used for sugar cane cultivation, while marginal lands were used for other crops and livestock for domestic consumption, mainly by the slaves. The plantation system had a tremendous impact on the composition of Jamaica's population, economy, culture, social interaction, language and land tenureship, which is still evident today.

EXPORT AND DOMESTIC CROP SECTORS

The post emancipation period saw the decline in production of sugar and a concomitant rise in the export of other commodities. Bananas emerged as the other major export commodity in this period and revenues earned sometimes exceeded those made from sugar, which still remains the dominant agri-food export. In recent times, the continuous damage to the banana crop by successive hurricanes and tropical storms led to the suspension of the export of this commodity by the largest exporter in late 2008. Therefore all production is now being consumed locally.

Cocoa, coffee, citrus, coconut, pimento, ginger, tobacco and rum exports also grew significantly during the post-emancipation period and became of such economic importance that associations were formed for most of these commodities to protect the interests of producers and market them internationally. The importance of these commodities to the Jamaican economy, with the exception of tobacco, has continued until present. However, the export sector has not emphasised value addition, mainly due to the nature of the trade agreements and marketing arrangements under which the commodities are sold, thus mirroring the plantation system of yesteryear.

The engagement in commodity export-oriented production has led to a dualistic agricultural sector, where a limited amount of crops are cultivated on large farms for export and domestic crops continue to be produced on small parcels of land. The pattern of land distribution for agricultural production is evidenced by findings from the Agricultural Census of 2007, which shows that 140 farms (or less than 1 per cent) are greater than 200 hectares, while 180,000 farms (or 78.7 per cent) are less than 1 hectare.

The export sector tends to be more organised and efficient than the domestic crop sector and commodities such as sugar and bananas are sold in the markets of developed countries in their ▷

BELOW: Exports of non-traditional commodities such as ackee have outpaced those of traditional exports. Photo: Tony Matthews

RIGHT: Domestic crops are produced on small parcels of land and sold at local markets or at road-side locations throughout Jamaica. Photo: Jamaica Tourist Board

primary form under preferential arrangements. However, due to successful challenges to Europe's sugar and banana preferential trade regimes, the survival of these sub-sectors will lie in their ability to take advantage of the domestic market, as is being done by the latter, and move up the value chain.

Other export commodities such as Jamaican Blue Mountain coffee and fine flavoured cocoa are sold at premium prices in the international markets due to their high quality. Jamaica is recognised as one of the eight exclusive producers of fine flavoured cocoa internationally. With greater investment, there exists great scope for the expansion of production and the creation of local value added products from fine flavoured cocoa.

Key spice exports, pimento and ginger, are sold through the Ministry of Agriculture & Fisheries' Export Division to commodity traders on the international market. Jamaican ginger, known for its exquisite pungency and flavour, has been exported since the mid 16th century, and the island is recorded as being one of the world's three largest producers between the 1930s and 1960s. However, production has contracted significantly since that period, although Jamaican ginger continues to be in high demand internationally as a key ingredient in confectionary, drink and baked products. Therefore, opportunities exist for greater levels of investment in the production of this crop.

The domestic sector consists of farmers cultivating vegetables, legumes, fruits, roots, tubers, cereals and condiments, mainly on hillsides for local consumption. A proportionately small amount of total production is exported to markets ▷

MAIN PICTURE: The domestic agricultural sector consists largely of farmers cultivating vegetables, legumes, fruits, roots, tubers, cereals and condiments for sale at local markets such as Coronation Market in Kingston. Photo: Klaus Wolf

BELOW: Jamaican Blue Mountain coffee is sold at premium prices in the international markets due its high quality. Photo: Jamaica Trade & Investment

of developed countries in North America and the United Kingdom. In recent times, exports of non-traditional commodities such as papaya, ackee, fish, conch, pumpkin, sweet potatoes, dasheen, mangoes and yam contributed to 47 per cent of Jamaica's agricultural export revenue in 2008 and their growth has outpaced that of traditional exports.

Condiments such as hot pepper (scotch bonnet and Jamaica/West Indian red) are used to make famous hot pepper sauces. However, when hot peppers are combined with escallion and pimento, they form the base for the world renowned and flavourful jerk sauce, known and loved by people all over the globe as a key seasoning for their meats.

Opportunities exist for the expansion of domestic crop production for the local market and the untapped export market for ethnic foods. Commercial fruit tree crop production for domestic consumption, value added and exports also presents another area for long-term investment.

LIVESTOCK

Besides crop production, the country also has a thriving livestock sector comprising of beef and dairy cattle, poultry, sheep, pig and goat sub-sectors.

The cattle industry has benefited from the work of Dr Thomas P. Lecky who revolutionised the Jamaican dairy and beef industries through the development of four tropically adapted breeds of cattle: Jamaica Hope for milk, the Jamaica Red Poll, Jamaica Brahman and Jamaica Black for beef. The Jamaica Hope is popular among cattle farmers as the main milk-producing cattle in Jamaica. Jamaica Red Poll is now the main meat producing cattle in

BELOW: The Jamaica Red Poll is now the main meat producing cattle in Jamaica. Photo: Jamaica Information Service

RIGHT: Jamaica has yet to fully exploit its full fisheries potential. Photo: Brian Rosen

Jamaica, as well as other Caribbean and Latin American countries.

Livestock, particularly poultry, is the main source of protein in the Jamaican diet and is therefore critical to food security. The structure of the livestock sector reflects that of the crop sector where there are many small farmers and a few large players, particularly for the poultry, beef and dairy sub-sectors.

Jamaica is near self-sufficient in poultry and pork, but imports much chevon (goat meat), mutton, beef (choice cuts and trimmings) and dairy products to satisfy local demand.

There exists, however, great potential for expansion of sheep production as over 95 per cent of local consumption is derived from imports. The revitalisation of the beef and dairy sector also presents good investment opportunities for prospective investors.

FISHERIES

The Fishing Industry in Jamaica is comprised of over 18,000 fishers, 95 per cent of which are small scale, operating from 187 fishing beaches with over 4,800 registered vessels.

There are five main types of fishing operations carried out on the island:

- Industrial fisheries, for conch, lobster and fish, mainly for export
- Artisanal fisheries at high sea, banks, inshore and inland, mainly for domestic consumption
- Aquaculture, including tilapia, penaeid shrimp, oysters, ornamental fish and others, for export and local consumption
- Sport fishing for marlins and fishing trips with tourists
- Collection of seaweeds, land crabs, etc.

Total fisheries production in 2008 was 15,355 tonnes, with marine fisheries accounting for 62 per cent of production and inland fisheries, 38 per cent. Current fisheries production satisfies less than 12 per cent of the local demand for fish and fisheries products.

Sustainability of Jamaican fisheries has been threatened by over-fishing of onshore fishing grounds. With the exception of industrial conch and lobster fisheries and the artisanal fisheries on Pedro Bank, all fisheries are operated on an open-access basis which significantly contributes to the problem of over-fishing. Interestingly, Jamaica has not fully exploited its full fisheries potential as evidenced by the high incidences of illegal fishing and poaching by foreign vessels within the Economic Exclusive Zone (EEZ), which covers approximately 235,000 square kilometres. ▷

Opportunities also exist for investment in aquaculture, which is currently concentrated in two parishes. Based on current domestic fish consumption, there is the potential to double or triple its present size, especially in western parishes.

FORESTRY

The Forestry Agency reports that over 30 per cent of Jamaica, or approximately 335,900 hectares, is classified as forest. Of this total, approximately 88,000 hectares is classified as "closed broadleaf forest" with a closed canopy and minimal human disturbance. Most of the remaining forest is classified as "disturbed broadleaf" (showing varying degrees of human disturbance) or natural dry open forest. Although the latter is often referred to as woodland or scrub, dry limestone forests are a key component of Jamaica's forest ecology and economy. Another 30 per cent of the country is classified as "mixed use", which describes areas of "disturbed broadleaf" forest mixed with another land use/forest cover. The remaining 39 per cent of the area of Jamaica is classified as non-forest.

The annual rate of deforestation is estimated at 0.1 percent or 300 hectares of forest. Major causes of deforestation are bauxite mining, natural diseases and pest and disease infestation of trees and removal of trees for various economic activities such as agriculture, housing, road construction and industrial purposes. The Forestry Agency is countering deforestation and forest degradation through programmes and projects that encourage reforestation and enrichment plantings.

Investment opportunities exist in commercial pine and high value hardwoods (such as mahogany, teak and cedar) for value added products, commercial *Cupressus spp.* (Christmas tree), forest recreation and eco-tourism. Currently, only 20 per cent of hardwood needs are derived from local production. In addition to hardwood, other potential sources of earnings from forestry include medicinal and aromatic plants from which essential oils can be extracted.

Poultry plays a significant role in the Jamaican diet and is one of the main sources of protein. Photo: Klaus Wolf

THE WAY FORWARD

Agriculture was the leading sector up to Jamaica's pre-independence period when it was surpassed by the bauxite/alumina industry in the 1950s. Diversification of the Jamaican economy and other challenges relating to adverse weather conditions (namely, droughts, hurricanes, storms), disease outbreaks, low productivity, declining production, liberalisation of the economy due to structural adjustment and the implementation of World Trade Organisation's rule-based regime, have all contributed to the decline of the sector. However, the sector remains a key foreign exchange earner and the third largest employer of labour for the economy.

The future of the agricultural sector in Jamaica rests in its ability to exploit existing market segments, both locally and internationally in the fresh and processed foods markets for various

commodities. Opportunities also exist for Jamaica's products in the fair trade and organic foods markets. However, costs relating to certification and attainment of standards present barriers to entry to these markets for producers.

There exists a wide range of markets and market segments for Jamaican agricultural commodities and by-products. Opportunities to access major markets in Europe, United States, Canada and the Caribbean exist under the Economic Partnership Agreement, Caribbean Basin Initiative, Canada Caribbean (CARIBCAN) Agreement and Caribbean Single Market. Locally, the tourism sector and domestic market, which together account for over 4 million people annually, also provide ready markets for fresh produce and value added products.

Emphasis and support for value addition will increase growth of the sector in the medium to long term. The country must take advantage of 'Brand Jamaica' that utilises the concept of nation branding as a tool for achieving competitive advantage for Jamaica's products in order to increase growth in existing and new markets. Targeted marketing of Jamaica's foods, complemented by an effective nation branding strategy will catapult Jamaica's agriculture into a new dimension, thus ensuring the sustainability of the sector for the long term.

Further details on market and investment opportunities can obtained from: Agro-Invest Corporation , c/o Ministry of Agriculture and Fisheries, Hope Gardens, Kingston 6. ∎

The history of coffee in Jamaica

CHRISTOPHER GENTLES

In the late 1600s and early 1700s, coffee houses became popular in England. They were the meeting places where prominent men went to transact business. These coffee houses proliferated to the extent where every level of the society had some coffee house that catered to that particular grouping. This generated a huge demand for coffee from the colonies.

The Governor of Jamaica, Sir Nicholas Lawes, introduced coffee to Jamaica from some coffee arabica seeds and plants that he had acquired from Martinique. The House of Assembly at the time supported coffee cultivation as a way of cultivating and inhabiting the hilly interior of the island, as this was seen as a move that would increase the stability of the economy and, therefore, the security of the island.

The high duty on coffee being imported into England prevented this from being a profitable venture at first, but eventually when the duty was reduced in 1790, coffee cultivation became extremely lucrative. Many French and Haitian planters, who fled from Haiti after the revolution, brought to Jamaica great skills in running coffee plantations. Haiti, after all, was one of the prime producers of coffee. In 1809, Jamaica, itself, became one of the world's largest exporters producing as much as 83 millions pounds.

After the abolition of slavery in 1838, coffee production fell sharply. Many of the large coffee plantations were abandoned out of fear that the production would never be profitable with paid labour. Many of the freed slaves also started plots of coffee either on the abandoned farms or on farmlands close to original plantations. By 1865, the production had declined to six million pounds.

It was soon discovered that coffee planted in the mountains developed a unique aroma and more delectable flavour. The coffee grown in the Blue Mountain regions of Jamaica became renowned in the European coffee houses for delicate balance, superb aroma, smooth, naturally sweet and creamy taste, with mild notes of herbs, chocolate and sugar cane. Much of the cultivation took place between 500m and 1500m.

Jamaica High Mountain coffee was also recognised as very special and the pricing of this coffee reflects the esteem in which the markets hold this coffee.

Coffee production fell to a record low during the years after the Second World War, and the Inspector General of Agriculture for the West Indies, A.J. Wakefield wrote the report entitled, 'The Rehabilitation of the Coffee Industry in Jamaica'. As a result of this report, Parliament formed the legislation called the Coffee Industry Regulations Act of 1948, which led to the development of the Coffee Industry Board in 1950.

The Coffee Industry Board was given significant powers in order to regulate the coffee industry, and the resources to centralise the purchasing and processing of cherry coffee. Pulperies were built at strategic locations in the High Mountain and Blue Mountain regions, and the Coffee Industry Board set up a network of co-operatives to assist the farmers with the organisation and co-ordination to plant, cultivate and consistently reap high quality coffee.

In the early sixties, much of the exports of Jamaican coffee went to England. It was reputed that the Queen of England insisted on having Jamaica Blue Mountain Coffee. The Japanese were intrigued by this and started to purchase coffee from England. It was soon discovered, however, that much of the coffee was being transhipped to Japan. Some of the coffee was shipped directly to the Japanese from Jamaica, and after some promotions it was recognised that the characteristics of the Jamaica Blue Mountain Coffee was perfectly suited the delicate palates of the Japanese.

By the late 1970s, the demand for Jamaica Blue Mountain Coffee significantly outpaced its supply. In 1983, the government amended the Coffee Industry Regulations to define that Jamaica Blue Mountain Coffee must be grown within a specifically defined geographical region, and must be pulped within this very same region.

In the 1980s, the government decided to deregulate the Coffee Industry and issued licences to private companies to process and market Jamaican coffee for private companies and individuals, who produced more than 10,000 cherry boxes.

The Coffee Industry Development Company (CIDCO) was founded in 1981 in order to facilitate increasing acreage and productivity of Jamaica Blue Mountain and High Mountain Coffee. It was

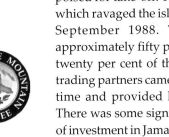

very effective in motivating the farmers and guiding the investment of the loan funds for the development of the coffee industry.

Many private individuals, companies and professionals found coffee production to be an attractive option, which was previously seen as the purview of small farmers. It seemed at this point in the 1980s that the coffee industry was poised for take-off. Then came Hurricane Gilbert, which ravaged the island from east to west on 12th September 1988. This caused the loss of approximately fifty per cent of the coffee crop and twenty per cent of the coffee trees. The Japanese trading partners came to Jamaica's assistance at the time and provided hurricane restoration loans. There was some significant recovery, but the level of investment in Jamaica High Mountain Coffee fell off after the disaster. The recession in the Japanese economy in 1992 reduced the demand for Jamaica High Mountain Coffee, and the production fell to a record low of 45,000 boxes in 2007-8.

In 1999, there was a decision by the government to separate the commercial arm of the coffee industry from the regulatory arm. This was

CLOCKWISE FROM TOP LEFT: Hillside coffee plantation; harvesting the crop; preparing the berries; Jamaica High Mountain Coffee ready for export.

critical in establishing objectivity in the assessment of coffee of privately licensed coffee dealers and the government-controlled operations. The commercial division was renamed the Wallenford Coffee Company. The Coffee Industry Board, the regulatory arm, regulates the industry, by defining the standards for Jamaican coffee, the best practices for growing and processing of Jamaican coffee.

Jamaica has challenges protecting its world famous brand and the Coffee Industry Board has registered the Jamaica Blue Mountain Coffee and Jamaica High Mountain Supreme trademark all over the world. Despite this there are consistent challenges as impostors seek to brand and package their coffee as Jamaican. The Coffee Industry Board is working with the Swiss Federal Institute of Intellectual Property (API) and the Jamaica Intellectual Property Office to have Jamaica Blue Mountain Coffee and, later, Jamaica High Mountain Coffee protected as geographical indicators. ■

Maximising the earning potential of Jamaica's creative economy

MARK THOMPSON

At the forefront of the national effort to position Jamaica's world renowned creative industries as a key generator of revenue for the local economy is the work of the Creative Industries Unit of Jamaica Trade and Invest (JTI) – the national investment and export promotion agency.

The creative industries encompass those sectors that are born out of individual creativity, skill and talent, such as the motion picture/film industry, recording industry, music publishing, music and theatre production, fashion and design and the visual and performing arts.

JTI's Creative Industries Unit is committed to tapping into the potential for wealth and job creation that is inherent in the many cultural and artistic expressions of the people, who are undoubtedly inspired by the island's beauty and rich heritage.

It is this natural and breathtaking beauty of the island with its variety of scenic locations combined with some of the most knowledgeable and talented facilitators of the film business, which have made Jamaica the Caribbean's preferred destination for film production.

Film, as one of the many vibrant creative industries, is bristling with the potential to spur economic growth. Since 1984, the Jamaica Film Commission housed within the Creative Industries Unit at JTI, has serviced over 3,000 film projects ranging from feature films and documentaries, to music videos.

Among the films shot in Jamaica are *20,000 Leagues Under The Sea* (1954), *A High Wind in Jamaica* (1965), *All The Brothers Were Valiant* (1953), *Belly* (1998), *Children of Babylon* (1979), *Clara's Heart* (1985), *Club Paradise* (1985), *Cocktail* (1987), *Dancehall Queen* (1996), *Dr. No* (1962), *Goldeneye* (1989), *How Stella Got Her Groove Back* (1998), *Instinct* (1998), *Legends of the Fall* (1993), *Prelude to a Kiss* (1991), *The Harder They Come* (1972), *The Mighty Quinn* (1989) and *Third World Cop* (1998).

The role of the Jamaica Film Commission is to facilitate all elements of the film production process through the provision of services such as location scouting, the acquisition of film licences and the administration of attractive incentives to production companies, both local and overseas.

The Commission is also charged to promote and market Jamaica as the premier location for filming and investment opportunities, and to facilitate a national presence at film industry trade shows. By so doing, it seeks to create business linkages for Jamaica's local industry with film-making organisations and providers of market opportunities from around the world.

Another key function of the Commission is to develop and facilitate the process of bi-lateral trade agreements within the global film industry, with the historic UK Co-production Treaty being one such example. The first of its kind in the Caribbean, the agreement gives mutual incentives to Jamaica and UK filmmakers, allows for joint productions and establishes a foundation for wider cultural exchanges.

In the area of music, Jamaican creativity and ingenuity has given rise to some of the world's greatest artistes, producers and sound engineers. Reggae music commands the respect of the world and a major industry has been built up on the island around the promotion, performance and recording of artistes from Jamaica and beyond.

The Creative Industries Unit has been empowering leadership in the music industry and facilitating the strengthening of industry associations to guide the development process for the long-term benefit of the music and the country. The Unit is actively engaged in the provision of linkages between potential buyers and local industry players and maintains a national presence at music trade shows to facilitate the professional showcasing of Jamaican talent and product. Additionally, its suite of services include reducing bureaucracy in the import/export of sector goods, identifying grant funding and low interest financing options, lobbying for sector incentives in order to increase investment and foreign exchange and providing education in areas affecting the sector.

As it relates to fashion and design – one of the fastest growing of the creative industries – and the visual and the performing arts, the Creative Industries Unit is focused on market penetration activities and unearthing opportunities for greater international exposure. The Unit is also working closely with the relevant industry groups and players to identify investment opportunities.

As Jamaica showcases its unique style, exquisite artistry and strong culture, the Creative Industries Unit of Jamaica Trade and Invest stands ready to facilitate local and international companies and individuals who are interested in maximising the full business potential of Jamaica's creative industries.

CONTACT
The Creative Industries Unit, Jamaica Trade and Invest (JTI), 18 Trafalgar Road, Kingston 10, Jamaica.
Phone: (876) 978-7755; 978-3337. Fax: (876) 946-0090.
Email: info@jti.org

TOLL FREE: Jamaica – 1-888-INVESTJA (468-4352)
International – 1-877-JAMVEST (526-8378)

www.jamaicatradeandinvest.org
www.filmjamaica.com
www.soundsofjamaica.com

Film, as one of the many vibrant creative industries, is bristling with the potential to spur economic growth. Photo: Jamaica Trade & Investment

Education

ALFRED SANGSTER

The early beginnings for the masses of the slave population began with the Free Church missionaries and a key player in the early struggle for freedom was the Baptist Deacon Sam Sharpe. He was leader of the slave rebellion of 1831, hanged for his role and his statue that of one of Jamaica's national heroes stands proudly in Sam Sharpe Square in Montego Bay.

Progress was slow but a mix of church initiatives along with enlightened planters led to the development of primary schools and secondary trust schools such as Mannings, Munro and Hampton, Wolmer's the Mico Teachers College.

The Kingston Technical High School (1896) and the Jamaica School of Agriculture (1910) were early initiatives in technical education. Most of the churches continued to build both primary and secondary schools and some teachers colleges. But the spaces were still limited.

The 'New Deal for Education' (1966) led by then Minister Edwin Allen dramatically increased the numbers of schools which could provide a bridge between the large numbers in the primary system and the smaller numbers at the secondary level with the construction of fifty Junior Secondary Schools funded by a World Bank loan which was itself a pioneering first initiative.

IMPORTANT HISTORICAL DEVELOPMENTS

The early connection of children from the primary to the secondary system at 11-plus was through the Common Entrance Examination (1958). It was performance based and the reality was that children who had the benefit of a paid education (prep schools) not surprisingly outperformed children from the primary schools. The ▷

RIGHT: *Prize giving ceremony at Moore Town Primary and Junior High School. Photo: Josh Hunter*

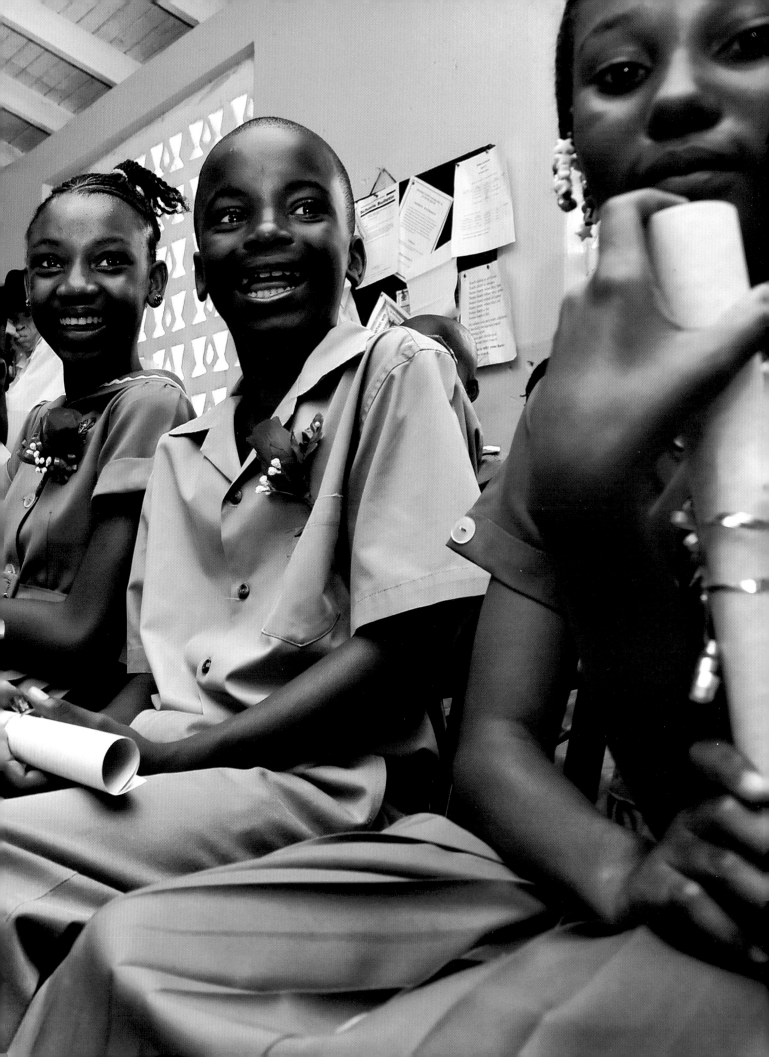

The need for gainful employment for the outputs at both the secondary and tertiary levels remains an important factor in the overall expectations of students at all levels. Photo: Tony Matthews

government in seeking a measure of social justice mandated that the placements of children to the secondary schools should be in the ratio 70:30 – primary/prep (1962). This was not a popular decision with the middle class at the time. Later as primary education improved the ratio was abandoned. But it was still a matter of trauma as only a fraction of those who took the test could move into the secondary system. This was improved later by the introduction of the Grade Six Achievement Test (GSAT), which provided for most students from the primary system entering into secondary. This was possible as successive administrations along with churches built more schools to cope with an expanding student population as well as to provide increased opportunities for secondary education.

Free education was dramatically announced in 1973 by the then Prime Minister Michael Manley. The facility lasted for some years and was reversed by a later government. It has been a matter of mixed policies with successive governments and currently operates in a mixed mode of free tuition with a smaller ancillary fee.

The establishment of the Caribbean Examinations Council (CXC) was a pioneering, regional initiative formally established in 1973 with the first exams in 1979. It has successfully established a regional secondary school examination system which caters to tens of thousands of Caribbean students in over forty different subject areas. It replaced the overseas UK-based school leaving examinations.

When free education was first announced a decision taken at the same time was to upgrade the Junior Secondary Schools with the establishment of a set of New Secondary Schools which had a different curriculum and examination from the traditional High Schools (commonly known as Name Brand Schools). Thus, a separate, parallel and inferior secondary school system was created which was only unified many years after. There is a great deal of catching up still to be done. However, these schools have done remarkably well and now boast their CXC examination results in the traditional subjects and are making their mark in the Inter Secondary School Sports (ISSA) competitions.

The first Community College to be established was the Excelsior Community College by visionary Wesley Powell. The model was soon followed and now there are some five of these colleges across the island offering a wide variety of programmes at different levels.

The Human Education and Resource Training (HEART) Programme introduced by Prime Minster Seaga in 1962 was geared to 'rescue' students who had not performed well at the secondary level. It provided a second opportunity, but was also geared to a specific skill training opportunity – such as cosmetology, hotel training, garment making, automotive skills, computer skills and more, which might not have been available in the traditional secondary schools. The programme provided opportunities for thousands of young students who might well have been deemed as failures

HIGHER EDUCATION

The Establishment of the University (College) of the West Indies (1948) was a critical decision tied to the UK government's post-war colonial territories initiative. UWI has since grown to be one of the signal regional success stories with campuses or links in all the Commonwealth Caribbean territories.

The University of Technology was so named in 1995 by the changing of the name of the College of Arts Science and Technology established in 1958.

Northern Caribbean University – a private university – was established from the foundations laid by the Seventh-Day Adventist West Indies College.

A number of institutions have now coined the term 'university' and offer various degree programmes. Many of these programmes are associated with overseas universities. Among these are: University College of the Caribbean (UCC), International University of the Caribbean (IUC), Mico University College, Teachers' Colleges and the Jamaica Maritime Institute. In addition several universities from the United States and Britain have moved into the country offering mainly MBA programmes at quite high cost.

Established in 1987, the University Council of Jamaica was created to address the need for the registration of institutions offering higher level qualifications. The UCJ not only registers institutions but also accredits programmes. It has become a flagship institution and a leader of the quality assurance movement in the Caribbean through founder Executive Director Dr Ethley London.

CHALLENGES FOR THE FUTURE

The educational system faces a number of challenges. Some of these are:

WEAKNESS IN THE BASIC PRE-PRIMARY SYSTEM

A major study entitled *Transformation* suggested that, "$60 billion was needed to fix the system." This was as if to say that money was all that was needed. In addition, the project said virtually nothing about the critical needs of a basic education gap which the present government is working hard to address.

THE PLACEMENT OF GSAT STUDENTS

The guideline in the GSAT examination at age 11-plus is that high performers get their first choice of school. The result is that the Traditional High Schools (Name Brand Schools) get the best students in the examinations and the New Secondary Schools cry "unfair" as they get low achievers and have a considerable amount of remedial work to do.

OVERALL PERFORMANCE OF STUDENTS AT THE PRIMARY AND SECONDARY LEVEL

It has been recognised that there is a need to improve performance generally at both the primary and secondary levels and there are indications of improvements in skills such as reading and the three R's.

Unfortunately a number of analysts use the performance of the schools in English and Maths as a method of ranking the schools. While these subjects are important there is a lot more to a school education and there needs to a better method of judgment. Items such as sports, drama, enterprise and specific circumstances need to be taken into account.

Another concern is the overall performance of boys and the distractions of the media and the challenge of crime and violence to the learning process.

JOBS FOR GRADUATES

The need for gainful employment for the outputs at both the secondary and tertiary levels remains an important factor in the overall expectations of students at all levels.

EDUCATIONAL ACHIEVERS

There is a great deal of migration of skilled Jamaicans and they have contributed to the development of other countries. There is of course a plus in that many of these graduates send remittances home, which helps the Jamaican economy. ■

Transforming health for national development

SANDRA GRAHAM

J amaica boasts an extensive outlay of health facilities that include over 330 health centres, 24 public hospitals, the University Hospital of the West Indies, a Caribbean teaching institution which is partially funded by the Government of Jamaica, ten private hospitals and more than 495 pharmacies. The public health sector accounts for 5,000 hospital beds compared to the 200 beds in the private sector. Each year, approximately 1.5 million visits are made to health centres and over 700,000 to Accident & Emergency Departments of public hospitals to access services. Patients make no 'out-of-pocket' payments since user fees have been abolished first for children in 2007 then extended to all public patients in April 2008.

The twenty-four public hospitals are spread across the fourteen parishes and four health regions. The hospitals are designated A, B, and C based on the range of services that are offered. The Regional Hospitals and the country's national referral hospital (the 233-year-old Kingston Public Hospital) provide the most extensive range of services including renal dialysis, ophthalmology, diagnostic, radiology, surgical and pharmaceutical services.

There are five specialist hospitals providing services in obstetrics/gynaecology, psychiatry, cardio-thoracic/pulmonary, rehabilitative, and oncology. In addition, there is a national referral hospital for children. Some of these specialist hospitals treat patients who are referred from other Caribbean countries.

As impressive as this outlay might be, especially for a small developing nation of 2.67 million people, it is secondary to the country's enviable track record of providing quality care at affordable cost. This is a track record that started more than thirty years ago and is attributed to the Primary Health Care Concept which was developed and introduced to Jamaica's health sector prior to the 1978 Alma Ata Conference in Russia. Indeed, the country's experience was pivotal in defining the primary health approach that was adopted by the Conference.

The country's health indices provide compelling testimony of the success of the health sector. The United Nations Development Program's 2008 Human Development Report puts Jamaica's life expectancy at 72.2 years, which compares favourably with other developing nations and is within striking distance of developed countries.

COUNTRY	LIFE EXPECTANCY
Select Developing Countries	
Bahamas	72.3
Barbados	76.6
Dominican Republic	71.5
Guyana	65.2
Jamaica	72.2
Trinidad and Tobago	69.2
Select Developed Countries	
Canada	80.3
United Kingdom	79.0
United States of America	77.9

Source: Compiled from the 2008 Human Development Report

THE HUMAN INFRASTRUCTURE

Like other developing countries, Jamaica faces the challenge of retaining its highly trained and experienced health workers. For decades, the country has sought to augment its human resources in health through a mix of strategies including increasing training in targeted areas such as nursing and bi-lateral agreements with countries such as Cuba to import skills.

Since 2004, over JA$350 million has been spent to support the training of nurses, doctors and in those disciplines supplementary to medicine such as pharmacy and radiology. In addition, a further JA$100 million is being spent to undertake short-term training in the Assistive Health Care Category of workers such as Laboratory Technician Assistants, Pharmacy Technicians, Psychiatric Aides, Operating Theatre Technicians and Anaesthetics Technicians. These workers will free the highly skilled workers to concentrate on those tasks that cannot be delegated.

In 2008, the government shifted the responsibility for training health workers from the Ministry of Health to the Ministry of Education. The Ministry of Health will concentrate on developing a national health workforce policy and plan. The majority of Jamaica's health workers are ▷

FACING PAGE: University Hospital of the West Indies is in Kingston is partially funded by the government. Photo: Klaus Wolf

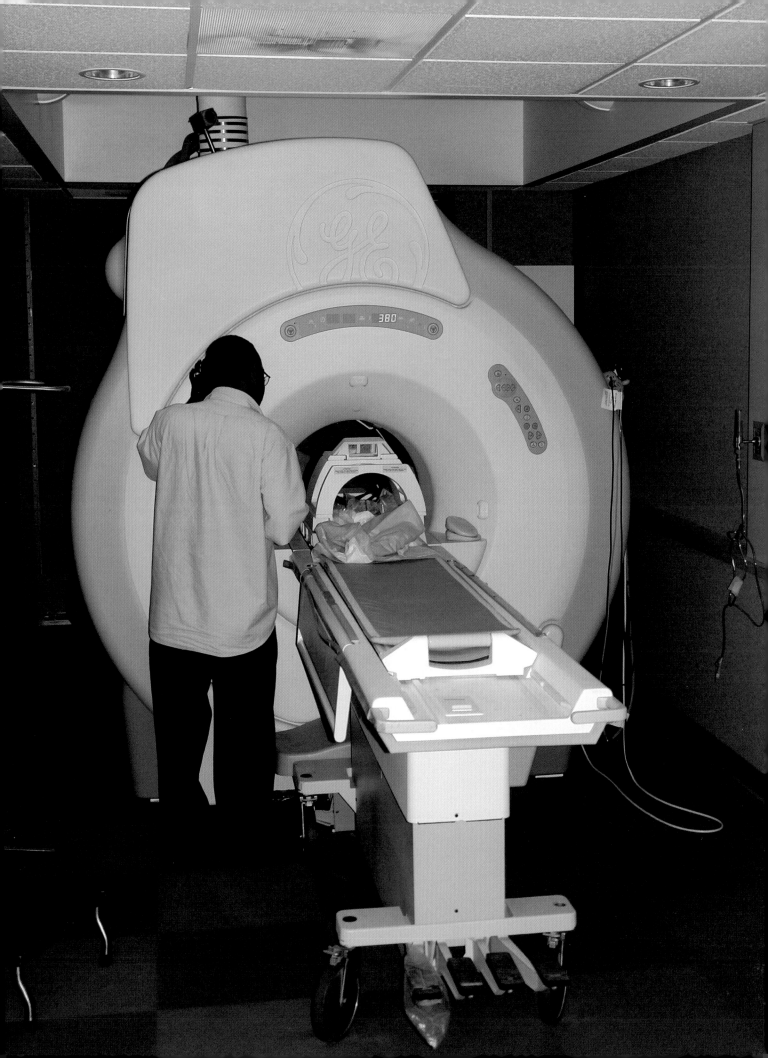

The 233-year-old Kingston Public Hospital is the country's main trauma centre

trained in Jamaica at the University of the West Indies, University of Technology and the Northern Caribbean University. Several community colleges and private post secondary institutions also provide training in nursing.

THE PHYSICAL INFRASTRUCTURE

During the 2009/10 financial year, the government will continue with the $500 million repair and renovation of health centres across the island in keeping with the programme of renewing primary health care. This focus on health centres is preceded by a comprehensive hospital restoration project which saw upgrading and infrastructure work being undertaken at six of the islands public hospitals to the tune of US $92 million up to the late 1990s. The project was funded jointly by the Government of Jamaica and the Inter-American Development Bank.

THE TECHNOLOGICAL INFRASTRUCTURE

The development of the technological infrastructure is an integral part of the transformation process. The Government of the Republic of Korea has provided technical support in the amount of US $1.5 million to develop Jamaica's National Health Information System. The System will be installed and ready for testing by October 2009.

HEALTH TOURISM

In addition to modernising the overall health infrastructure, Jamaica is interested in targeting the approximately eight million uninsured population in the United States who are likely to seek health care overseas.

Jamaica has some distinct competitive advantages including its geographic location, language, favourable climate and the health infrastructure. Many Jamaicans living abroad have been accessing health care back home especially dental services. The service is on par with what is available in their adopted country and the cost is much more affordable. The vast outlay of the public health sector coupled with modern private sector offerings in areas such as radiology and dentistry is a good platform on which to build a vibrant and viable health tourism industry.

Although by no means a giant in the area of medical research, Jamaica has done enough to demonstrate that it has what it takes to create a niche in herbal remedies. For example, the groundbreaking research work that was done at the University of the West Indies in developing the glaucoma drug Canasol from ganja is an

Nurses graduating from the Cornwall Nursing School

important development that augurs well for the future of the country's health sector.

Jamaica is in a race against time. The success of the country in achieving 'first world' status by 2030 and the Millennium Development Goals by 2015 will, to a large extent, be determined by the pace and outcomes of the transformation of the health sector.

HOSPITALS IN PUBLIC HEALTH SECTOR BY REGIONAL HEALTH AUTHORITIES

The South East Regional Health Authority (SERHA) comprises the parishes of Kingston, St Andrew, St Thomas and St Catherine. The St Joseph's Hospital is a new acquisition of the Government and is not as yet under the management of SERHA although it falls within its geographical boundaries.

INSTITUTION	PARISH
Kingston Public Hospital	Kingston
Victoria Jubilee Hospital	Kingston
Spanish Town Hospital	St Catherine
Princess Margaret Hospital	St Thomas
Linstead Hospital	St Catherine
Bellvue Hospital	Kingston
National Chest Hospital	St Andrew
Sir John Golding Rehabilitative	St Andrew
Hope Institute	St Andrew
St Josephs Hospital	St Andrew

In addition, the University Hospital of the West Indies is in Kingston and is partially funded by the Government of Jamaica.

The North East Regional Health Authority (NERHA) comprises the parishes of St Ann, St Mary and Portland.

INSTITUTION	PARISH
St Ann's Bay Hospital	St Ann
Annotto Bay Hospital	St Mary
Port Antonio Hospital	Portland

The Southern Regional Health Authority (SRHA) provides health care in the parishes of Clarendon, Manchester and St Elizabeth.

INSTITUTION	PARISH
Mandeville Regional Hospital	Manchester
May Pen Hospital	Clarendon
Black River Hospital	St. Elizabeth
Percy Junor Hospital	Clarendon
Lionel Town Hospital	Clarendon

The Western Regional Health Authority (WRHA) covers the parishes of St James, Hanover, Westmoreland and Trelawny.

INSTITUTION	PARISH
Cornwall Regional Hospital	St James
Savanna-la-Mar Hospital	Westmoreland
Falmouth Hospital	Trelawny
Noel Holmes	Hanover

PRIVATE HOSPITALS

INSTITUTION	PARISH
Medical Associates	St Andrew
Nuttall Hospital	St Andrew
Andrew's Memorial Hospital	St Andrew
Hargreaves Memorial Hospital	Manchester
Tony Thwaites Wing	Private wing at the University Hospital of the West Indies, St Andrew
Montego Bay Hospital	St James
MoBay Hope	St James
Faith Maternity	St James
Doctors' Hospital	St James
Royal Hospital	Westmoreland

PATIENT UTILISATION AT PUBLIC HEALTH FACILITIES 2002-2006

HEALTH CENTRE VISITS

2002	2003	2004	2005	2006
1,543,905	1,586,630	1,535,530	1,514,415	1,525,680

A&E VISITS

2002	2003	2004	2005	2006
695,239	746,844	775,727	694,354	715,707

NUMBER OF SURGERIES

2002	2003	2004	2005	2006
47,803	52,860	50,238	46,090	52,074

Source: Ministry of Health Annual Report 2006

Jamaica, the telecommunications hub of the region

DENISE WILLIAMS

When you think of Jamaica, images of its breathtaking physical beauty, cultural richness and sporting excellence – including the fastest man in the world, Usain Bolt – may come to mind. There is another side of Jamaica that is equally impressive. The island is also one of the best places to conduct business, and is currently ranked 24th in the world as the best destination for investments.[1] One of the main reasons for this ranking is a direct result of major developments in the telecommunications sector on the island over recent years.

Within the last five years, the telecommunications sector received a major boost from the exponential growth of the mobile sector with the advent of companies such as Digicel and Claro, as well as the rejuvenation of the island's first telecommunications company, Cable and Wireless, now operating as LIME. These major players have continued to expand and modernise their networks, introduce new services, adopt emerging technologies and employ a variety of marketing strategies that have catapulted mobile saturation to almost 90 per cent. As a result, Jamaica is now a world leader in terms of mobile connectivity.

The most fundamental change in the sector within recent times, however, is the arrival of true broadband to the island via the Columbus Communications group operating as Flow in Jamaica. Broadband makes available a wider range of frequencies to transmit information. It allows large amounts of multiple types of data traffic (voice, video and data) to be transmitted simultaneously over the same network. When we think in broadband terms we are thinking, speed, capacity and reliability.

Columbus Communications owns and operates an elaborate sub-sea fibre optic infrastructure called the Americas Region Caribbean Optical-ring System (ARCOS) that has critical implications for communications for the region. Jamaica is now directly connected to this ring that comprises more than 14,000 km of active undersea fibre optic cable.

This development heralds a new paradigm in the telecommunications landscape on the island. Jamaica is now the only country in the region with a direct undersea fibre-optic connection to both North America (via Boca Raton) and South America (via Colombia). These undersea systems have moved Jamaica's data connectivity on par with any developed country. Through the infrastructure, Flow now offers Jamaica, for the first time, various broadband-enabled services such as digital cable television, high-speed Internet and IP telephony services to both the retail and wholesale markets serving a mix of commercial and residential customers.

What is also notable is that the infrastructure affords the island unprecedented capacity, resiliency, redundancy and reliability for data communications. The implications for Jamaica are staggering as Flow's network provides the island with a high performance, low latency, direct route to the USA and South America, resulting in data and Internet connectivity that adds resiliency and increased capacity.

This means that unlike the major disruption after Hurricane Ivan a few years ago, where Jamaica was cut off from the rest of the world due to significant damage to the island's only undersea cable at the time, there are now three other robust undersea fibre optic connections leading out of the island on the Flow network, providing options that allow businesses to build resiliencies in their network infrastructure.

In effect, the island now has unprecedented broadband access, a critical requirement for effective business communications and business management. In practical terms, the island is now more attractive for investment and new business, particularly for companies focusing on data communications including call centres and financial institutions. What is more important is that these companies can now access bandwidth at much more cost-effective rates, with greater capacities and superior quality.

As a direct result, Jamaica is now ranked as one of the top locations in the world as an offshore destination, and is the only English-speaking Caribbean destination on the list. Jamaica is the Caribbean's leading contact centre destination for several reasons including a liberalised sector, the opportunity to save on costs, while maintaining standards and quality, and a well developed telecommunication infrastructure.

It is easy to see the effect of these developments. There has been a burst of investments. Fifteen new

Major developments in the telecommunications sector have made Jamaica and attractive investment destination.
Photo: Klaus Wolf

Business Process Outsourcing and Contact Centres have been established in Jamaica in recent times, representing significant foreign direct investment and employment creation. For North American companies, who are the major clients for outsourcing, Jamaica is an attractive English-speaking, near-shore location that offers comparable benefits to places like India. Companies such as Affiliated Computer Services, SITEL Caribbean Ltd, West Corporation and Alliance One Inc. have discovered that Jamaica is a fertile market to grow their business. Jamaica also boasts home-grown outsourcers such as e-Services Group International and Westcom Jamaica Ltd.

Jamaica's strength as an investment location is grounded in a number of factors. The fact that the island has almost limitless connectivity is a prime asset. In addition, its large English-speaking population, its competitively priced labour force, accessibility to a diverse labour pool, and its ideal location for trading with the rest of the Western Hemisphere. Its proximity to the United States, its historic and emerging relationship with the Latin American bloc and its proximity to the Panama Canal all make the island extremely attractive to investors.

Investment implemented from Jan-Dec 08[2]

COMPANY	CAPEX / Jobs
Premier Customer Care (BPO)	US $200,000 / 20
Carisbrook Business Solutions (BPO)	US $600,000 / 60
Enterprise Technology International (software)	US $500,000 / 12
Symptai/Symsure International (software)	US $2,000,000 / 18
West Indies Call Centre (BPO)	US $400,000 / 104
Alliance One/Teleperformance (BPO)	US $2,700,000 / 600
Jamaica Network Access Point (Telecoms)	US $1,200,000 / 12
Real Decoy (software)	US $50,000 / 9
MER Jamaica (Telecoms)	US $5,000,000 / 25
KRYS Financial (software)	US $1,000,000 / 8
CARIHOME Entertainment (software)	US $1,000,000 / 11
ACCENT Marketing (BPO)	US $1,000,000 / 60
Salary.com (BPO)	US $650,000 / 25
Professional Marketing Associates (BPO)	US $100,000 / 26
Innovative Solutions (BPO)	US $125,000 / 11

There were four software companies, eight contact centres and two telecoms companies implemented during the year.

Expansions undertaken from Jan-Dec 08[3]

e-Services: The company acquired a building in the Newport West region which will eventually employ 500 people.

Vista Print: The company is still proceeding with its US $30 million facility, which will eventually employ 1000 people.

Alliance One / Teleperformance: The company expanded to a 60,000 sq ft facility in the Montego Bay Freezone and there is even further expansion planned.

FLOW: The company is still undergoing significant build out of its infrastructure.

Claro: Since the takeover of MiPhone, the company is still spending robustly to build out its network.

The future for telecommunications in Jamaica looks bright. The island is now connected to the world via an infrastructure that has been described as a "network of the future". The island can now handle whatever innovations that will come to Jamaica from a capacity standpoint. Welcome to Jamaica, no problem man, indeed! ∎

1. Source: 2009 AT Kearney Global Services Location Index; 2. Source: PIOJ Industry Report, ICT sector, 2009 – unpublished Jamaica Trade and Invest, report; 3. Source: Jamaica Trade and Invest unpublished report, author Don Gittens, 2009.

Media and publishing in Jamaica

JANNETH MORNAN-GREEN

The history of media in Jamaica is long and colourful with indigenous Jamaican media offerings dating back to the early 1700s. The media's development and survival continue to be fuelled by the desire of the Jamaican people for freedom and self-determination.

Freedom of expression is protected under Jamaica's Constitution and is one of the fundamental human rights. Press freedom is also constitutionally guaranteed and generally respected.

The island's "robust free press" has its roots in the publishing of the "Weekly Jamaica Courant" in 1718, the second regular newspaper founded in the Americas. This publication, like numerous others that followed, had a commercial focus but also included the various Acts and other edicts of government, as well as significant local events including hurricanes and court trials. The establishment of a printing press in Jamaica laid the foundation for a vibrant, modern publishing industry.

Growth in the media industry was evident in the 1800s with the establishment of three newspapers in the then booming Western Jamaican town of Falmouth. These included the *Cornwall Courier*, the *Falmouth Post* and the *Falmouth Gazette*.

The launch of the *Gleaner* in 1834 by the Cordova brothers, however, was to be an important milestone in the development of Jamaican media and the country's history. The then "advertising sheet" whose appearance coincided with the abolition of slavery, has evolved into the region's oldest operating newspaper. It also produces a number of other publications including the *Children's Own* (1950), *The Star*, an evening ▷

One of the many newspaper vendors in Kingston. Photo: Tony Matthews

tabloid (1951) as well as the overseas editions. These have developed into major vehicles for chronicling events and activities that have shaped Jamaica's history from colonialism to the country's independence from Britain in 1962 and continuing self-government through Parliamentary democracy.

Further development in media in Jamaica came not only with the establishment of other newspapers, magazines and periodicals over the years, but significantly with the introduction of radio broadcasting through the effort of 'ham' operator John Grinan in 1939, the year that marked the start of the Second World War. Grinan's radio, which used the call letters 5P5PZ, was later handed over to the then government to assist the war effort.

In the space of a year, it was renamed ZQI and operated until 1949 when a licence was granted to the Jamaica Broadcasting Company, a subsidiary of the British-owned Re-diffusion group. The station later evolved into Radio Jamaica and Re-diffusion using the call letters RJR, which it continues to retain.

In 1953, Radio Jamaica became the first radio station in the British Commonwealth to broadcast regularly-scheduled programmes on the FM band. RJR has continued to expand with the introduction of other subsidiaries including FAME-FM and in 1997 Radio Jamaica Limited acquired the former government-owned Jamaica Broadcasting Corporation's (JBC) Radio II as well as JBC TV. Formerly the country's only television station, JBC TV was introduced by the government in the 1950s. As a member of the modern RJR Group, the station has been renamed Television Jamaica (TVJ).

The government has since launched the Public Broadcasting Corporation of Jamaica (PBCJ), which focuses on public education, information and entertainment on radio and television via cable transmission. The government-owned Jamaica Information Service (JIS) also provides information electronically and in print.

Today, Jamaica boasts multiple media houses and media products. Numbered among these are newspapers, including the *Daily* and *Sunday Gleaner*, *The Star*, *The Daily* and *Sunday Observer*, the *Sunday Herald*; community newspapers such as the bi-weekly *Western Mirror*, produced in the tourism capital of Montego Bay and the *North Coast Times* based in the resort town of Ocho Rios. ▷

Jamaica boasts multiple media houses and media products.
Photo: Tony Matthews

Journals and specialty magazines originating on the island include the *Jamaica Journal, Skywritings,* the *Jamaican, Jamaica Eats, Health, Home and Garden,* among others. Overseas newspapers such as the *New York Times* and the *Miami Herald* as well as news magazines, namely *Time, The Economist* and *Newsweek* are also available in pharmacies, bookshops and some hotels.

The island's population of some 2.6 million is served by over twenty radio stations offering both national and local programming ranging from variety to 'talk', all reggae to all gospel; three television stations (TVJ, LOVE 101 and CVM) as well as a host of cable stations that provide both international and local programmes. Approximately 40 per cent of the population, or 1,000,000 residents, have access to the Internet. Television sets are to be found in over 70 per cent of Jamaican households (World Bank, 2006) and well over a million radio receivers.

With the emergence of modern information-communication technologies, including the Internet to which residents have unrestricted access, the media landscape in Jamaica reflects a healthy mix of traditional as well as "new" media. These offerings are not only available to those who reside on the island but can be accessed via the Internet by millions of others across the world.

The introduction by the University of the West Indies (Mona, Jamaica) in 1974 of the Caribbean Institute of Mass Communication (CARIMAC), the region's first official media training institute, later renamed the Caribbean Institute of Media and Communication, has made it possible for numerous media and affiliated practitioners to be trained in areas ranging from Text and Graphic Production (Print), Broadcasting Skills (Radio and TV), to Social Marketing and Public Relations. They serve the media and related needs of Jamaica and the Caribbean region.

The island continues to nurture a free, vocal and active media and to encourage free expression by its citizens as evidenced in the numerous daily radio talk shows, letters to the editor and via the modern avenues of social media. Recently, 'Reporters Without Borders' ranked Jamaica at number 24 of 167 countries for press freedom.

To further "modernise the laws ..." governing libel and slander, the present government has established the "Libel and Slander Committee" to recommend, among others, "changes necessary to promote good governance ...," as well as "support the principles of freedom of the press" and "prevent the laws relating to libel, slander and defamation being used to suppress information to which the public is reasonably entitled."

PUBLISHING

The move to establish Jamaica's and the Caribbean region's first printing press in the early 1700s signalled the turning of a new page in the publishing business on the island. The advent of the Gleaner Company in 1834 also marked a significant milestone in the history of publishing in Jamaica.

While in its early stages the industry may have focused, among other things, on "spreading mercantile notices," books and pamphlets were also produced. *The Gleaner*'s subsequent founding and financing of Pioneer Press, the region's first commercially successful publishing company, provided an opportunity for the publication of indigenous Jamaican material until it closed in 1958.

Today, Jamaica continues to boast some of the largest publishing companies in the Caribbean.

These produce a variety of material ranging from the general to educational, children's publications to literary titles.

The National Library of Jamaica, the designated depository for all materials published on the island, lists among the major national publishing houses: Arawak Publications, Ian Randle Publishers (IRP), Carlong Publishers, the Gleaner Company, Jamaica Publishing House, LMH Publishing Limited, The Mill Press, Pelican Publishers, Sangster's Book Store, Sunzone Books, Twin Guinep Publishers, the University of the West Indies Press, Creative Links/Trailblazers Ink and Mid-Island Educators. Publishing is also done by a number of individuals and organisations including the government-owned Jamaica Information Service (JIS) and the Ministry of Education.

Of these, the eighteen-year-old IRP is the largest book publishing house in the Caribbean region producing mainly scholarly and academic books in general areas of Caribbean history, sociology, politics, anthropology, economics and development, law, arts and culture. Carlong Publishers remains the leading primary and secondary school textbook publishers while The Press, University of the West Indies (UWI), Mona, mainly produces academic works. The focus of LMH Publishing is trade and titles of general interest.

While there has been sustained interest in publishing and growth in the number and capacity of the publishing houses on the island, there is still

Television Jamaica is one of three TV stations serving the island. Photo: Tony Matthews

much scope for investment in the industry. As increased value is placed on intellectual property, it is expected that this will continue to drive the industry's development. Advances in information-communication technologies along with the resulting new media is also revolutionising and improving the trade by enhancing printing, publishing, distribution and marketing.

With tremendous improvement also in the quality of the printing facilities offered on the island, publishers may choose to print publications locally using any of several printing houses.

The Book Industry Association of Jamaica (BIAJ), founded in 1989, facilitates the integrated and balanced development of the industry. It comprises all related sectors and promotes "joint development initiatives, improved standards of service" while lobbying Government on critical issues. The organisation includes publishers, printers, authors, distributors and booksellers like Novelty Trading. The BIAJ is represented on all book-related advisory bodies, specifically: The National Council of Libraries, Archives and Information System (NACOLAIS), the National Book Development Council (NBDC), the Textbook Advisory Committee to the Ministry of Education, Youth and Culture and the National Copyright Task Force. ■

El pueblo que surgió de muchos pueblos

REX NETTLEFORD

Hace mucho que se viene describiendo a Jamaica como un microcosmos del planeta. En un pasado no muy lejano, se esforzaba por recordar al mundo que era mucho más que sol, arena y mar. "Es mucho más que una playa: es un país", rezaban los anuncios dirigidos a visitantes potenciales. Y sigue siendo un país, un país con una historia rica en la que no han faltado las rupturas y el sufrimiento, pero donde destacan la voluntad y una capacidad probada de sobrevivir e ir más allá.

Sin duda dicha historia es consecuencia de un colorido torrente de llegadas: caucasianos de Europa, negros del África subsahariana (mayormente de África Occidental), asiáticos de la meseta del Decán en la India y mongólicos del Valle cantonés de China. Algo más tarde llegó gente del Mediterráneo del Este. Todos fueron viniendo durante cuatro siglos para desempeñar diversas funciones que, no se puede negar, albergaron los dilemas de la diferencia. Hubo desde administradores de la corona, aventureros y propietarios de plantaciones, hasta mano de obra explotada (propiedad durante dos siglos de quienes los importaron) y trabajadores en régimen de servidumbre una vez que la abolición de la esclavitud dio lugar una seria escasez de mano de obra. Tras sus pasos llegaron los industriosos emigrantes del Mediterráneo del Este, quienes sin duda habían oído que Jamaica, que ya tenía una identidad propia para muchos fuera de la isla, podía ofrecerles una vida mejor y más tolerable que la que llevaban en sus países.

Prodigiosamente, esta diversidad de almas dotadas de sus dispares culturas (con sus idiomas, artes, cocinas y filosofías) supuso un reto para las multitudes políglotas de pueblos transplantados, quienes se fueron labrando modelos adecuados de convivencia social. Así fueron mezclándose, compartiendo, explorándose unos a otros, "cruzándose" y creando un sentido y una sensibilidad jamaicana de pura cepa que actualmente es la herencia común de todos, ya sean hombres o mujeres, de origen caucasiano o de antepasados africanos, chinos, libaneses o de las Indias Orientales, o bien de alguna de las varias combinaciones étnicas que aportan textura y dinamismo mestizo a la población jamaicana.

Todo esto se puede equiparar, en muchas maneras, con el esplendor tan diverso y calidoscópico del paisaje natural. No sólo con respecto a la flora, sino también a la variedad de estructuras del suelo, las cadenas montañosas, los altozanos ondulantes, las colinas con sus cimas, los valles, arroyos, manantiales, ríos y el Mar Caribe que, ahora embravecido, ahora tranquilo y calmo, los rodea. Aunque la belleza no es garantía absoluta de una existencia sin problemas. Los desastres naturales han sido frecuentes y los desórdenes sociales, como ocurre en cualquier otro lugar del mundo, han amenazado con contradecir la tan repetida invocación "*Jamaica, no problem*".

Los temperamentos son asimismo igual de variados. Las actitudes anglosajonas de estoicismo rivalizan con caracteres, supuestamente africanos, que son efervescentes y vivaces a la par que templados. Junto a estos, la inescrutable calma asiática de India y China coexiste con gusto intertextual para producir un conglomerado de almas de múltiples capas, polifacético, contrario y contradictorio. A veces, el explosivo clima de las elecciones ha puesto en vilo a la duradera y prometedora democracia parlamentaria de Jamaica. Esta aparente impredecibilidad no deja de ser fascinante.

Se dice que todas las grandes civilizaciones son resultado del mestizaje. La Jamaica contemporánea representa el mestizaje de Europa, África, Asia y el Mediterráneo del Este, en suelo extranjero, con los pobladores nativos americanos originarios, los tainos. Todos son responsables de la diversidad cultural, la riqueza y la energía de Jamaica. Sus diversos caracteres se manifiestan claramente en la música, la danza, el arte visual y culinario y el sentido del estilo de las personas comunes, quienes se ofrecen a sí mismos y ofrecen al mundo una colorida *troupe* formada no sólo por artistas y deportistas (en pista y campo, en críquet y fútbol), sino también por líderes políticos al estilo de Westminster, además de académicos bien formados y profesionales muy preparados. Todos ellos son, individual y colectivamente, descendientes de sus muchos y diferentes ancestros.

Aquí se evidencian Europa y su plenitud de rasgos culturales, que van desde la capacidad de gobierno anglosajona pasando por la vitalidad celta (de galeses y escoceses), a las reflexiones ancestrales de los judíos sefardíes; el África superviviente de la Travesía Transatlántica, que aporta su arte musical y teatral, su animismo religioso, su aversión innata a la opresión racial y su sentido de la comunidad; el encuentro consolidado de India con sus costumbres hindúes y musulmanas (culinarias, festivas y filosóficas); China y su aportación de disciplina y esfuerzo concentrados, equiparada por una similar contribución levantina que se puede apreciar entre los "sirios".

Tales son los principios reguladores subyacentes de los cambios inevitables que acompañan al mundo actual "globalizado", así como al nacimiento de la revolución tecnológica de las comunicaciones electrónicas. Esta última ha sido exportada por los Estados Unidos a través de sus noticieros y programas con participación popular y de entretenimiento, que se han reconfigurado, reinterpretado y adaptado debidamente a los gustos propios de la mayoría de la población jamaicana.

Los encuentros a través de la implicación mutua, la conformidad y la resistencia, la colaboración y la confrontación, el ingenio irreverente y el solemne enfado han dado lugar a elementos distintivos jamaicanos de importancia social y cultural. Dichos elementos se manifiestan en la lengua que la mayoría de los jamaicanos hablan habitualmente junto con el inglés estándar, en la religión (completa con sus santos y pecadores, lo sagrado y lo profano, el bien y el mal, Dios y el Demonio), en los patrones de parentesco que celebran las líneas de descendencia (ya sea con o sin confeti), en las manifestaciones artísticas (tradicionales, contemporáneas y clásicas) y en un sentido y una sensibilidad de delicado equilibrio.

Así que "el habla jamaicana", influenciada en gran parte por el léxico inglés estándar y la gramática y estructura africanas (acano), está considerada como una de las principales lenguas criollas del hemisferio occidental. El evangelismo sionista, la *pukkuminia* (pocomania) y el culto Convince son variantes de expresiones religiosas "sincréticas" derivadas de combinar la liturgia cristiana y el ritual africano conservado, como la *kumina* y el rito *kikongo*. Más recientemente aparece el movimiento rastafari, que recurre de forma innovadora al Antiguo Testamento y a la teología judaica sobre «Dispersión, Exilio y Regreso» en el camino a la redención y en la búsqueda de la justicia social, la libertad y la dignidad humana, algo que la ortodoxia cristina, heredada de los colonizadores europeos, nunca llegó a cumplir. El parentesco incluye el cuidado mutuo entre primos bien lejanos o las adopciones no consanguíneas

sin necesidad de una autorización legal formal. De esta forma se garantiza el ideal de cohesión familiar, la hermandad de las personas y la práctica del cuidado y la compasión, especialmente entre las mujeres jamaicanas (las portadoras de la cultura), independientemente de su clase, raza o credo.

Las artes se inspiran en fuentes ancestrales de África, Europa y Asia para crear música, danza teatro, drama y teatro coral de calidad mundial, y no simples manifestaciones exóticas, como algunos equivocadamente las consideran. La música popular jamaicana, desde el *mento* al *ska*, del *rocksteady* al *reggae* y el *dancehall*, ha generado artistas como Bob Marley, Jimmy Cliff, Peter Tosh y Toots Hibbert, con Beenie Man y Buju Banton, entre otros, en tiempos más recientes. Todos se pueden enorgullecer de un alcance global amplio y todos se han beneficiado de la confluencia de las muchas tradiciones y culturas que los generaron y aportaron exclusividad a Jamaica.

La llegada de los diversos pueblos ha nutrido las creaciones artísticas de la sociedad de otra forma también. Este fenómeno trajo al Caribe Sur el carnaval anterior a la Cuaresma, actualmente un acontecimiento posterior a la Cuaresma en el calendario jamaicano. Pero aquí, y ya desde principios del siglo XIX, se viene celebrando además el *jonkonnu* o mascarada, donde las fiestas europeas interactúan con la mascarada africana durante la Navidad para producir un festival distintivamente jamaicano. Variantes del mismo siguen encontrando expresión en el baile y el teatro musical, y en los programas culturales de Jamaica tras la Independencia.

Por otro lado, los indios (orientales) han contribuido de forma significativa con el arte del festival de Hosay. Se trata de una celebración mahometana en la que participan gustosamente tanto los jamaicanos hindúes como los cristianos, mientras los jamaicanos africanos tocan los tambores y los indios bailan.

Tal es el resultado del mestizaje a lo largo del tiempo en el espacio limitado que comparten los diversos pueblos llegados. Todo el mundo es, al fin y al cabo, parte del resto, independientemente de la raza, el color, la clase, el credo o la inclinación política. Sin embargo, esto no excluye la perseverancia de diferencias entre los jamaicanos. Aún más grande que dicha diversidad es la capacidad demostrada de tratar de forma creativa y positiva con los dilemas que dichas diferencias engendran, lo cual hace que sea verdad, de forma indiscutible e incontrovertible, el dicho de que todos los jamaicanos tienen una parte africana, una parte europea, una parte asiática y una parte nativa americana, sin dejar de ser al mismo tiempo totalmente jamaicanos.

De la multitude, un seul peuple

REX NETTLEFORD

La Jamaïque est depuis longtemps décrite comme le microcosme du globe. Et ceci malgré ses efforts, il n'y a encore pas si longtemps, de rappeler au reste du monde que l'île n'est pas que sable au soleil. « C'est bien plus qu'une plage – c'est un pays », clamaient il y a quelques années les campagnes de promotion destinées aux touristes potentiels. La Jamaïque demeure en effet une nation au riche passé, marqué il est vrai par la séparation et la souffrance, mais aussi et surtout par une volonté et une capacité de survie et d'épanouissement.

Son histoire a bien entendu été forgée par le flot d'immigrants « arc-en-ciel » venus d'Europe caucasienne, du continent sub-saharien (notamment d'Afrique noire occidentale), du plateau indien du Deccan et de Chine cantonaise – ainsi que, plus récemment, du bassin méditerrannéen oriental. Durant quatre siècles, l'île vit s'établir les uns et les autres dans des rôles qui, il faut le reconnaître, devaient entretenir les dilemmes de la différence. Ses pionniers furent des administrateurs royaux, des aventuriers et des planteurs, mais aussi une main-d'œuvre exploitée (qui fut pendant deux siècles la propriété de ceux qui l'avaient importée) et des engagés venus pallier l'intense manque de main-d'œuvre qui suivit l'abolition de l'esclavage. S'y joindront plus tard des entrepreneurs émigrés de Méditerranée orientale pour qui la Jamaïque, déjà une marque parmi tant d'autres à l'échelle internationale, offrait la promesse d'une existence meilleure et plus tolérable que celle qu'ils connaissaient.

La diversité humaine et la différence culturelle (s'exprimant entre autres par les langues et les arts, les coutumes alimentaires et la philosophie) eurent pour remarquable effet d'amener cette masse polyglotte de populations transplantées à établir des modèles de vie sociale appropriés. Ceux-ci ont promu l'échange, le partage, la découverte de l'autre et la « cross-fertilisation », créant une sensibilité jamaïcaine spécifique qui est aujourd'hui l'héritage commun de chacun et chacune, qu'il ou elle soit d'origine caucasienne, de souche africaine, indienne, chinoise ou libanaise, ou issu de l'un des divers mélanges ethniques qui, ensemble, font la texture et le dynamisme du peuple jamaïcain.

De bien des manières, cette diversité fait écho à la splendeur kaléïdoscopique du paysage naturel, à laquelle contribue non seulement la flore, mais aussi la variété des structures du terrain, ses chaînes de montagnes, ses collines aux formes ondulées, aux crêtes rugueuses, ses vallées, ses ruisseaux, ses sources, ses rivières et, tout autour, la Mer des Caraïbes – tantôt furieuse, tantôt calme. La beauté n'est cependant pas la garantie d'une existence sans difficultés. L'île n'est pas épargnée par les catastrophes naturelles et les troubles sociaux, qui existent ici comme partout ailleurs, menacent de contredire la célèbre invocation, « *Jamaica, No Problem* ».

Les tempéraments sont, eux aussi, variés. A la réserve anglo-saxonne s'oppose l'exhubérance, l'ardeur et le détachement du soi-disant caractère africain. S'y ajoute le calme asiatique (indien et chinois), impénétrable, qui coexiste avec une relish intertextuelle pour former un agrégat démographique complexe, aux facettes multiples, à la fois contraire et contradictoire. L'inflammabilité électorale secoue parfois la démocratie parlementaire jamaïcaine, qui demeure continuellement prometteuse. Cette apparente imprévisibilité s'avère néanmoins fascinante.

On dit que toute grande civilisation est le fruit d'un croisement. Et la Jamaïque d'aujourd'hui incarne le croisement de l'Europe, de l'Afrique, de l'Asie et de la Méditerranée orientale, une cross-fertilisation à laquelle participent également les tous premiers immigrants amérindiens (les Taïnos). C'est de ces peuples que le pays tire sa diversité, sa richesse et son énergie culturelle. Ces traits s'expriment à travers la musique, la danse, les arts plastiques et l'art culinaire, ainsi que par un sens du style commun à tous les Jamaïcains, produisant une foule arc-en-ciel d'artistes et de sportifs de haut niveau (athlètes, joueurs de cricket et footballeurs), mais aussi de personnalités politiques de style britannique, de grands universitaires et d'ingénieurs spécialisés, descendant tous – collectivement et individuellement – de ces nombreux ancêtres.

Si l'Europe se manifeste à travers une plénitude de traits culturels, de la gouvernance anglo-saxonne à la vitalité celtique (galloise et écossaise) et aux rêveries ancestrales des

Séfarades, l'Afrique survivante du *Middle Passage* apporte quant à elle sa musique et ses arts vivants, son animisme religieux, son dégoût foncier de l'oppression raciale et son sens de la communauté ; l'Inde encourage la rencontre grâce à ses traditions hindoues et musulmanes (culinaires, festives et philosophiques), tandis que la Chine insuffle sa concentration sur la discipline et le travail, à laquelle fait écho une contribution levantine non dissemblable que l'on dénote chez les « Syriens ».

Ainsi influencés sont les principes régulatoires qui sous-tendent les inévitables changements imposés par la mondialisation et l'assaut de la révolution technologique des communications électroniques exportée par l'Amérique du Nord par le biais de ses bulletins d'informations, de ses talk-shows et de ses émissions de divertissement, qui sont reconfigurés, réinterprétés et dûment adaptés à ses propres goûts par la masse de la population jamaïcaine.

Les rencontres formées par l'engagement mutuel, la soumission et la résistance, la collaboration et la confrontation, l'humour irrévérencieux et la solennité crispée, ont produit des traits distinctifs de portée sociale et culturelle qui s'expriment aujourd'hui à la fois dans la langue que parlent la plupart du temps la majorité des Jamaïcains parallèlement à l'anglais standard, dans la religion (où s'opposent les saints et les pécheurs, le sacré et le profane, le bon et le mal, Dieu et le diable), dans les modèles de parenté, où l'on célèbre la progéniture avec ou sans confettis, dans les manifestations artistiques (traditionnelles, contemporaines et classiques), ainsi qu'à travers une sensibilité délicatement équilibrée.

Fortement influencé par le lexique de l'anglais standard et par la grammaire et la structure de l'africain (akan), le *Jamaica Talk* est désormais considéré comme l'une des langues créoles majeures de l'hémisphère occidental. Le revivalisme zioniste, le Pukkumina (ou Pocomania) et le culte Convince sont des variantes des expressions religieuses « syncrétisées » issues du mélange de la liturgie chrétienne et du rituel africain tel qu'il est préservé dans le Kumina et le rite kikongo. Plus récemment est apparu le mouvement Rastafari, qui s'inspire de manière originale de l'Ancien Testament et de la trajectoire théologique judaïque de la diaspora, de l'exil et du retour sur la voie de la rédemption, dans une quête de justice sociale, de liberté et de dignité humaine qui avait fait défaut à l'orthodoxie chrétienne, legs d'une Europe colonisatrice. Un système de parenté fondé sur le soutien mutuel entre cousins à de nombreux degrés ou l'adoption non

consanguine sans cadre de sanction juridique formel, assure l'idéal de cohésion familiale, la fraternité entre les hommes, et l'exercice de la compassion, en particulier parmi les femmes jamaïcaines, gardiennes de la culture, toutes classes, races et croyances confondues.

La création artistique s'inspire des sources ancestrales africaines, européennes et asiatiques pour entretenir une production musicale et théâtrale (danse, art dramatique et chant choral) de stature internationale plutôt qu'à simple caractère exotique, comme certains le croient parfois à tort. La musique populaire jamaïcaine, du mento au ska, du rocksteady au reggae et au dancehall, a produit des artistes tels que Bob Marley, Jimmy Cliff, Peter Tosh ou Toots Hibbert, auxquels viennent aujourd'hui s'ajouter, parmi les musiciens de crus plus récents, Beenie Man et Buju Banton. Tous peuvent s'enorgueillir d'une vaste portée internationale, et tous ont bénéficié de la confluence des traditions et des cultures qui les ont engendrés et qui ont donné à la Jamaïque sa personnalité unique.

La diversité culturelle a créé autre chose qui, là encore, alimente l'activité artistique de la société. Si le phénomène a donné aux Antilles du Sud leur carnaval d'avant-carême (aujourd'hui une fête pascale de fin de carême dans le calendrier jamaïcain), il a donné à la Jamaïque, dès le début du XIXe siècle, le Jonkonnu (ou mascarade), où s'entremêlent, à l'époque de Noël, réjouissances européennes et mascarade africaine pour produire un festival tout à fait particulier à la Jamaïque. Celui-ci donne lieu à des variations qui continuent de trouver leur expression dans la danse et le théâtre musical et dans les programmes culturels de la Jamaïque post-indépendance.

Les Indiens ont pour leur part apporté une importante contribution à l'art du festival Hosay – une célébration mahometienne fêtée par les Jamaïcains hindous et chrétiens, qui voit les Jamaïcains-Africains accompagner aux percussions les danses des Indiens.

Tel est le fruit de la cross-fertilisation dans cet espace limité que se sont partagés les différents arrivants au cours des âges. Chacun, après tout, fait partie des autres, indépendamment des questions de race, de couleur, de religion ou de persuasion politique. Ceci ne doit cependant pas dissimuler le fait que persistent des différences parmi les Jamaïcains. Mais au-delà de ces différences s'impose la capacité d'aborder de manière créative et positive les dilemmes qu'elles engendrent, apportant sa véracité et son irréfutabilité à l'adage que tous les Jamaïcains sont un peu africains, un peu européens, un peu asiatiques, un peu amérindiens, et entièrement jamaïcains.

Aus vielen Völkern ein Volk

REX NETTLEFORD

Jamaika wird seit Langem als ein Mikrokosmos auf Erden bezeichnet. Trotzdem musste es in der jüngsten Vergangenheit der Welt oft ins Gedächtnis rufen, wie viel mehr es zu bieten hat als nur Sonne, Sand und Meer. „Es ist mehr als nur ein Strand – es ist ein Land", riefen die Werbeplakate potenziellen Besuchern entgegen. Tatsächlich ist Jamaika ein Land mit einer langen und reichen Geschichte, zwar voller Leiden und Schmerz, aber auch mit dem Willen und der ausgewiesenen Fähigkeit zum Überleben.

Dies ist natürlich eine direkte Folge seiner ‚Regenbogen-Ankömmlinge' aus Europa, den afrikanischen Ländern südlich der Sahara (hauptsächlich Westafrika), von Indiens Dekkan-Plateau oder Chinas Kanton. Später kamen dann noch Einwanderer aus dem östlichen Mittelmeerraum hinzu. Sie alle kamen im Verlauf von vier Jahrhunderten, um verschiedene Funktionen zu erfüllen, die allerdings bekanntermaßen die unterschiedlichsten Probleme auslösten. Unter den Ankömmlingen befanden sich sowohl königliche Verwalter, Abenteurer und Plantagenbesitzer als auch ausgebeutete Arbeiter (die zwei Jahrhunderte lang im Besitz derer waren, die sie importiert hatten) und verpflichtete Vertragsarbeiter, als die Abschaffung der Sklaverei in einem starken Mangel an Arbeitskräften resultierte. Danach folgten unternehmerische Einwanderer aus dem östlichen Mittelmeerraum, denen sicher zu Ohren gekommen war, dass Jamaika, für viele auf der Welt schon eine Marke für sich, ein besseres und angenehmeres Leben zu bieten hatte, als sie von zu Hause kannten.

Bemerkenswerterweise stellte die Seelenvielfalt der polyglotten Horden verpflanzter Völker und deren verschiedenste Kulturen (ob in Sprache oder Kunst, Ernährung oder Philosophie) eine Herausforderung dar und führte zu einer bedarfsgerechten Gestaltung des Zusammenlebens.

Dies bedeutete, dass sie sich vermischten, austauschten, näher kennenlernten, ‚einander befruchteten' und ein gebürtiges und einheimisches jamaikanisches Bewusstsein schufen, welches heute das gemeinsame Erbe aller Jamaikaner ist, egal ob sie europäischer, afrikanischer, ostindischer, chinesischer, libanesischer oder einer anderen ethnischen Abstammung sind, welche die Struktur und Dynamik der jamaikanischen Bevölkerung ausmachen.

In vielerlei Hinsicht passt all dies zu der äußerst mannigfaltigen und kaleidoskopischen Pracht der natürlichen Landschaft, nicht nur mit Blick auf die Flora, sondern auch auf die Vielseitigkeit der Bodenstruktur, Gebirgszüge, wogenden Hügel, hahnenkammähnlichen Berge, Täler, Ströme, Quellen, Flüsse und dem umgebenden – manchmal wilden, manchmal ruhigen – Karibischen Meer. Schönheit allein jedoch ist keine absolute Garantie für eine problemlose Existenz. Naturkatastrophen kommen häufig genug vor und soziale Unruhen, wie sie überall auf der Welt auftreten können, drohen zeitweise, den oft wiederholten Spruch „Jamaica, No Problem" zu negieren.

Die Temperamente sind ebenso vielfältig. Die steife Oberlippe der Angelsachsen wetteifert mit der überschäumenden, ausgelassenen und zum Teil ebenso kühlen Attitüde, die den Afrikanern nachgesagt wird, genau wie mit den unergründlichen Asiaten (Inder und Chinesen), die ruhig beieinander leben. Alle zusammen ergeben eine vielschichtige, vielseitige, gegensätzliche und widersprüchliche Ansammlung von Menschen. In Wahlzeiten führt dies mitunter zu angespannten Situationen für Jamaikas andauernd vielversprechende parlamentarische und demokratische Regierungsführung. Doch das macht die scheinbare Unberechenbarkeit nicht weniger faszinierend.

Man sagt, alle großen Zivilisationen seien das Ergebnis gegenseitiger Befruchtung. Und das heutige Jamaika repräsentiert diese Vermischung der Einflüsse aus Europa, Afrika, Asien, dem östlichen Mittelmeerraum und der ursprünglichen Siedler, den amerikanischen Ureinwohnern (Tainos). Sie alle tragen zu Jamaikas Vielfalt, Fülle und Energie bei. Diese Eigenschaften zeigen sich in Musik, Tanz, visueller und kulinarischer Kunst sowie dem persönlichen Stil der einfachen Menschen, die sich und der Welt ein Regenbogenteam offerieren aus Künstlern oder Sportlern (in Leichtathletik, Cricket und Fußball), aber auch politischen Führern im Stil von Westminster, gut ausgebildeten Akademikern und hoch qualifizierten Fachkräften – alle individuell und gemeinsam Nachkommen ihrer vielen verschiedenen Vorfahren.

Europas kulturelle Einwirkungen sind

offenkundig– von der angelsächsischen Regierungsführung über die Vitalität der Kelten (Waliser und Schotten) bis hin zu den Einflüssen der sephardischen Juden – und vermischen sich mit denen der anderen Kulturen: aus Afrikas Überleben der Mittelpassage stammen die musikalischen und darstellenden Künste, der religiöse Animismus, der angeborene Widerwille gegen Rassenunterdrückung und der Gemeinschaftssinn; Indien stärkt die Gesellschaft durch seine hinduistischen und muslimischen Bräuche (kulinarisch, festlich und philosophisch); China entsendet seinen Fokus auf Disziplin und harte Arbeit und einen ähnlichen Beitrag leisten die Levante und die „Syrer".

So die Regelwerke, die den unausweichlichen Veränderungen der heutigen globalisierten Welt zugrunde liegen, welche den Ansturm der elektronischen Kommunikationsrevolution nach sich zieht – über aus Nordamerika exportierte Nachrichtensendungen, Talk-Shows und Unterhaltungsprogramme, die dann von der Masse der Bevölkerung neu konfiguriert, neu interpretiert und entsprechend angepasst werden.

Das Zusammentreffen von wechselseitigem Engagement, von Fügsamkeit und Widerstand, Kollaboration und Konfrontation, respektlosem Witz und ernster Feierlichkeit haben charakteristische jamaikanische Elemente sozialer und kultureller Bedeutung hervorgebracht – in der Sprache, die die Jamaikaner neben dem Standardenglisch täglich sprechen, in der Religion (komplett mit Heiligen und Sündern, dem Geistlichen und dem Profanen, Gut und Böse, Gott und Teufel), in der Verwandtschaft, wo die Nachkommen mit oder ohne Konfetti gefeiert werden, in der Kunst (traditioneller, moderner oder klassischer) und in einem fein ausgewogenen Sinn für Gefühl und Verstand.

Das durch das Vokabular des Standardenglischen und die Grammatik und Struktur des Afrikanischen (Akan) beeinflusste ‚Jamaica Talk' hat sich zu einer der wichtigsten kreolischen Sprachen der Westlichen Hemisphäre entwickelt. Zion Revivalism, Pukkumina (Pocomania) und Convince Cult sind Varianten ‚synkretistischen' religiösen Ausdrucks, resultierend aus einer Mischung aus christlicher Liturgie und afrikanischen Ritualen, erhalten etwa in Kumina-Zeremonien, dem Kikongo-Ritus und in jüngster Zeit in der Rastafari-Bewegung; diese basiert auf dem Alten Testament und dem jüdischen theologischen Konzept von Zerstreuung, Exil und Rückkehr auf dem Weg zur Erlösung, auf ständiger Suche nach sozialer Gerechtigkeit, Freiheit und Menschenwürde, wie sie die vom kolonisierenden Europa eingeführte christliche Orthodoxie nicht liefern konnte. Verwandtschaftsbeziehungen sind eng; auch weit entfernte Cousins kümmern sich umeinander und nicht-blutsverwandte Adoptionen können ohne formelle gesetzliche Bestimmungen stattfinden, wodurch Familien zusammengehalten werden, die Menschen als Brüder zusammenleben und wodurch Mitgefühl und Barmherzigkeit besonders bei den jamaikanischen Frauen, den Kulturträgern egal welcher Klasse, Rasse oder Herkunft, großgeschrieben wird.

Künstler bedienen sich der Ahnen aus Afrika, Europa und Asien, um Musik, Theater, Tanztheater und chorisches Theater von Weltklasseniveau zu produzieren, und dies nicht nur als Exotikum. Die Populärmusik Jamaikas – von Mento über Ska und Rocksteady bis hin zu Reggae und Dancehall – hat Größen wie Bob Marley, Jimmy Cliff, Peter Tosh und Toots Hibbert sowie, in jüngerer Vergangenheit, Beenie Man und Buju Banton hervorgebracht. Sie alle erfreuen sich weltweiter Beliebtheit und profitieren von den Einflüssen der vielen Traditionen und Kulturen, aus denen sie hervorgegangen sind und die Jamaika einzigartig machen.

Und noch etwas hatten die verschiedenen Ankömmlinge im Gepäck, das die künstlerischen Ergüsse der Gesellschaft antreibt: Jonkonnu. Was den Bewohnern der südlichen Karibik der Karneval in der Vorfastenzeit war (jetzt ein feststehender Termin in Jamaikas Osterkalender), brachte außerdem ab dem frühen neunzenten Jahrhundert diese Weihnachtsfeierlichkeit – Jonkonnu (oder Maskerade) – hervor, bei der europäische Feiernde mit afrikanischen Kostümierten zu einem unverwechselbar jamaikanisches Fest zusammenkommen. Seine verschiedenen Variationen finden Ausdruck in Tanz- und Musiktheater sowie in den Kulturprogrammen des unabhängigen Jamaikas.

Mit dem Hosay-Fest haben die Einwanderer aus (Ost)Indien einen bedeutenden Beitrag geleistet – es handelt sich um ein mohammedanisches Fest, an dem sowohl hinduistische als auch christliche Jamaikaner mit Elan teilnehmen, die Afro-Jamaikaner dazu trommeln, während die Inder das Tanzbein schwingen.

Dies ist das Ergebnis der gegenseitigen Befruchtung der verschiedenen Ankömmlinge. Schließlich ist jeder ein Teil des anderen, ungeachtet der Rasse, Farbe, Klasse, Herkunft oder politischen Einstellung. Dabei sollen die bestehenden Unterschiede nicht geleugnet werden. Doch größer als diese Unterschiede ist die erwiesene Fähigkeit der Jamaikaner, daraus resultierende Probleme kreativ zu lösen. Und so wird wieder einmal unwiderlegbar bestätigt, dass alle Jamaikaner teils afrikanisch, teils europäisch, teils asiatisch und teils indianisch sind – dabei aber uneingeschränkt jamaikanisch.

Gente di tutto il mondo, un solo popolo

REX NETTLEFORD

La Giamaica viene definita da tempo il microcosmo del Pianeta Terra, anche senza l'aiuto degli slogan diffusi in un passato non molto lontano che ripetevano al mondo intero che non è solo sole, sabbia e mare, ma molto, molto di più. "È più di una semplice spiaggia: è un paese" sanciva la pubblicità rivolta ai potenziali turisti. Si tratta davvero di un paese con una storia molto ricca, che narra sì di divisioni e di sofferenze, ma soprattutto della volontà e della dimostrata capacità di sopravvivenza (e non solo) dei suoi cittadini.

Tutto ciò è, ovviamente, il risultato dell'imponente flusso di immigrati dai colori dell'arcobaleno, dai bianchi europei, ai neri dell'Africa subsahariana (per lo più dell'Africa occidentale), ai "marroni" provenienti dagli altipiani indiani del Deccan e ai mongoli cinesi della valle cantonese. Più tardi giunsero genti dal Mediterraneo orientale: arrivarono tutti nel corso di quattro secoli, per svolgere funzioni svariate, nelle quali si annidavano, in fieri, problematiche di differenza. Si trattava di amministratori reali, di avventurieri e proprietari di piantagioni, di manodopera da sfruttare (per più di due secoli di proprietà di chi l'importava), nonché di forza lavoro a contratto quando l'abolizione della schiavitù provocò un'improvvisa ed intensa carenza di manodopera. Questi furono poi seguiti da immigrati intraprendenti che giunsero dal Mediterraneo orientale e che avevano, senza dubbio, sentito dire che la Giamaica, che godeva già di una certa fama nel mondo intero, poteva offrire loro una vita migliore e più tollerabile di quella che conducevano nel proprio paese.

La straordinaria diversità delle genti, che avevano portato con sé una cultura propria, fatta di lingua e di arte, di cucina e di filosofia, ha indotto queste orde poliglotte di trapiantati a ideare delle nuove forme di vita sociale adatta alle loro molteplici esigenze. Essa ha consentito loro di mescolarsi, di mettere in comune, di esplorarsi a vicenda, di procedere a "fecondazioni incrociate" e di creare un insieme di ragione e sentimento tutto nato e cresciuto in terra giamaicana che ora compone il patrimonio culturale di tutti, a prescindere dall'origine dei propri antenati: che questi fossero bianchi o africani, delle indie orientali, cinesi o libanesi, oppure discendenti di una delle innumerevoli misture etniche che rappresentano tutte insieme la trama e il dinamismo incrociato della popolazione giamaicana.

Ciò rispecchia, in diversi modi, lo splendore eterogeneo e caleidoscopico del paesaggio naturale del paese, non soltanto per quanto riguarda la flora, ma anche la varietà delle strutture del terreno, le catene montuose, i dolci poggi ondulati, le colline a cresta di gallo, le vallate, i corsi d'acqua, le sorgenti, i fiumi e il Mar dei Caraibi, a volte furioso, a volte calmo e tranquillo. La bellezza non è una garanzia assoluta di un'esistenza senza problemi. Le calamità naturali si sono fatte spesso sentire, e i disordini sociali, come in qualsiasi altra parte del mondo, minacciano di rinnegare la ricorrente invocazione "Giamaica, No Problem".

Il temperamento dei suoi abitanti è altrettanto variegato. La tipica impassibilità anglosassone compete con altrettanto evidenti tendenze caratteriali più esuberanti e vivaci, ma a volte anche compassate, attribuite al sangue africano. A queste si affianca una calma asiatica imperscrutabile (indiana e cinese), che a sua volta convive con un gusto intertestuale di riprodurre un'aggregazione di anime multistrato, variamente sfaccettata, contraria e contraddittoria. La passione che si sprigiona in fase elettorale a volte mette a dura prova il governo democratico parlamentare giamaicano, considerato in perpetuo promettente. L'apparente imprevedibilità è comunque affascinante.

Si dice che tutte le grandi civiltà siano il frutto di una fecondazione incrociata. La Giamaica di oggi rappresenta la fecondazione incrociata di Europa, Africa, Asia e Mediterraneo orientale, e dei primi colonizzatori nativi americani (i Tainos): il risultato è una diversità culturale, una ricchezza e un'energia che fanno della Giamaica un posto unico al mondo. Tali caratteristiche emergono evidenti nella musica, nella danza, nelle arti visive e culinarie e nella naturale eleganza della gente comune, che offre al mondo e a se stessa un variegata gamma non soltanto di artisti e di sportivi (pensate all'atletica leggera, al cricket e al calcio), ma anche di leader politici in stile Westminster, di professori colti e di professionisti di alto livello, tutti, sia individualmente che collettivamente, discendenti di antenati molto diversi tra loro.

Se l'influsso europeo è evidente nella pienezza delle sue caratteristiche culturali che partono dall'arte di governo anglosassone, passano attraverso la vitalità celtica (gallese e scozzese) fino a giungere all'atavica riflessività degli ebrei sefarditi, l'Africa sopravvissuta alla tratta atlantica offre arti musicali e dello spettacolo, animismo religioso, ed un'innata avversione per l'oppressione razziale, nonché un forte senso di comunità. L'India, a sua volta, rafforza la fusione degli usi e costumi indù e islamici (culinari, filosofici e inerenti alle festività), mentre la Cina rivive nell'importanza attribuita alla disciplina e al lavoro, che viene a sua volta rafforzata da un non dissimile contributo levantino frequente tra i "siriani".

Tali sono i principi che costituiscono le fondamenta per gli ineluttabili cambiamenti che provengono da un mondo ormai globalizzato e dall'assalto della rivoluzione della tecnologia delle comunicazioni elettroniche esportata dall'America del Nord attraverso i suoi notiziari, i suoi talk-show e i suoi spettacoli, seppur riconfigurati, reinterpretati e debitamente adattati dalla massa della popolazione ai propri gusti.

I rapporti con i nuovi arrivati, caratterizzati da impegno reciproco, remissività e resistenza, collaborazione e scontro, irriverente arguzia e severa solennità, hanno dato vita ad elementi di rilievo sociale e culturale tipicamente giamaicani che risultano evidenti nella lingua parlata più di frequente dalla maggior parte dei giamaicani accanto all'inglese standard, nella religione (completa di santi e peccatori, del sacro e del profano, del bene e del male, di Dio e del diavolo), nei rapporti di parentela che portano a celebrare l'arrivo della progenie dentro e fuori il vincolo matrimoniale, e in manifestazioni artistiche (tradizionali, contemporanee e classiche): il tutto in un delicato equilibrio tra ragione e sentimento.

Pertanto, la "parlata giamaicana", profondamente influenzata dal lessico dell'inglese corrente e dalla grammatica e dalla struttura africana (Akan), è diventata una delle lingue creole principali dell'emisfero occidentale. Il revivalismo ebraico-sefardita, la pocomania e l'antico culto "Convince" sono varianti delle espressioni religiose sincretistiche risultanti dalla mescolanza della liturgia cristiana e dei rituali africani conservati nel cumina, il rito kikongo, seguito più di recente dal Rastafari, il quale si rifà, in modo del tutto innovativo, al Vecchio Testamento e alla traiettoria teologica ebraica dell'esilio, della diaspora e del ritorno sulla via della redenzione, in cerca di giustizia sociale, libertà e dignità umana, che l'ortodossia cristiana, ereditata da un'Europa colonizzatrice, non era riuscita ad offrire. I rapporti di parentela che implicano un'assistenza reciproca tra cugini di grado molto lontano, ovvero le adozioni tra non consanguinei senza il beneficio di una sanzione legale formale, rappresentano l'ideale della coesione familiare, la fratellanza universale e l'espressione di aiuto e compassione specialmente tra le donne giamaicane, depositarie della cultura di questo paese, a prescindere dalla classe e dalla razza di appartenenza o dal loro credo religioso.

L'arte, ispirata a fonti ancestrali africane, europee ed asiatiche, produce musica, danza, teatro e cori di livello molto prestigioso, e non semplicemente dai caratteri esotici, come alcuni potrebbero erroneamente intenderla. La musica popolare giamaicana, dal mento alla ska, dal rock steady al reggae e al dance hall, ha prodotto personaggi come Bob Marley, Jimmy Cliff, Peter Tosh e Toots Hibbert, fino ai più recenti Beenie Man e Buju Banton, per nominarne solo alcuni, i quali, tutti beneficiari e figli della confluenza delle più svariate tradizioni e culture, possono vantare fama mondiale e l'onore di aver reso la Giamaica un paese unico al mondo.

I vari immigrati sono responsabili di un'altra cosa che si è tramutata, ancora una volta, in una valanga artistica nella società giamaicana. Se il fenomeno ha regalato ai Caraibi meridionali il carnevale pre-quaresimale (oggigiorno un evento post-quaresima nel calendario giamaicano), esso ha donato alla Giamaica, fin dall'inizio del XIX secolo, il "jonkonnu" (ovvero mascherata), in cui gli europei in festa interagiscono con le maschere africane nel periodo natalizio per produrre un festival unicamente giamaicano. Questo, con le sue infinite variazioni, continua a trovare espressione nella danza e nel teatro musicale, nonché in programmi culturali della Giamaica post-indipendenza.

Nel frattempo, gli indiani (orientali) hanno apportato contributi significativi all'arte del festival di Hosay, la celebrazione musulmana abbracciata con allegria da giamaicani sia indù che cristiani, che vede i giamaicani africani che si occupano dei tamburi, e gli indiani della danza.

Quelli descritti sono i risultati della fecondazione incrociata tra diversi immigrati, verificatisi nel corso del tempo in uno spazio di ridotte dimensioni. In fondo, tutti sono parte di tutti gli altri, a prescindere dalla razza, dal colore, dalla classe sociale, dal credo religioso o dalle opinioni politiche. Ma ciò non esclude il persistere di notevoli differenze tra i giamaicani. Tuttavia, più che le differenze, è la comprovata capacità di gestire con creatività e positività i dilemmi creati da tali differenze che rende assolutamente vero ed incontrovertibile il detto che tutti i giamaicani sono in parte africani, in parte europei, in parte asiatici e in parte nativi americani, restando, allo stesso tempo, assolutamente giamaicani.

来自多元，一个民族

REX NETTLEFORD 著

很久以来，牙买加都被描述为"行星地球的缩影"。在不久以前，牙买加就告诉世界这里不仅仅有阳光、沙滩和大海。向潜在游客宣传牙买加的广告词这样说道："牙买加不仅仅是一个海滩，它是一个国家！"这个国家有着丰富的历史，众所周知的是其国家分离、受苦受难的历史，然而，它却向人们展示了其生存和超越的意志与能力。

当然，这是高加索欧洲、撒哈拉以南的非洲（主要是西非）不同肤色的移民，以及印度德干高原的布朗人和中国广东地区的黄种人纷纷涌入牙买加的结果。此后，还有东地中海地区的移民来到牙买加。他们在四个多世纪中都扮演着各种暗含着不同困难的角色，从王室的统治者、冒险家、种植园主到被剥削的劳动力（持续两个多世纪其财产都受到剥削）以及在奴隶制的废除导致劳动力短缺的时候签订了合约的劳动者。那些深信在世界上享有盛誉的牙买加生活要比家里好得多的东地中海的移民企业家随后也来到了牙买加。

显然，多样的民族赋予了他们多样的文化（包括语言与艺术、饮食与哲学），这对由移民组成的多语言部落来说，构建和谐的社会生活也是一种挑战。他们可以相互的融合、分享和探索，结合并培养出土生土长的牙买加人的意识形态和感情。如今，这样的意识

形态和感情是所有人共有的遗传性，无论他们是高加索人的血统，或是非洲、东印度、中国和黎巴嫩人的血统，还是多个民族的混合血统，不同肤色和不同民族的人们结合组成了牙买加的人口。

在许多方面都存在着相互的融合，多样的自然风光也是如此，这里不仅有丰富的动植物群，还有多样的土地结构、山脉、连绵起伏的小山、鸡冠状的丘陵、山谷、溪流、泉水、河流以及四周时而汹涌澎湃时而平缓幽静的加勒比海。在这样的美景中并不是绝对没有问题存在的。自然灾害时常发生，与地球上其他地方一样也会出现社会混乱的情况，这让人们常常祈祷的"牙买加，没问题"面临威胁。

他们甚至连性格也都不一样。态度坚定不移的盎格鲁-撒克逊人报以热情洋溢、高昂的斗志与人竞争，并与冷静的非洲人的性格大致相似。除此以外，高深莫测的亚洲人（印度人和中国人）和谐共存并相互影响的特性使其产生了多层次、多方面、相反的、相互对立的性格的集合。选举的激烈性有时会让牙买加前途光明的民主议会管理氛围变得很紧张。虽然如此，外表上的高深莫测仍让他们散发着一股迷人的魅力。

据说，所有伟大的文明社会都是多民族相互融合的结果。当代的牙买加是欧洲、非洲、亚洲、东地中海以及国外的原美国本土移民的融合。因此，牙买加蕴藏着丰富多彩且充满活力的文化特色。这些特色突出表现在音乐、舞蹈、精湛的烹饪技巧，以及普通人民的意识形态上，他们为这个世界和自己造就了各色人才，不仅有艺术家、运动员（径赛和田赛、板球和足球），还有威斯敏斯特式的政治领导、受过良好教育的大学生和训练有素的专业人士，在个体和整体上，他们都有着不同的祖先。

欧洲丰富的文化特色包括从盎格鲁撒克逊人的管理能力到凯尔特人（威尔士人和苏格兰人）的生存能力和西班牙系犹太人祖传的思维能力，这些特色是显而易见的；非洲在大西洋中央航线上产生了其音乐和表演艺术、宗教上的万

物有灵论、对种族压迫的天生厌恶感和社会意识形态；而印度的印度教和穆斯林习俗（烹饪、节庆和哲学方面的习俗）之间的冲突加剧；中国则将其重心放在思想修养和辛勤劳作上，这种做法与叙利亚人表现出的地中海东部沿岸民族做出的努力相同。

这就是以调节原理为基础的不可避免的变化，这些变化与如今"全球化"社会和由北美洲通过其新闻广播、谈话节目和娱乐节目输出的电子通信技术改革的冲击一起到来，虽然这些节目是根据人们的爱好重新安排、重新说明和适时地改编过的。

相互约定、依从与抵抗、合作与对抗、轻佻与庄重之间的冲突产生了具有社会和文化意义的独特的牙买加元素，它们突出地表现在语言（大部分牙买加人通常都使用标准英语）、宗教（包括圣人和罪人、神圣和亵渎、善良与邪恶、神灵和魔鬼）、纯良或仁爱的亲属关系、多元化的艺术表现形式（传统的、当代的和经典的）以及和谐感与情感中。

因此，"牙买加语言"受到了标准英语词汇与非洲语法和结构的巨大影响，被认为是西半球主要的克利奥尔语言之一。基督教会复兴（Zion Revivalism）、pukkumina（Pocomania 传统音乐）和信仰崇拜，是基督教仪式和非洲宗教仪式相结合产生的融合宗教各种不同的表现形式。非洲宗教仪式在 Kumina 音乐、班图教派以及最近出现的拉斯塔法里教之中得以保存。拉斯塔法教不仅创新地吸纳了《旧约》，也在寻求社会正义、自由和人类尊严的救赎过程中采用了犹太教的驱散、放逐和回归的神学轨迹，还吸收了秉承于殖民欧洲却未能在牙买加传播开来的正统基督教。亲属关系包括远亲或无正式法律约束的非血缘亲子之间的互相关爱，保证了家庭的团结、人与人之间的手足情谊，特别是对不分等级、种族或信仰的牙买加妇女和文化传递者的关爱和同情。

来源于其非洲、欧洲和亚洲祖先的艺术衍生出一流的牙买加音乐、舞蹈、戏剧和合唱乐团。从门特传统民间音乐（mento）、斯卡音乐（ska）、慢拍摇滚乐到雷鬼乐和 dancehall 的牙买加流行音乐催生了一批伟大的音乐家如鲍勃·马利（Bob Marley）、吉米·克里夫（Jimmy Cliff）、彼得·托许（Peter Tosh）和图斯·海伯特（Toots Hibbert），其中比尼·曼（Beenie Man）和布珠·班顿（Buju Banton）是近些年较知名的歌手。他们都以其具有广泛的全球知名度而自豪，并受益于使牙买加具有独特性的多种传统和文化。

各地的移民再次推动了牙买加社会的艺术发展。如果说这样的进步给加勒比海南部地区带来了斋期前的狂欢节（在牙买加日历中是斋期后的复活节），那么它给牙买加带来的东西则是可以追溯至 19 世纪的 jonkonnu（假面舞会）——圣诞期间欧式狂欢与非洲假面舞会相结合而产生的牙买加独特节日。它的变化也在独立后的牙买加的舞蹈、音乐剧和文化项目中得以体现。

同时，（东）印度人也为 Hosay 节日艺术做出了重要的贡献。Hosay 节是伊斯兰教徒的庆典，由印度人和牙买加基督教徒共享——牙买加非洲人击鼓奏乐，印度人翩翩起舞。

这就是拥有各种不同文化的移民在牙买加有限的领土上相互融合所产生的结果。抛开种族、肤色、社会等级、宗教或政治派系，每个人都是其他人的一部分。然而，这并不否认牙买加人之间存在差异，与之相比，更重要的是如何能创新并积极地处理因差异造成的窘境。因此，我们可以肯定地说所有的牙买加人身上都有着部分非洲血统、部分欧洲血统、部分亚洲血统、部分本土美洲血统，但是却是绝对的牙买加人。

High Commissions and Embassies

BELGIUM

Jamaican Mission to the European Union

Embassy of Jamaica
Avenue Hansen-Soulie, 77
1040 Brussels, Belgium

Tel: (322) 230-1170, (322) 230-1317, (322) 230-4536
Fax: (322) 234-6969
Email:
emb.jam.brussels@skynet.be

Ambassador: Her Excellency
Marcia Y. Gilbert-Roberts
Minister/Counsellor: Mr
Esmond Reid

CANADA

High Commission of Jamaica
Standard Life Building
275 Slater Street
Suite 800
Ottawa
Ontario KIP 5H9

Tel: (613) 233-9311
Fax: (613) 233-0611
Email: hc@jhcottawa.ca

High Commissioner: Her
Excellency R.V. Evadne Coye,
CD
Counsellor: Ms Hillary
Williams

COLOMBIA

Embassy of Jamaica
Avenida 19 No. 106A-83
Oficina 304
Santafé de Bogotá, D.C.

Tel: 571- 612-33-89/612-33-96 &
612-35-98
Fax: 571-612-34-79
Email: emjacol@cable.net.co

Charge D'Affaires & Consul
General - Mrs Elaine Sanchez

CUBA

Embassy of Jamaica
Calle 22 No. 503, E/5ta y 7ma
Miramar, Playa
Ciudad de La Habana

Tel: 537-204-2908/204-6959
Fax: 537-204-2531
Email: embjmcub@enet.cu

Ambassador: His Excellency
A'Dale Robinson
Attaché: Ms Elizabeth King

DOMINICAN REPUBLIC

Embassy of Jamaica
Ave. Enriquillo No. 61, Los
Cacicazgos, Santo Domingo

Tel: 809-482-7770-1
Fax: 809-482-7773
Email: emb.jamaica@tricom.net

Charge D'Affaires and Consul
General: Mr T. Allan Marley

FRANCE

Permanent Delegation of
Jamaica to UNESCO
1 rue Miollis
75352 Paris, France

Tel: 33 145 683 360 or 33 145
683 223
Fax: 33 143 068 451

Representative: H.E. Marcia
Gilbert-Roberts
First Secretary: Mrs Angela
Prendergast

GERMANY

Embassy of Jamaica
Schmargendorfer Strasse 32
12159 Berlin

Tel: 00-49-308599450 or 1
Fax: 00-49-3085994540
Email: info@jamador.de

Ambassador: Her Excellency
Joy Wheeler
Counsellor: Ms Carol Lee

JAPAN

Embassy of Jamaica
Toranonon Yatsuka Building,
2F
1 - 11 Atago 1 - Chorme
Minato-Ku
Tokyo 105 - 002

Tel: 813-3435-1861
Fax: 813-3435-1864
Email:mail@jamaicaemb.jp
Website: www.jamaicaemb.jp

Ambassador: Her Excellency
Claudia Barnes
First Secretary/Consul: Ms
Sonya White

NIGERIA

High Commission of Jamaica
Plot 247 Muhammadu Buhari
Way,
Central Area District,
Abuja

Tel:/Fax: 234 9780 6809/234 070
2786 3243
Email:
jamaicanembassy@yahoo.com

High Commissioner: His
Excellency Robert Miller
Attaché: Mrs Angella
Robinson-Okpananchi

ORGANISATION OF AMERICAN STATES (OAS)

Permanent Mission of Jamaica
to the OAS
1520 New Hampshire Avenue
N.W., Washington, DC 20036

Tel: 202-452-0660
Fax: 202-452-0081
Email: jamaica@oas.org
Email: jamaicaoas@earthlink.net

Permanent Representative: His
Excellency Anthony Johnson
Minister/Deputy Permanent
Rep.: Mrs L. Ann Scott

PEOPLE'S REPUBLIC OF CHINA

Embassy of Jamaica
Jian Guo Men Wai Diplomatic
Compound, No 1 Xiu Shui
Street, Building 6, Room 6-2-72
Chaoyang District
Beijing, 100600

Tel: 8610 653 2670 – 1/8610
6532 0667
Fax: 8610 6532 0669
Email:
embassy@jamaicagov.cn
Website: www.jamaicagov.cn

Ambassador:His Excellency
Courtney Rattray
Minister/Counsellor: Mrs Julia
Hyatt

SOUTH AFRICA

High Commission of Jamaica
Private Bag X5, Hatfield 0028
3rd Floor, MIB Building
1119 Burnett Street
Hatfield, Pretoria

Tel: 27 12 362 6667 / 27 12 366
8500
Fax: 27 12 366 8510 / 27 12 362
6666
Email: info@jhcpretoria.co.za

High Commissioner: His
Excellency Audley Rodriguez
Counsellor: Ms Shorna Kay
Richards

TRINIDAD AND TOBAGO

High Commission of Jamaica
2 Newbold Street, Port of Spain
Tel: 868-622-4995
Fax: 868-622-9043/9180
Email: jhctnt@tstt.net.tt

High Commissioner: Her
Excellency Sharon Saunders
Counsellor: Miss Cherett
Campbell

UNITED KINGDOM

High Commission of Jamaica
1-2 Prince Consort Road
London SW7 2BZ
Tel: 207-823-9911
Fax: 207-589-5154
Email: jamhigh@jhcuk.com

High Commissioner: H.E. the
Hon. Burchell Whiteman, OJ
Minister/Deputy High
Commissioner: Ms Joan Thomas

UNITED MEXICAN STATES

Embassy of Jamaica
Schiller 326, Piso 8, Chapultepec
Morales, Delegacion Miguel
Hidalgo, 11570 Mexico

Tel: 55 5250-6804, 55 5250-6806
Fax: 55 5250-6160
Email: embajadadejamaica@
prodigy.net.mx

Ambassador: Her Excellency
Sheila Sealy-Monteith
First Sec.: Ms Keisha Kal Witter

UNITED NATIONS – GENEVA

Permanent Mission of Jamaica
to the Office and Specialised
Agencies of the UN
36 rue de Lausanne, 1st Floor
1201 Geneva
Tel: 4122-7315-780/789
Fax: 4122-7384-420
E: mission.jamaica@ties.itu.int

Permanent Representative: His
Excellency Peter Black
Minister Counsellor: Miss
Cheryl Spencer

UNITED NATIONS – NEW YORK

Permanent Mission of Jamaica
to the United Nations
767 Third Avenue
9th and 10th Floors
New York 10017

Tel: 212-935-7509
Fax: 212-935-7607
Email: jamaica@un.int

Permanent Representative: His
Excellency Raymond Wolfe
Minister/Deputy Permanent
Representative: Mrs Angella
Brown

UNITED STATES OF AMERICA

Embassy of Jamaica
1520 New Hampshire Avenue
N.W.
Washington
DC 20036

Tel: 202-452-0660
Fax: 202-452-0036
Email:
contactus@jamaicaembassy.org
Email:
ambassador@jamaicaembassy.org

Ambassador: His Excellency
Anthony Johnson
Minister: Mrs Sharon Miller

VENEZUELA

Embassy of Jamaica
Edificio "Los Frailes"
Piso 5, Calle
La Guairita, Urb. Chuao
Caracas

Tel: (582) 21991-69055 or (582)
129916133
Fax: (582) 91-5708, (582)
9524487, (582) 952 7536, (582)
1299 1060 55
Email:embjaven@cantv.net

Ambassador: Her Excellency
Delrose Montague
Counsellor/Consul: Mrs Faith
Mullings-Williams

Consular Representatives

ANTIGUA AND BARBUDA

Jamaican Consulate
6 Temple Street
P.O. Box 2372

Jamaican Consulate
St John's
Tel: (268) 460 6184
Fax: (268) 460 6183
Email: lawrhudd@candw.ag
Hon. Consul: Vacant

ARGENTINA

Jamaican Consulate
Bermejo 1250
(1609) Boulogne sur Mer
Prov. De Buenos Aires
Tel: 5411 4719 7448
Fax: 47 65 7255
Email: ebanuchi@hotmail.com
E: consul@consuladodejamaica.com
Honorary Consul: Enrique G.
Banuchi

ARUBA

Jamaican Consulate
Papilon 121 F
Santa Cruz
Tel: 011-297-8-30226/26093
Fax: 011-297-8-57490
Email: dannyjmk@yahoo.com
Honorary Consul: Daniel T. Wilson

AUSTRALIA

Jamaican Consulate
P.O. Box 421, Earlwood
Sydney, NSW 2206

Office Address:
8 Leonora St, Earlwood
Sydney NSW 2206
Tel: 02-9787 4948
Fax: 02-9787 4948
Email: marcobb@y-3net.com.au

Hon. Consul Marco Breakenridge

BAHAMAS

Jamaican Consulate
P.O. Box N-3451, Nassau
Tel:/Fax: 242-394-8538
Email: patharry@coralwave.com
Hon. Consul: Patrick Hanlan

BELGIUM

Jamaican Consulate
Commerzbank Belgium NV
Uitbreidingstraat 46, 2600
Antwerpen
Tel: 32 3 287 3390
Fax: 32 3 281 0989
Email: honcons.jambel@tiscali.be

Hon. Consul: Jacques Nyssen

BELIZE

Jamaican Consulate General
4 Eve Street, P. O. Box 1250
Belize City
Tel: 501-822 2183
Fax : 501-822 0797
Email: dujondujon@btl.net

Consul General: Nicholas Dujon

BERMUDA

Jamaican Consulate
55 Court Street, Hamilton, HM 12
Tel: (441) 292-5264
Fax: (441) 295-5646
Email: honconjam@northrock.bm

Hon. Gov't Rep.: Winston G. Laylor

BOLIVIA

Jamaican Consulate
Calle 15, Calacoto, Torre Ketal
Piso 4, Oficina 404
La Paz
Tel: 591-2-211-2993
Fax: 591-2-279-9290
Email: panamasec@entel.net
Email:
eherrera@panamericansec.com.bo

Hon.Consul: Enrique Herrera Soria

BOTSWANA

Jamaican Consulate
Gabarone, Botswana, P.O. Box
47053
Tel: 267 365 0256
Email: ewaugh@bca.bw
Hon. Consul: Esau Waugh

BRAZIL

Jamaican Consulate
Bastos-Tigre, Coelho da Rocha, e
Lopes Advogados, Al. Jaú, 1754 - 4°
andar, 01420-002 – Sao Paulo, SP
Tel: 55 11 3067-3414
Fax: 55 11 3067-3413
E: marapia@bastostigre.com.br
Hon. Consul: Mrs Maria Pia
Faulhaber Bastos-Tigre

CANADA

EDMONTON

Consulate of Jamaica
Marcus Garvey Center for Unity,
12526 126th Avenue
Edmonton, Alberta, T5L 0X3
Tel: (780) 481-0499
Fax: (780)452-0383
Email: ceneita@shaw.ca
Hon. Consul: Mrs Coleen E. Neita

TORONTO

Jamaican Consulate-General
303 Eglinton Avenue East
Toronto, Ontario M4P 1L3
Tel: 416-598-3008/3035/2369
Fax : 416-598-4928
Email: congentoronto@on.aibn.com
Consul General: Mrs Ann Marie
Bonner
Consul: Nigel Smith

VICTORIA

Consulate of Jamaica
206-4430 Chatterton Way, Victoria,
BC, VX8 5J2
Tel: (250) 479- 9800
Fax: (250) 479- 1642
E: jamconvictoria@shaw.ca
Hon. Consul: Michael Marley

VANCOUVER

Jamaican Consulate
Royal City Centre Mall - Main
Floor, 154A-610 Sixth Street, New
Westminster, Greater Vancouver,
B.C. V3L 3C2
Tel: (604) 515-0443
Fax: (604) 521-6322 or 515 -0443
Email: Jamaicanconsulate
vancouver@hotmail.com
Hon. Consul: Dr Astley E. Smith

WINNIPEG

Jamaican Consulate
127 Eastcote Drive, Winnipeg,
Manitoba, R2N 2Y4
Tel: 204 256-9137
Fax: 204 257 6318
Email: chnemb@mts.net
Email: cnembhardt@mts.net
Hon. Consul: Mrs Carmen H.
Nembhardt

CAYMAN ISLANDS

Jamaican Consulate
342a Dorcy Consul
Industrial Park, Georgetown, Grand
Cayman
Tel: 1 (345) 949-9526
Fax: 1(345) 945-7294 / 1 (345) 949-
6322
Email: jamaica@candw.ky
Hon. Consul (Acting): Ms Elaine
Harris

CHILE - SANTIAGO

Jamaican Consulate
Isidora Goyenechea 3250, Oficina
401, Los Condes, Santiago
Tel: 562-335-2692
Fax: 562-335-2693
Email: mail@jorquiera.cl
Hon. Consul: Carlos Jorquiera

CHINA

HONG KONG - Special
Administrative Region
Jamaican Consulate
Penthouse, East Ocean Centre,
98 Granville Road, TST East,
Kowloon
Tel: (852)3552-8538
Fax: (852)2267-1088
Email:jamconsulate@yahoo.com.hk

Hon. Consul: Mrs Evelyn Lu

SHANGHAI
Jamaican Consulate
16/F Zhongda Square, No. 989
Dongfang Road, Shanghai 200122
Tel: 86-21-68752899
Fax: 86-21-68763299
Email: gl_intl@163.net
Hon. Consul: Zhou Yuejin

COLOMBIA
Jamaican Consulate
Optica San Andres
Local 2, Transversal 2
San Andres Island
Tel:/Fax: 578 512- 3037
E: robinsonai@hotmail.com
Hon. Consul: Samuel Robinson
Davis

COSTA RICA
Consulate of Jamaica
c/o Robinson Transport Services
San Jose de Matute Gomez, 100 mts.
Norte y 100Esta casa 2309, San Jose
Tel: 506 253-5605, 506 253-5486
Fax: 506 234-9135
E: jamaicanconsulate@ice.co.cr

Hon. Consul: Gene Alejandro
Robinson Davis

CYPRUS
Jamaican Consulate
9 Dhemitsanis Street, P.O. Box 4862,
Nicosia
Tel: 357-224 58298
Fax: 357-22-761-671
Hon. Consul: Pantelis Leptos

CZECH REPUBLIC
Jamaican Consulate
Ondøíèkova 7
130 00 Praha 3
Tel: 00420 222 727 041
Fax: 00420 222 727 041
Email: formanek@gocanada.cz

Hon. Consul: Peter P. Formanek

DOMINICAN REPUBLIC
PUERTO PLATA
Jamaican Consulate
Suite B-1-13
Centro Commercial Y de
Convenciones de Playa Dorada
Puerto Plata
Tel: 809-320-2224-5-7
Fax: 809-320-2242

Hon. Consul: Enrique E De
Marchena Kaluche

SANTO DOMINGO
Jamaican Consulate
c/o Jamaican Embassy
Ave Enriquillo No. 61
Los Cacicazgos
Santo Dominigo
Tel: 1 (809) 482 7770-1
Fax: 1 (809) 482 7773
Email: emb.jamaica@tricom.net

Hon. Consul: Volker Hans Wilhelm
Rehbein

ECUADOR
QUITO
Jamaican Consulate
c/o Falconi Puig & Asociados
Avenida Amazonas 477 y Roca
Edificio Río Amazonas, Oficinas
900, P.O. Box 17-03-423, Quito
Tel: (593)-(2)-2561808
Fax: 593-2-2500295
Email: mail@falconipuig.com
Email: mfalconi@falconipuig.com

Hon. Consul: Miguel Falconi Puig

GUAYAQUIL
Jamaican Consulate
Avenida Malecon de Entre - Ríos,
Conjunto Mediterráneo, Villa No. 8,
Guayaquil
Tel:/Fax: 593-4-2830346
Email:
consuladojamaicagye@yahoo.com

Hon. Consul: Ana Maria Pinchin
Gonzalez de Ching

EL SALVADOR
Jamaican Consulate
KM. 10 Carretera a La Libertad, San
Salvador
Tel: 503-2278-1111
Fax: 503-2278-1919
Email: adolfosalume@hotmail.com

Hon. Consul: Adolfo Salume

ETHIOPIA
Jamaican Consulate
Debrezeit Road, Higher 20, Kebele
45, House # 921, P.O. Box 5633,
Addis Ababa
Tel: 251-1-6543-22
Fax: 251-114-654-747

Hon. Consul: Gebre E. Gebru

FINLAND
Jamaican Consulate
Wrede & Co, Kasarminkatu 27
00130 Helsinki
Tel: 358-9-6962 400
Fax: 358-9-602-595
Email: kenneth.wrede@wredeco.fi

Hon. Consul: Kenneth Wrede

FRANCE
NICE
Jamaican Consulate
50, Blvd. Victor Hugo, Hotel
Splendid, 06048 Nice
Tel: 33-6-6044- 6727
Fax: 33-4-9341-2800

Hon. Consul: Dieter S.W. Freidrich

PARIS
Jamaican Consulate
60 Avenue Foch
75116 Paris
Tel: 331-4500-6225
Fax: 331-4500-2063

Hon. Consul: Albert Bickel

GERMANY
BRANDENBURG
Jamaican Consulate
Selchowstrasse 4 A
14199 Berlin
Tel: 0049 30 82 09 64 58
Fax: 0049 30 82 45 088
Email: Gerclan@aol.com

Hon. Consul: Hermann Gerbaulet

HAMBURG
Jamaican Consulate
Ballindamm 1
20095 Hamburg
Tel: 0049 40 30 299 232
Fax: 00149 40 30 299 288
Email: kellinhusen@behnmeyer.de

Hon. Consul: Jens Kellinghusen

GREECE
Jamaican Consulate
Dodekanisou 86
Petroupoli 13231, Athens
Tel: (302) 10505-3321
Fax: (302) 10501-8206
Email: GR456@aol.com
Hon. Consul: William N. Argeros

GRENADA
Jamaican Consulate
Office of the Resident Tutor
University of the West Indies
P.O. Box 439, St George's
Tel: (809) 440-2451
Fax: (809) 440-4985
E: bevathome@caribsurf.com

Hon. Consul: Mrs Beverley Steele,
CBE

GUATEMALA
Jamaican Consulate
"Costibal" Km 14.1, Carretera a El
Salvador, Aldea, Puerta Parada
Mailing Address: P.O. Box 38-C
Guatemala City 01915
Tel: 502-6634-1528/2223-4
Fax: 502-6634-2225
Email: valeva95@yahoo.com
Email: valeva@intelnett.com

Hon. Consul: Mrs Natasha A.
Valladares Evans

HONDURAS
Jamaican Consulate
Final Av, Los Proceres,
P O Box 152, Tegucigalpa
Tel: (504) 2-369-655/(504) 2-365-932
Tel:/Fax: (504) 2-365-826
E: eduardo.Kafie@lufussa.com
Hon. Consul: Eduardo Kafie

HUNGARY
Jamaican Consulate
Zajon u. 10, 1112 Budapest
Tel:/Fax: 00 36 1 319 64 86, 00 36 1
319 64 87
Email: abatizi@sunrise.hu

Hon. Consul: Dr Andras Batizi

INDIA

Jamaican Consulate General
Meridien Tower, 9th Floor, 10
Windsor Place, New Delhi – 110
001
Tel: 2335 5411/2341 7122
Fax: 011 2335 5432/2341 6275
E: Khemka@del3.vsnl.net.in

Hon. Consul General: Nand
Khemka

INDONESIA

Consulate of Jamaica
Rumah Maduma, Jl. Dr. Sahraj No.
52, Jakarta, 12970
Tel: 62-21-831-1184
Fax: 62-21-831-1185
Email: maduma@indo.net.id
Hon. Consul: Soy Martua Pardede

IRELAND

Jamaican Consulate
1 Wellington Road, Ballsbridge,
Dublin 4

Hon. Consul: Patrick James Mara

ITALY

Jamaican Consulate General
1 Via G Sgambati
Rome 00198
Tel: 39 06 854-6626; 39 06 852-494
Fax: 39 06 840-80042
Email: jamaicarome@email.it
Email: tonyalfano@email.it

Hon. Consul General: Dr Salvatore
T. Alfano

JAPAN - KOBE

Jamaican Consulate
Ueshima Coffee Company Limited
(U.C.C)
7-7-7, Minatojima-Nakamachi
Chuo-Ku, Kobe 650-8577
Tel: (81) 78-304-8887
Fax: (81) 78-304-8865
Email: masaru-nagasawa@ucc.co.jp

Hon. Consul Tatsushi Ueshima
Contact: Masuru Nagasawa

JORDAN - AMMAN

Jamaican Consulate
P. O. Box 1, Amman
Tel: 00962-6-4646020
Telex: TEC 21300 JO
Fax: 00962-6-778164/4641164

Hon. Consul: Faud T. Kattan

REPUBLIC OF KOREA

Jamaican Consulate General
5th Floor, Samsung-dong,
Kangnam-gu, Seoul, 135-881
Tel: 82-25541915
Fax: 82-2565-5636
E: ywyoon21@hotmail.com

Hon. Consul-General: Yung Woo
Yoon

LEBANON

Jamaican Consulate
Mme Curie Street, Minkara Centre
Bldg., 3rd Fl., Hamra, P. O. Box
5584, Beirut
Tel: 747-244/5/6, 352425, 340736
Fax: 961 340 735

Hon. Consul: Khalil Zantout

MALAYSIA

Jamaican Consulate-General
25th Floor, Bangunan AmBank
Group, 55 Jalan Raja Chulan
50200 Kuala Lumpur
P.O. Box 12402
50776 Kuala Lumpur
Tel: 603-207-82801/82841/603 2078
2633 ext 6510/6511
Fax: 603-203-23031
Email: dah@ambg.com.my

Hon. Consul-General: Dato Azlan
Hashim

MONACO

Jamaican Consulate
14 Quai Antoine 1ER
98000 Monte Carlo
Tel:/Fax: 377 93 50 50 50
Fax: 33-493 412 800
Hon. Consul: Dieter S.W. Freidrich

NETHERLANDS

Jamaican Consulate
Herengracht 316
1016 CD Amsterdam
Tel: 310628 20 63 08
Fax : 312 062 209 76
Email: cojam@xs4all.nl

Hon. Consul: Jacques H. Huysser

CURAÇAO

Jamaican Consulate
Habaaiweg No 68, Willemstad
Curacao, Netherlands Antilles
Tel: 5999-462-6561
Fax: 5999-462-6561

Hon. Consul: Rafaelito Hato

PERU

Jamaican Consulate
Av. Jorge Basadre 255, Of. 501
San Isidro, Lima 27
Tel: (511) 442 8828
Fax: (511) 442 0504
Email: jcbarrenechea@peru-
legal.com

Hon. Consul: Dr Julio Cesar
Barrenechea Gamio

PHILIPPINES

Jamaican Consulate General
Tesoro Building, 5th Floor, 1325 A.
Mabini Street, Ermita, Manila 1000
Tel: (632) 524-39-36 to 40
Fax: (632) 522-1580
Consul General: Miguel M.A.
Guerrero

NICARAGUA

Jamaican Consulate
Estatua Montoya 3C Norte 1C
Este #11, Managua
Tel: (505) 266-2963
Fax: (505) 268-2965
Email: piero@cablenet.com.ni
E: pbergman@fonocenter.com

Consul: Piero Erick Bergman Morea

NORWAY

Jamaican Consulate
Professor Dahlsgt. 26, Oslo
Tel: 47 22 56 00 40
Email: haagen@oust.no

Hon. Consul: Haagen Oust

PANAMA

Jamaican Consulate
Edificio Via Espana 500, No. 10, Via
Espana
Panama City
Tel: (507) 263 4001
Fax: (507) 263-4002
Email:rmatalon@cwpanama.net
E: rmatalon@jampatty.com
Hon. Consul: Mrs Rebeca Matalon
Castel

PARAGUAY

Jamaican Consulate
Avenida Venezuela, 1255e, Florida
y Sol, Asuncion
Tel: 595-21-290-558
Fax : 595-21-291-361
E: plastima@conexion.com.py

Hon. Consul: Marcos Ismachowiez,
OBE

POLAND

Jamaican Consulate
c/o Kimar Export-Import Company,
Ul. Sandomierska 23 m. 7, 02-567
Warszawa
Tel:/Fax: (48-22) 646-59-63
Email: kimar@qdnet.pl

Hon. Consul: Mrs Maria
Dembowska

PORTUGAL- LISBON

Jamaican Consulate
R Ocidental Do Mercado
57 - 1 Esq, 2900 Setubal
Tel: 351 265 529170/2
Fax: 351-265 238595
Email: oneill@oneill.pt

Hon. Consul: Jose Luis Da Costa
Resende

SPAIN

Jamaican Consulate
Villanueva 35 Piso 2o puerta 4a,
28001 Madrid
Tel:/Fax: 3491-220-0041
Email: Ignacio.sampere@jamconsul.es

Hon. Consul: Ignacio Sampere Villlar

SINGAPORE

Jamaican Consulate
Resource Pacific Holdings PTE Ltd.,
Macondray Corporation PTE Ltd,
78 Shenton Way, 328-01, 079120
Tel: (65) 6227 7855/(65) 6323 1800
Fax: (65) 6 323 2939
Email: hida@arc.com.sg
Hon. Consul: Dr Melanie Chew

ST KITTS & NEVIS

Jamaican Consulate
Claxton's Arcade Building, 1st
Floor, Cnr Fort and Cayon Street,
Claxton's Arcade, P.O. Box 165,
Basseterre
Tel: (869) 465-8551
Fax: (869) 465-8551.
E: claxtonproperties@yahoo.com

Hon. Consul: Mrs Jacqueline
Claxton

ST LUCIA

Jamaican Consulate
29-31 Micoud Street, P.O. Box 81,
Castries
Tel: 758-452-3040
Fax: 758-452-2499
Email: chongco@candw.lc
Hon. Consul: Tyrone Chong

ST VINCENT & THE GRENADINES

Jamaican Consulate
P.O. Box 1525, Fair Hall Housing
Scheme #61
Tel:/Fax: 784-457-4728
E: svgjamcon@vincysurf.com
Email: htevesham@msn.com

Hon. Consul: Mrs Morine Williams

SURINAME

Jamaican Consulate
c/o CARIMECO Management
Consultants, Prinsessestraat 73
Paramaribo
Tel: 597-479-210
Fax: 597-479-268
Hon. Consul: Dr Deryck
Heinemann

SWEDEN

Jamaican Consulate
Knackepilsgrand 39, 16576
Hasselby, Stockholm
Tel: 468-38-0797
Fax: 468-739-0034
E: jamaican.consulate@swipnet.se
Hon. Consul: Lennart O. Anderson

THAILAND

Jamaican Consulate
Ground Floor, Loxley Building
102 Na Rangong Road
Klongtoey, Bangkok
Tel: 66-2-240-3285
Fax: 66-2-240-3286
Email: jingjai@loxley.co.th
Hon. Consul: Dr Jingjai

TURKEY

Jamaican Consulate
Harbiye Cad. No: 283, Harbiye
Istanbul
Tel: 00 90 212 549 07 00
Fax: 00 90 212 549 07 10
Email: jamaicanconsul@gmail.com

Hon. Consul: Mehmet Aykut Eken

TURKS & CAICOS ISLANDS

Office of the Hon. Representative of
the Government of Jamaica
Suite No. 9, Eden Courts, Leeward
Highway, Providenciales
Tel: 649 946 4655
Mobile: 649 331 4655
E: jamaicanconsul@tciway.tc
Hon. Consul: Allan Eden-
Hutchinson

UNITED STATES OF AMERICA

CALIFORNIA – San Francisco
Jamaican Consulate
52 Donna Way, Oakland, CA 94605
Tel: (510) 562-4391
Fax: (510) 915-0227
E: newtgordon@sbcglobal.net
Hon. Consul: Prof. Newton C.
Gordon, DDS, MS

FLORIDA – Miami
Jamaican Consulate-General
842 Ingraham Building, 25 South
East Second Avenue
Miami, FL 33131
Tel: (305) 374-8431-2
Fax: (305) 577-4970
Email: jamconmi@bellsouth.net

Consul-General: Mrs Sandra Grant
Griffiths
Consul: Ms Desreine Taylor

GEORGIA – Atlanta
Jamaican Consulate
5405 Memorial Drive, Building H,
Suite 1, Atlanta, GA 30083
Tel: 404-297-7696,
Fax: 404-508-4712
Email: jaconsulateatl@bellsouth.net

Hon. Consul: Vin Martin

HOUSTON – Texas
Consulate of Jamaica
6001 Savoy Drive, Suite 509
Houston, Texas, 77036
Tel: (713) 541- 3333
Fax: (713) 782- 4323
Email: ful2law@aol.com

Hon. Consul: Khalfani Omari Fullerton

ILLINOIS – Chicago
Jamaican Consulate
4655 S. Dr. Martin Luther King
Drive, Suite 201
Chicago, Illinois 60653
Tel: (773) 373-8988
Fax: (773) 663-2496
Email:
jamaicanconsulatechicago.org
Email: conjam1@netzero.com

MASSACHUSETTS – Boston
Jamaican Consulate
451 Bluehill Avenue
Dorchester, MA 02121
Tel: 617-266-8604
Fax: (617)266-0185 ext. 212
Email: pfarr@uhmgt.com

Hon. Consul: Kenneth Guscott
Hon. Vice Consul: Ms Patricia Farr

NEW HAMPSHIRE – Concord
Jamaican Consulate
235 Mountain Road
Concord, NH 03301
Tel: 603-230-9843
Fax: 603-230-9542
Email: opolack@aol.com

Hon. Consul: Dr Ofelia Dudley-Polack

NEW YORK – New York
Jamaican Consulate-General
767 Third Avenue, 2nd and 3rd
Floors, New York, NY 10017
Tel: 212-935-9000
Fax: 212-935-7507
E: cg@congenjamaica-ny.org

Consul General: Mrs Geneive
Brown Metzger
Deputy Consul General: Mrs Tracey
Blackwood

PENNSYLVANIA – Philadelphia
Consulate of Jamaica
Welcoming Center West, 246 South
52nd Street, Philadelphia, PA 19143
Mailing Address:
P.O. Box 13117
Philadelphia, PA 19101
Tel: 215 313 9508
Email: ablinstead@aol.com

Hon. Consul: Alston B. Meade, Ph.D

VIRGINIA – Richmond
Jamaican Consulate
P.O. Box 15101
Richmond, VA 23227
Tel:/Fax: (804) 262 – 4453
Email: agusfran@gmail.com

Hon. Consul: Mrs Beryl Walters-Riley

WASHINGTON – Seattle
Jamaican Consulate
c/o J.P. Francis & Associates, Inc.,
8223 South 222nd Street
Kent, Washington 98032
Tel: 206-872-8950
Fax: 206-872-8953
Email: EDwyer7636@aol.com

Hon. Consul: Mrs Enid L. Dwyer

URUGUAY

Jamaican Consulate
Nicaragua 1243
11.800 Montevideo
Tel: 598-2-924-0433
Fax: 598-2-924-1727
Email: esojo@josemduran.com

Hon. Consul: Eduardo Sojo Duran

Jamaica Tourist Board offices

JAMAICA

KINGSTON
64 Knutsford Blvd, Kingston 5
Tel: 876 929 9200-19
Fax: 876 929 9375
vipcard@visitjamaica.com

MONTEGO BAY
Cornwall Beach Complex
Glocester Ave
Montego Bay
St. James
Tel: 876 952 4425-6
Fax: 876 952 3587
vipcard@visitjamaica.com

UNITED STATES

MIAMI
5201 Blue Lagoon Drive
Suite 670
Miami, Florida 33126
Tel: (305) 665-0557
Fax: (305) 666-7239
Toll Free: 1 800 233 4582
vipcard@visitjamaica.com

CANADA

TORONTO
303 Eglington Ave East
Suite 200
Toronto, Ontario M4P 1L3
Tel: 416-482-7850
Fax: 416-482-1730
Toll Free: 1-800-465-2624
vipcard@visitjamaica.com

UNITED KINGDOM

LONDON
1-2 Prince Consort Rd
London, England SW7 2BZ
Tel: +44 0207 225 9090
Fax: +44 0207 225 1020
vipcard@visitjamaica.com

GERMANY

BERLIN
Schmargendorferstr. 32, 12159 Berlin- Friedenau
Federal Republic of Germany
Tel: +49 (0) 30 85 99 45 18
Fax: +49 (0) 30 85 07 92 87

HOLLAND

WOERDEN
Postbus 2073, 3441 DB Woerden, Netherlands
Tel: +31 (0) 34 843 0829. Fax: + 31(0) 34 848 2307

SPAIN

BARCELONA
c/o Sergat Espana SL, Avenida Pau Casals, 4
Barcelona 8021
Tel: +34 9 3414 0210
Fax: +34 9 3201 8657

ITALY

ROME
c/o Brian Hammond Associates
Via Nazionale 243, 00184 Roma
Tel: +39 06 4890 1255
Fax: +39 06 4890 7384

INDIA

NEW DELHI
c/o TRAC Representations
A-16, 6th Floor, Himalaya House, Kasturba Ghandi
Marg, New Delhi - 110001
Tel: 91-11-23352550. Fax: 91-11-23350270

JAPAN

TOKYO
Strategic Tower Bldg. 2F
2-11-1 Shibuya, Shibuya-ku, Tokyo 150-0002, JAPAN
Tel: (81) 3-3400-2974. Fax: (81) 3-3400-2973

International dialling code for Jamaica from UK 001 876
North America and Caribbean 1- 876